MICHAEL DUC

COUNTDOWN
TO FIRST CERTIFICATE

STUDENT'S BOOK

OXFORD
UNIVERSITY PRESS

COUNTDOWN
TO FIRST CERTIFICATE

framework

A BRIEF GUIDE TO THE FIRST CERTIFICATE EXAMINATION

What does the paper consist of?

PAPER 1 READING

Four parts *(35 questions in total)*

Part 1	Multiple matching
Part 2	Multiple-choice questions
Part 3	Gapped text
Part 4	Multiple matching

PAPER 2 WRITING

Two tasks of between 120–180 words each.

Part 1   A compulsory formal or informal transactional letter.

Part 2   One task from a choice of four (one of the tasks in Part 2 can be on one of five set books).

What do you need to do?

PAPER 1 READING

Read all the texts and answer the questions.

Part 1   Choose one from a list of headings or summary sentences.

Part 2   Choose one option from a set of four.

Part 3   Choose one from a list of missing paragraphs or sentences.

Part 4   Choose one or more items from a list and match the item(s) to parts of the text.

Write your answers in the correct boxes on an answer sheet.

PAPER 2 WRITING

Do the compulsory task and one other.

Part 1   Read input material which will be no more than 250 words and may include graphics and pictures.

Part 2   Choose one task from – an article, a non-transactional letter, a report, a discursive composition or a narrative composition (story).

Select a set book task if appropriate.

Write your answers in the question booklet.

What will help you?

PAPER 1 READING

- Read as widely as you can in your preparation for the exam.
- Read the whole text through quickly to get a general idea of what it is about before looking at the questions.
- Don't worry about words you don't know in the text as you should still be able to complete the task.
- Underline the words in the text and question which help you to find the answer.
- Read all the options, headings, sentences, etc. to see if they could be correct and eliminate them before choosing your answer.

PAPER 2 WRITING

- Read the question carefully and underline the key words.
- Always plan your writing by making notes for each paragraph.
- Think carefully about who you are writing for. Write in a formal or informal style as appropriate.
- Keep your writing relatively simple – you will make fewer mistakes.
- Remember to use paragraphs and keep within the word limit.
- Read your work carefully and check for any spelling, punctuation or grammar mistakes.

PAPER 3 USE OF ENGLISH
(1 hour 15 minutes)

PAPER 4 LISTENING
(40 minutes approximately)

PAPER 5 SPEAKING
(14 minutes approximately)

Five parts *(65 questions in total)*

Part 1 Multiple-choice cloze with emphasis on vocabulary.

Part 2 Open cloze testing grammar and vocabulary.

Part 3 Key word transformations testing grammar and vocabulary.

Part 4 Error correction with emphasis on grammar.

Part 5 Word formation testing vocabulary.

Four parts *(30 questions in total)*

Part 1 Multiple-choice questions (8 unrelated extracts of 30 seconds each).

Part 2 Note taking or blank filling – questions on a monologue or dialogue involving different speakers (about 3 minutes).

Part 3 Multiple matching – matching speakers with statements (5 related extracts of 30 seconds each).

Part 4 Questions on a monologue or text involving different speakers (about 3 minutes).

Four parts

Part 1 The interview (3 minutes)

Part 2 Individual long turn (4 minutes)

Part 3 Two-way task (3 minutes)

Part 4 Three-way discussion (4 minutes)

Two candidates are examined by one examiner and an assessor.

Read all the texts.

Part 1 Choose one word or phrase from a set of four.

Part 2 Fill each gap with one word only.

Part 3 Rewrite the sentence using between two and five words, one of which must be the given word.

Part 4 Decide if the fifteen lines of the text contain an incorrect (extra) word or not.

Part 5 Change the words given into a suitable form to fit into the text. Spell the words correctly.

Write your answers on the answer sheet.

Listen to all four parts twice.

Part 1 Choose one option from a set of three.

Part 2 Write a maximum of three words to take notes, complete statements or questions.

Part 3 Match five speakers with statements.

Part 4 Answer one of the following: true/false statements, yes/no answers; three-option multiple choice; who said what?, etc.

Write your answers filling in the correct boxes on the answer sheet.

Part 1 Give personal information, talk about: present circumstances, past experiences, future plans.

Part 2 Compare and contrast two pictures, talk for one minute, give information, express opinions. Comment after your partner's long turn.

Part 3 Negotiate with your partner, turn-take sensitively, exchange information and opinions, agree and/or disagree, sometimes reach a decision together.

Part 4 Respond to the examiner's questions, develop the discussion topics.

- In the Multiple-choice cloze, look carefully at the words which come before and after each space as these will affect your choice.

- Remember that contractions should not be used in the open cloze as they count as two words.

- In the key word transformations, make sure that the words fit in grammatically and that the second sentence has a similar meaning to the first.

- In the error correction and word formation tasks, always read through the whole text before answering.

- In Part 1, the instructions, questions and options are all read out on the tape. In Parts 2, 3 and 4, you will be given sufficient time to read the questions before you hear the extracts.

- Read through the questions carefully before listening in order to focus your thoughts on the topic and to find out what sort of information you need to listen for.

- Listen carefully for key words to help you choose the correct answer. Don't be misled by distractors.

- Practise speaking English outside the classroom as much as possible.

- If you don't understand a question the examiner asks, ask him or her to repeat it.

- If you don't know a word, paraphrase it.

- Try to avoid one-word answers and use a range of words and phrases instead of repeating yourself.

- Remember to show you are listening to what your partner is saying, e.g. by nodding and commenting when appropriate, as in Part 3.

- Speak clearly so that the examiner can hear you.

Look at these pictures of an actress in four different films and answer the questions.

1 What kind of character do you think she is playing in each film?

2 What do you think helps to create these different images?

3 Do you ever judge people by the way they look? Why?

4 What other qualities can make a person attractive?

1 Multiple matching

Many of the texts in the First Certificate exam come from magazines and newspapers rather than books. It is a good idea to read as widely as you can in your preparation for the exam.

For every reading task, read the whole text through quickly to get a general idea of what it is about before looking at the questions.

Don't worry about words you do not know in the text, as you should still be able to complete the task.

A Look at the title of the text and discuss with your partner what the text may be about. Read the text quickly to see whether your predictions were correct. Take no notice of gaps 0–6.

The **mask** of **beauty**

0	*H*

The green ocean sparkles in the sunshine and tall palm trees wave gently in the wind. Young women roller-skate along the pavement, a young sun-tanned lifeguard walks along the beach. This is Huntingdon Beach, just south of Los Angeles,
05 where everyone seems to be young and beautiful.

1	

It is also the home of successful surgeon, Dr Stephen Marquardt, who believes that he has discovered a scientific formula for measuring beauty. And in a city like Los Angeles, where being attractive means everything, this kind of
10 knowledge could be worth a fortune.

2	

He is by no means the first person to try to discover exactly what makes people attractive. The ancient Greeks were among the first to look into the question. Plato believed that it should be possible to define a beautiful face in terms of
15 mathematics. Over the centuries, others continued the hunt for the formula, but without any real success.

3	

Dr Marquardt, however, says he has now found the answer. He has developed a practical way of measuring beauty, which he calls 'the mask'. This is a series of lines and shapes
20 making up a face. There are specific, set distances between all the features and the outside shape, and it shows the exact proportions that the ideally beautiful face should have.

4	

By laying the mask over a photograph of a face, it is possible to see how attractive someone is – the more a face fits the
25 mask, the more beautiful it is said to be. The fact that the mask can measure the beauty of men, women and people of different races makes it a particularly useful instrument.

5	

It is alarming to think that, if we all start changing the way we look, there may soon be thousands of individuals
30 wandering the streets of Los Angeles looking exactly the same. But it is even more alarming that people may begin to think they are unattractive if their face does not have the proportions of Dr Marquardt's mask.

6	

This would be a great mistake, because there are two sorts
35 of beauty – one is the beauty of the mask, the measurable beauty of the face. The other sort is the kind that we see when we love someone, a much more powerful, enduring beauty that comes from the heart. This is the beauty expressed by poets, the beauty that does not fade, and it is something that no plastic surgeon on earth can give you. ■

B Look at the list of headings A–H and then read the text again more slowly. After each paragraph look down the list and choose the heading that fits best. There is one extra heading you do not need. There is an example at the beginning (0).

Concentrate on the main ideas of the paragraph and look out for words that are similar to those in the list of headings.

The exact words in the headings are usually not repeated in the paragraphs.

A **An adaptable tool**

B **The latest solution**

C **An unsuccessful search**

D **Forever beautiful**

E **An important discovery?**

F **The face without lines**

G **Worrying thoughts**

H **Land of youth and beauty**

2 Language study

be, like, be like, look like

A Read the following questions.

1 How is she?

2 What is she like?

3 What does she like?

4 What does she look like?

Which do we use when we want to ask:

a about someone's health?

b for a physical description?

c for a more general description of character?

d about someone's likes and dislikes?

B Match the following questions 1–5 with answers a–e. *Example: 1b*

1 How's your mother?

2 What does Peter look like?

3 What does Peter like?

4 What is Susan like?

5 Who does Susan like?

a She's very warm and affectionate.

b She's fine, thanks.

c Pubs, TV, football, that sort of thing.

d Peter, I think.

e He's tall and thin, just like his brother, in fact.

C In pairs, ask and answer questions about each other's friends and family.

GRAMMAR ZOOM

Do you believe that any of these things can tell you what a person's character is like? Discuss your ideas with your partner.

their star sign	their accent	their clothes
their handwriting	their job	

1 Multiple-choice cloze

> The multiple-choice cloze is mainly a test of vocabulary but there may also be some grammatical items.
>
> Read all the text before deciding on your answer in order to understand what it is about.
>
> You should look carefully at the words that come immediately before and after the space as these will affect your choice. In the example (0), *interested* is the only word in the group that could be followed by the preposition *in*.

Read the following text and decide which answer A, B, C or D best fits each space.

Example: (0) D

Studying the brain

In the early 19th century, people became very (0)......*D*...... in phrenology. The aim of this new science was to provide a new and easy (1).................... of judging someone's character. (2).................... to scientists, the human brain was (3).................... up into different areas which controlled qualities like intelligence, kindness, selfishness and so on. They also thought that if someone was particularly (4).................... at music, for example, the part of the brain that (5).................... with music would be bigger, so there would be a small bump on the head at that point. This (6).................... that it was possible to judge someone's character by measuring the shape of their head.

Interest in the (7).................... grew rapidly, and scientists produced 'maps' of the brain to help people interpret the shape of heads. Special machines were (8).................... to make accurate measurements, and some of these can still be (9).................... in museums today. In time, people began to (10).................... that phrenology was not a proper science, but it is interesting to note that the basic idea, that there was a link between brain and personality, was in fact correct.

	A	B	C	D
0	fond	keen	enthusiastic	interested
1	instrument	tool	way	formula
2	According	Depending	Referring	Relating
3	separated	organized	shared	divided
4	clever	good	strong	able
5	dealt	controlled	heard	managed
6	resulted	led	caused	meant
7	matter	subject	item	theme
8	done	invented	discovered	found
9	thought	looked	noticed	seen
10	know	tell	realize	imagine

Adjectives and adverbs

1 Regular adjectives and adverbs

A Look at these sentences from the multiple-choice cloze text and answer the questions.

The human brain was divided up into different areas.

Interest in the subject grew rapidly.

1 Which words are adjectives and which is an adverb?

2 How do we normally form adverbs from adjectives?

3 What do we use adverbs and adjectives to describe?

B Underline the word in *italic* that correctly fits each sentence.

I'm not driving too slowly am I?

1 Although he's a *slow/slowly* driver, he has had a lot of accidents.

2 The teacher asked the class to check their compositions *careful/carefully*.

3 I thought it was a really *funny/funnily* film.

4 Emma can speak English *fluent/fluently*.

5 Most of the students passed the test *easy/easily*.

2 Irregular adjectives and adverbs

A **Not all adverbs are formed by adding -ly to the adjective form. Match the adjectives and adverbs in italic with words that could replace them from a–i.**

1	You shouldn't drive so *fast*.	a	fluent
2	The journey was very *fast*.	b	scarcely
3	I speak *good* German.	c	healthy
4	You speak English *well*.	d	fluently
5	He was sick, but he is *well* now.	e	quick
6	The player kicked the ball *very hard*.	f	quickly
7	I *hardly* know her.	g	stupid
8	I thought the exam was very *hard*.	h	with great force
9	You're behaving in a very *silly* way.	i	difficult

B **Answer the questions.**

1 In which sentences are *fast* and *hard* adjectives? In which are they adverbs?

2 What is the difference between *hard* and *hardly*?

3 What structure do we use instead of an adverb if an adjective ends in *-ly*?

4 What are the two meanings of *well* in sentences 4 and 5?

3 Comparisons quiz

You have one minute to complete the following task.

Look at the list of adjectives and adverbs. Write A, B or C next to each word depending on whether:

A they are compared using *-er, -est* (*cheap, cheaper, cheapest*)

B they are compared using *more ... than, the most* (*more interesting, the most interesting*)

C they are irregular (*good, better, best*).

cheap *A*	interesting *B*	good *C*
well	badly	soft
old	hot	famous
easy	pretty	comfortable
fast	bad	modern

In which of these words does the spelling change in the comparative forms?

4 Practice

Read these sentences comparing different makes of jeans. Then make comparisons about the ideas below.

Paul Smith jeans are by far the most expensive.

Lee Cooper jeans are slightly cheaper than Replay jeans.

Replay jeans cost a lot, but they don't cost as much as Paul Smith jeans.

1 three sportsmen / sportswomen. How good are they?

2 three TV programmes. How interesting are they?

3 three singers or groups. How much do you like them?

4 three film stars. How attractive are they?

WP 1

5 Key word transformations

Use the word in bold to complete the second sentence so that it has a similar meaning to the first. Write between two and five words.

Example:

0 Tom has almost no friends at all.

hardly

Tom has ..*hardly any*.. friends at all.

> **Read both sentences first, then look at the word in bold. Think about the meaning and the grammar. Use this checklist:**
>
> 1 What other words do I need?
>
> 2 Do the words fit in grammatically?
>
> 3 Does the second sentence have a similar meaning to the first?
>
> 4 Have I got too many words? NB: contractions like *don't, wouldn't*, etc. count as two words.

1 John is a really good guitarist and he writes his own songs too.

plays

John .... and he writes his own songs too.

2 He's a very fast driver, but he hasn't had any accidents.

drives

He ...., but he hasn't had any accidents.

3 The meal wasn't as cheap as I had expected.

more

The meal .... I had expected.

4 My sister can type much faster than me.

quickly

I can't .... my sister.

1 Talking together

A With a partner, label the items using the words in the box.

trainers	socks	boots
tie	skirt	sandals
shirt	cardigan	belt
jumper	jacket	jeans
blouse	trousers	cap

Student A   Compare the people in pictures 1 and 2. Say who they are, what they are doing and what they are wearing.

Student B   Compare the people in pictures 3 and 4. Say who they are, what they are doing and what they are wearing.

> **Paraphrasing**   PHRASE BOX
>
> *The children are all wearing the same kind of clothes for school. (uniform)*

B Decide with your partner which of the things above you would wear if you were going out with your friends for the evening.

2 Taking a long turn

The pictures in the next column show people wearing different clothes. With the same partner, take it in turns to talk for about 30 seconds about the pictures.

> HELP LINE
>
> If you don't know a word, try to paraphrase it. See the example in the Phrase Box.

3 Discussion

Join with another pair of students and take it in turns to ask and answer the questions.

> HELP LINE
>
> Remember that one-word answers such as *Yes* or *No* are not enough.

1 What do children wear to go to school in your country? (Do they wear formal or casual clothes?)

2 Do you think school uniforms are a good or a bad idea? Why?

3 When you buy clothes, what is more important: the price, the style, the colour, the brand name?

WP 2

In pairs, discuss the following statements.

I love fashion and always wear the latest designs.

Models always look great whatever they wear.

It's possible to dress well without spending lots of money.

1 True or false?

You will hear part of a radio programme about London Fashion Week. Read the following statements carefully. Listen and say whether they are true or false.

1   The London Fashion Show only has clothes by British designers.

2   The show takes place every two years.

3   Laura says that colourful clothes are currently in fashion.

Listen again and check your answers.

2 Multiple choice

You will hear part of a radio programme about some women who volunteered to try out some unusual designer clothes. For questions 1–4, choose the best answer A, B or C.

> HELPLINE
>
> Look at the questions quickly and use them to think about what you are going to hear.
>
> The questions will always follow the order of the tape.
>
> You will hear the extracts twice, so do not worry if you cannot answer a question the first time.

1   When Elaine was in the supermarket she thought
   A   she looked taller and more confident.
   B   she might be accused of treating the bird badly.
   C   the bird might die.   [1]

2   What did Elaine find it difficult to do?
   A   stop the bird falling off its perch
   B   reach up to the top shelves
   C   get things from the bottom shelves   [2]

3   Why did it take Julie a long time to reach the bar?
   A   The tail was difficult to pull along the floor.
   B   The dress was very tight around her legs.
   C   People kept stopping her to make comments.   [3]

4   Julie liked the colour of the dress because
   A   it meant that she was less noticeable.
   B   it was a colour that was in fashion.
   C   it made her look more attractive.   [4]

Listen again and check your answers.

In Part 2 of the writing paper, there are different kinds of writing tasks such as letters, stories, reports, articles and compositions. Each unit of the book will focus on a different task and will give you advice about how to plan and write your answer.

Read the question carefully and underline the key words. This will remind you to include all the necessary information when you begin writing.

Always plan your writing carefully by making notes for each paragraph.

Keep your writing simple – you will make fewer mistakes. After you have finished writing, read your work again carefully and check for any spelling, punctuation or grammar mistakes you may have made.

Watch the length. Your aim is to show what you can do accurately within the word limit.

Writing an article (1)

In Part 2 of the writing paper, you may be asked to write a description of a person or place in an article, letter, story or report.

1 Sample task

Read the sample task.

A magazine for young people has asked readers to send in articles describing a person they have known for a long time. Write an **article** (120–180 words) for the magazine.

2 Sample answer

Read the article and underline any adjectives used to describe Jenny.

Jenny – one of my best friends

Jenny Light is one of my oldest friends. We first met when we were at primary school, and we have been friends ever since. Now she is twenty years old and goes to university in Leeds.

Most people would say that she is very attractive. She has a pretty face with beautiful blue eyes and long brown hair. She's a tall slim girl, and looks good in almost anything. During the week when she's at university, she usually wears jeans and an old blue denim jacket or a baggy red Norwegian jumper and a pair of white tennis shoes, but when she goes out at the weekend she likes bright stylish clothes.

She's great fun to be with because her sense of humour is wonderful. However, she is also sensitive and always has time to listen if you have a problem.

We have always been friends, and I am sure that if she gets married or moves away, we will still be close and will see each other regularly.

(173 words)

3 Language study

Adjective order

In order to write a good description, you will need to use adjectives and adverbs effectively.

A Read the following list. Are the adjectives in the correct order? Look back at the sample answer to help you, and correct the order if necessary.

skinny short girl	*short skinny girl*
green lovely eyes	....
short black hair	....
a new cotton green jacket	....
a Swedish big green jumper	....
football black boots	....

B Learn this rhyme to help you remember the order of adjectives.

In my nice big flat
There's an old round box
For my green Swiss hat
And my woolly walking socks

C Using the information in the rhyme, complete the following rule about the order of adjectives. Put the words from the list below into the correct spaces.

country of origin   material
colour   size and weight
age   purpose and power
shape   opinion and general description

Generally, we put adjectives in the following order when using more than one:

1 adjectives of *opinion and general description*

nice, ...

2 adjectives of ....

big, ...

3 adjectives of ....

old, ...

4 adjectives of ....

round, ...

5 adjectives of ....

green, ...

6 adjectives of ....

Swiss, ...

7 adjectives of ....

woolly, ...

8 adjectives of ....

walking (socks), ...

D Now add at least two adjectives of your own to each example above.

E Put the words in brackets into the correct position.

1 She's just bought a .... leather sofa.
(new, horrible)

2 Daffodils are .... flowers. (big, yellow)

3 Shall we go to that .... restaurant tomorrow?
(Italian, nice, little)

4 I'm very pleased with my .... racket.
(tennis, graphite)

5 Boursin is a .... cheese. (small, French, round)

WP 3&4

Articles

Give the article an imaginative title to attract the readers' attention.

Think carefully who will read your article and write (in)formally, as appropriate.

If it is appropriate, add your opinion or a personal comment in the final paragraph to make it more interesting and informal for the readers.

Writing an article

A magazine for young people is running a competition and has asked readers to send in an article about an important person in their life.

Write your **article** for the magazine (120–180 words).

Notes...

Work through the notes and prepare your article.

Paragraph 1

Give some information about the person you have decided to describe. You could include some or all of the following:

- what their name is
- how old they are
- what they do
- when you met
- how you met

Paragraph 2

Say what they look like. You could write about:

- their height
- their build
- their face (eyes, nose, hair, etc.)
- their dress sense

If you use more than one adjective before a noun, take care to put them in the right order.

Paragraph 3

Write about their personality. If you use an adjective describing their character, give an example of what you mean.

Examples:

She is very loyal and would never talk about you behind your back.

He is very romantic and never forgets to send me flowers on my birthday.

Paragraph 4

Conclusion. Write a short sentence summarizing how you feel about the person and why they are important in your life. You could begin with one of these sentences:

I am very glad to have ... as a friend.

(S)he's important to me because ... and I am sure that we will ...

After you have planned each paragraph, write your article and then check your writing carefully for spelling, punctuation and grammar mistakes.

WORD POWER

1 Verbs and adjectives

Verbs of the senses are often followed by adjectives, not adverbs. Complete the sentences with one of the verbs below and an adjective of your choice.

look	seem	sound
taste	feel	smell

1   Are you sure you put sugar in this coffee? It ....

2   Have you met Anna's new boyfriend? He ....

3   I don't think I'd like to meet your boss. From what I've heard, she ....

4   This strawberry ice cream ....

5   She hasn't made any new friends yet, so she's ....

6   You ought to see a doctor if you don't ....

7   You .... Have you had a haircut?

8   The new perfume from Chanel ....

2 Words easily confused

try on, put on, wear, get dressed

Look at these sentences showing how we use these words.

I'm not sure if this shirt will fit me. Can I try it on?

I hate getting dressed on cold mornings – I'd rather stay in bed.

If you're cold, why don't you put on a jumper?

I hate wearing suits.

Complete the following sentences using the words in the correct form.

1   Hurry up, get out of bed and .... or you'll be late for school.

2   I must get some new clothes. I have nothing nice to ....

3   When I .... the jeans in the shop, I thought they looked good.

4   I'd like to have a shower and .... a clean shirt before we go out.

5   I thought the dress you .... at the party was lovely.

6   Here, let me help you .... your coat.

3 Physical descriptions

A   Match the sets of adjectives with the words they can describe.

1	hair colour	a	long, shoulder-length, short
2	hair type	b	curly, wavy, straight
3	height	c	mousy, auburn, ginger
4	hair length	d	expressive, bright, oval
5	age	e	scruffy, smart, casual
6	nose	f	plump, slim, chunky
7	eyes	g	tall, short, tiny
8	general build	h	in his / her early / mid / late twenties, middle-aged, elderly
9	other features	i	pointed, snub, flat
10	overall look	j	a mole, wrinkles, freckles

B   Add two more words to each group. Compare your answers with the rest of the class.

C   Look at these pictures and describe the people using some of the words above.

4 Describing personalities

A   Look through the list of adjectives that can be used to describe personalities. Next to each word, write A, B or C to show whether your ideal partner in life:

A   would need to be like this.

B   could be like this, but it's not important.

C   should definitely not be like this.

sensitive	funny	sensible
aggressive	intelligent	independent
hard-working	honest	ambitious
romantic	attractive	jealous

B   In pairs, describe someone famous. Talk about their physical appearance, character and personality. See if your partner can guess who you are talking about.

UNIT 1 ➤ LET'S REFLECT!

1 Multiple-choice cloze

Read the text and decide which answer A, B, C or D best fits each space.

Example: (0) A

* the right image

People's choice in clothes has always helped to (0)......... A .... others an impression of who they are, but (1).................... , a whole new industry has developed to help people create the (2).................... they want to present. Nowadays it is becoming more and (3).................... common for politicians and business people to hire professional image consultants to help them look their (4).................... .

The advice that image consultants give depends (5).................... what the client wants to look (6).................... and who he or she wants to appeal to. For example, an ambitious business executive will be advised to wear a smart dark (7).................... ; a politician who wants to appeal to young voters might be told to wear something (8).................... formal, such as jeans and a baseball cap.

TV appearances require special care. There are some patterns, for example checks, that must not be (9).................... because they can interfere with the picture. Both men and women also need advice on (10).................... , which is essential because of the bright studio lights.

0 A give	B lend	C put	D have
1 A newly	B recently	C hardly	D quickly
2 A image	B view	C picture	D sight
3 A even	B more	C also	D very
4 A least	B worst	C most	D best
5 A for	B from	C on	D about
6 A as	B for	C so	D like
7 A cloth	B suit	C trousers	D trainers
8 A less	B minus	C without	D fewer
9 A dressed	B tried	C put	D worn
10 A take-up	B set-up	C make-up	D run-up

(10 marks)

2 Key word transformations

Use the word in bold to complete the second sentence so that it has a similar meaning to the first. Write between two and five words.

1 What sort of weather did you have on holiday?
   like
   What .... on your holiday?

2 She gave a friendly smile and waved goodbye.
   way
   She .... and waved goodbye.

3 I am not very good at skiing, but I'd like to learn.
   not
   I do ...., but I'd like to learn.

4 My brother works harder than I do.
   as
   I do .... my brother.

5 The exam wasn't as hard as I had expected.
   than
   The exam .... I had expected.

(10 marks)

3 Spot the mistake

Correct each of the following sentences.

1 I didn't know you could speak English so good.
2 I've never been to India. How is it like?
3 I'm not very interested for fashion.
4 I'm tired because I've been working too hardly.
5 It can be dangerous if you too slowly drive.
6 He's quite thin because he hardly doesn't eat anything.
7 Manchester is much more bigger than Cardiff.
8 The film wasn't as good than the book.
9 My sister's the girl over there with dark long hair.
10 There's something wrong with this wine – it tastes horribly.

(20 marks)

4 Vocabulary

Complete the sentences with a suitable adjective. The first letter of each answer is given.

1 Alex's husband is terribly j.............. He gets upset if he sees her talking to another man.
2 Jack is so f.............. He always makes me laugh.
3 Hassan is a s.............. child. He would never do anything dangerous or risky.
4 Hilary is a very a.............. politician. She wants to be Prime Minister one day.
5 Laura likes reading r.............. novels about falling in love and getting married.
6 Simon is an a.............. man. He's always shouting at people and fighting.
7 I know Jack is h.............. and would always tell the truth.
8 My brother's very i.............. He'll probably be a university professor or a doctor.
9 I like Georgia because she's s.............. and cares about how people feel.
10 Caroline is certainly a.............. enough to be a model.

(10 marks)

Total: 50 marks

LEAD-IN ▶

A In pairs, ask each other these questions and note down your partner's answers by putting ticks (✓) in the boxes.

	YES	NO
1 Do you believe in ghosts?	☐	☐
2 Do you know anybody who has seen a ghost?	☐	☐
3 Do you know of any ghosts in your area?	☐	☐
4 Would you like to see a ghost?	☐	☐

B Answer these questions.

1 What does *haunted* mean?

2 What kinds of places are usually haunted?

1 Multiple matching

A You are going to read a text about some ghosts that are said to haunt some places in Britain. Read the text quickly and find the places and ghosts on the map of Britain.

B Answer questions 1–12 by choosing from sections A–O of the article. Some of the sections may be used more than once.

> **HELPLINE**
>
> Look for clues like the ones in the two examples, then underline the words in the article and in the question which help you to find the answers.

Examples: Which section tells you that:

you have <u>more chance</u> of <u>seeing a ghost</u> here? | 0 | B |

(In the article, Section B mentions England's *most haunted* house.)

these ghosts are <u>not British</u>? | 00 | M |

(In the article, Section M mentions *Roman soldiers*.)

Which section tells you that:

this ghost is religious?	1	
this ghostly vision carries one passenger?	2	
this ghost played a stringed instrument?	3	
this ghost wears a pleasant perfume?	4	
this ghost is enormous?	5	

former employees haunt these places?	6		7	

you are treated kindly by these ghosts?	8	
this ghostly image is a ship?	9	
you have to go underground to see this solitary ghost?	10	
this ghost was a construction engineer?	11	
this ghost was a monarch?	12	

C Which of the ghosts do you think is the most interesting? Why?

Things that go BUMP in the night...

Are you interested in ghosts? Do you need any advice about where to find them? Here's some information about ghosts in Britain. We're not promising you'll find any ghostly activities, but if you have time, you might like to carry out your own investigation!

2 Vocabulary

Divide into pairs. One student looks in the article for the people described in Task 1, the other for the places described in Task 2. When you have finished, ask your partner to answer your questions.

Examples:

What do you call someone who plays a violin?

What do you call a place where things are kept underground?

A Glasgow
The Theatre Royal is haunted by the spirit of a cleaning lady, Nora.

B Preston
The 13th-century Chingle Hall, three miles north west of Preston, is said to be England's <u>most haunted</u> house.

C Manchester
The Grey Man of the Great Western Hotel wears a grey sweater and is apparently most often seen in the cellars.

D Birmingham
The beautiful Jacobean mansion of Aston Hall has a heap of ghosts due to a murderous 17th-century owner. With any luck, you'll see a housekeeper in a green dress with a white collar, a grey lady and a servant who died in the attic.

E Gloucester
People say the courteous spirits at the Bishop's House help visitors on with their coats.

F Swansea
The Grand Theatre has a White Lady who leaves a scent of violets. She is thought to be the spirit of a young actress who left the theatre to board the ill-fated *Titanic*.

G Cardiff
Cardiff Castle has a giant ghost that is 3 metres tall.

H Bristol
Leigh Woods, by Clifton Gorge, is said to be haunted by Clifton Suspension Bridge builder, Isambard Kingdom Brunel.

I Torquay
Torre Abbey has the ghost of a brightly-lit coach and horses, driving a smiling Lady Cary down the avenue.

J Brighton
Brighton's seaside is home to the spectral 10th-century galley, the *Nicholas*, which sank with all hands (and pilgrim passengers) returning from Constantinople.

K Eastbourne
The Devonshire Park Theatre is haunted by a violinist in evening dress.

L Balcombe Tunnel
This Tunnel is haunted by four soldiers killed there during the First World War.

M York
The Treasurer's House is haunted by <u>Roman soldiers</u>.

N Edinburgh
A demonic drummer has banged about the castle since the 17th century and Holyroodhouse has the majestic apparition of Mary, Queen of Scots.

O Cupar
The Royal Hotel is haunted by a hooded monk.

TASK 1

Find words for someone:

1 who plays a violin.
2 who fights in wars.
3 who possesses something.
4 who plays a loud instrument.
5 who makes a religious journey.
6 who constructs something.
7 who can be the ruler of a country.
8 who stays in your house for a short time.
9 who is a religious person (two answers).
10 who works in someone's house (three answers).

TASK 2

Find words for a place:

1 where things are kept underground.
2 which is an underground passage.
3 where people with a lot of money live (three answers).
4 where a royal family might live.
5 where plays are performed.
6 where religious people live.
7 at the top of a house.
8 where people often go on holiday.
9 which is covered with trees.
10 which is wide and lined with trees or buildings.

---

3 Language study

Uncountable nouns

The words in the right-hand column of the table are uncountable nouns. Select the most suitable combination of words to complete the sentences below.

give (sb) have hear ask (sb) for tell (sb)	some a piece of a bit of a stroke of a lot of	luck advice information news

1 Can you .... me .... about train times to Edinburgh?

2 I want to .... you .... very exciting .... I'm getting married!

3 Let me .... you .... Never go into that house alone. It's haunted.

4 You'll have to .... the receptionist for .... about meal times in the hotel.

5 You can .... on this local radio station.

6 I've just .... I've won a prize!

LEAD-IN ►

In small groups, ask each other questions to find out:

1 what time everyone goes to bed during the week/at weekends.
2 who needs a lot of/not much sleep.
3 who is a light/heavy sleeper.

WP 1

1 Open cloze

A Read the article about sleep. Take no notice of the spaces.

Lack of sleep

Not getting enough sleep is apparently one of the most worrying problems of the late twentieth century. Lack of sleep makes us tired at work and bad-tempered (0) ....*at*......... home; it causes accidents, makes us feel depressed and damages our health. In (1) .... recent survey, 82% of shift workers said they did (2) .... get enough sleep and 72% of train drivers said they sometimes fell asleep while driving their train. According (3) .... experts, people are now getting about 1.5 hours less sleep per night (4) .... they used to. Studies show that most people need (5) .... seven and eight hours sleep a night but evidence suggests that they are certainly not getting it. There are many reasons for this: some shops stay open 24 hours a day; TV and radio keep us awake; life itself is busier. The streets (6) .... I live are full of traffic (7) .... three in the morning, and after that you can still hear some noise. On the other hand, perhaps sleeping is like eating and drinking. A certain amount is necessary but we can easily have more than (8) .... need. Just because we choose to sleep (9) .... hour or so longer than our daily average amount, for example when we are (10) .... holiday, it does not mean that we really need that extra sleep.

B Read the article again and work out what the missing words are.

Example: (0) at

> Look at the space first and decide what kind of word you think fits in grammatically, e.g. a noun, a verb, a preposition.
> Next, make sure that the meaning of the word is correct.
> Look at what comes both before and after the space.

Now look at page 170 and see if your answers are correct.

Present tenses

1 Uses

A Read these sentences and underline the verbs. Which tenses are used?

1 Most people sleep for about six or seven hours a night.
2 Some university students are doing research into sleeping habits.
3 Richard works at the local hospital.
4 Richard is talking to a patient now.

B Which sentence uses a particular tense to show that:

a this happens regularly or is always true?
b this is happening at this moment?
c this is happening now, but over a longer period of time?

2 Simple present or present continuous?
watch, listen, look

Read these two sentences.

My brother <u>watches</u> the news every night on TV.
The children <u>are watching</u> a cartoon on TV at the moment.

Put the verbs *listen* and *look* in the correct tense in these sentences. You will need to add an extra word.

1 Amy usually .... the news on the radio in the morning.
2 Sam .... a concert on the radio at the moment.
3 My sister always .... unusual things to bring back when she goes on holiday.
4 We .... Alima's purse. She can't find it anywhere.

WP 2

3 Verbs not normally used in the present continuous tense

like, need, want, prefer, hate, seem

A Make questions using the prompts in 1–6.

1 foreign food/like?
2 need/take/go camping?
3 want/do/after the lesson?
4 season/prefer? Why?
5 there/anything/really hate/do?
6 this exercise/seem difficult?

B In pairs, ask and answer these questions.

Example:

1 *What kind of foreign food do you like?*
  I love Italian and Chinese food.

4 Verbs of physical perception

Smell, see, taste, hear are often used with the modal *can.*

In pairs, ask and answer questions using the prompts below and one of these verbs. The answers are given below in the word-line.

Example:

What can you usually hear near a busy road?
The noise of traffic.

1 .... often .... when it's raining and the sun is shining?

2 .... always .... when a plane is taking off or landing?

3 .... usually .... when something is on fire?

4 .... often .... in a school playground?

5 .... sometimes .... if a cooker is not switched off properly?

6 .... sometimes .... when you eat French food?

7 .... always .... when you're at a disco?

8 .... usually .... after a flash of lightning?

children's voices gas the noise of traffic a rainbow garlic thunder loud music an aircraft engine burning

5 Night workers

The people in the pictures are all working at night. Make sentences like the ones in the example for each picture.

Example:

This woman is a fire officer. She fights fires for a living. At the moment she is reading a newspaper.

6 Dreamland

A In small groups, find out:

- how many of your partners can/can't remember their dreams
- if anyone dreams in colour
- if anyone has nightmares
- if anyone sleepwalks
- if anyone has the same dream over and over again
- if anyone ever dreams they are:
  1 falling   3 trying to escape   5 ill
  2 hungry   4 unable to speak   6 swimming

B What do you think the dreams in 1–6 mean?

Example:

If you dream you are falling, you are probably in a difficult situation at the moment but you will be all right in the end.

Look at page 170 and read the interpretations.

Look at page 170 and read the interpretations.

1 Taking a long turn

A These words could all be used to describe the pictures on the right. In pairs, decide which words can be used with each picture.

indoors	display
telescope	deafening
spectacular	exciting
bedroom	peaceful
open-air	fireworks

WB 3

B With the same partner, take it in turns to talk for about 30 seconds about one of the pictures on the right. Talk about the people in the picture. Say what they are doing.

> Do not interrupt when your partner is speaking.

2 Talking about yourself

Here are some other kinds of evening entertainment. Tell your partner if you like going to places or events like these. Use the expressions in the Phrase Box below.

> Give extra information if you can. Say why you like or dislike doing something.

- discos
- barbecues
- restaurants
- open-air cinemas
- beach parties
- open-air theatres

Expressing likes and dislikes

Personally, …

😊 *I really enjoy …(-ing).*
I love …(-ing).

🙂 *I quite like …(-ing).*
I don't mind …(-ing).

🙁 *I don't really like …(-ing).*
I don't find …(-ing) interesting.

3 Talking together

A Look at these pictures of people doing different activities at night. In small groups, describe what the people are doing. Remember to use the present continuous.

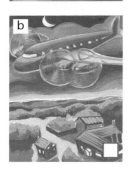

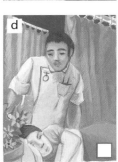

B Which of the activities above do you think are dangerous, frightening or difficult? Say why. Use the expressions in the Phrase Box to find out what other members of your group think.

Asking what your partner thinks
What / How about you? What do you think?

You will hear four of the people in the pictures in the Talking Together task on page 20. Number the pictures in the order you hear them mentioned.

Which words helped you decide?

1 Multiple choice

> In the exam, the instructions, questions and options are read out on the tape.
>
> Each question is followed by three options – A, B or C.
>
> While you listen, read the questions and options carefully. Think about what you will hear.
>
> As the extracts are played, listen carefully for key words which will help you to choose the correct option.

Listen to the four speakers again and tick (✓) how you think they feel. As in the lead-in, note down the words which help you decide. You will hear the three options on the tape.

Example:

1   a   I'm afraid.

b   I feel terrified.

c   I feel a little afraid.

C is the correct answer because the speaker says:

I'm not really afraid ... I still feel a bit worried.

2   a   I find the work exhausting.
b   I'm used to the work now.
c   I enjoy the work.

3   a   I really enjoy driving at night.
b   I find driving at night difficult.
c   Night driving isn't too bad.

4   a   I feel lucky to have this job.
b   I don't find the job interesting.
c   I'm always short of time in this job.

Listen again and check your answers.

WP 4

2 Everyday expressions

A   The speakers on the tape use these everyday expressions. Match the explanations 1–3 with the underlined expressions in a–c below.

1   hopefully

2   and I mean that

3   really

a   *... and I'm not very good at it, <u>I can tell you</u>.*

b   *... it gets a bit boring, <u>actually</u>.*

c   *But, <u>with any luck</u>, nothing too serious'll happen ...*

B   Use the expressions to complete the sentences below.

1   Well, ... I don't really enjoy being out on the road at night.

2   If we can leave on time, ..., we'll be home by midnight.

3   Driving in the fog and rain is a dangerous business, ...

3 Vocabulary

A   These words appear on the tape. Match them with the explanations on the right.

1   *have time on your hands*   a   continue to pay attention

2   *tend to*   b   do something without hurrying

3   *take your time*   c   be bored or have nothing to do

4   *keep your mind on*   d   do something often or normally

B   In pairs, ask and answer these questions.

1   Do you ever find yourself with time on your hands? When?

2   What do you tend to do if you feel bored?

3   Why is it important to keep your mind on the road when you are driving?

4   When is it often a good idea to take your time?

4 Word stress

These words appear in the speaking and listening frames. Read them out and mark the main stress.

Example: afráid

alone	worried	spectacular	serious
frightening	boring	dangerous	difficult
deafening	tiring	peaceful	deserted
interesting	exhausting		

Writing a report (1)

In Part 2 of the writing paper, you may be asked to write a report. It is important to remember who you are writing it for and why. This will affect your writing style and your choice of information.

1 Sample task

Read the sample task and answer the questions.

You have a part-time job in a local Tourist Information office. Your boss has asked you to visit a new cinema and restaurant which have both opened recently in your area and to write a **report** on them (120–180 words).

Task interpretation

1 Who are you writing this report for?
2 What will the two main sections of the report contain?
3 Which of the following pieces of information would be useful for your boss?
   a   the name and location of the cinema
   b   ticket prices
   c   what you thought of the film you saw
   d   what the cinema is like inside
   e   the name and location of the restaurant
   f   exactly what you had to eat
   g   good and bad points of the restaurant
   h   opening times and the day of week they close
4 Is there any other information which might be useful?

2 Sample answer

Read the report and answer the questions.

Analysis

1 What do you notice about the layout of the report?
2 Would it be better to begin with *Dear Sir ...* and to write your address at the top?
3 In which paragraphs does the writer present factual information?
4 In which paragraph does the writer express an overall opinion?
5 Is the language formal or informal?

Here is my report giving details of the new Plaza Cinema and Don Antonio's Restaurant.

1 Plaza Cinema, 22 Harwell Avenue

This five-screen cinema complex is situated in the centre. It is easy to reach by bus, and is also close to a public car park. The five screens are all fitted with stereo sound and comfortably seat up to 180 people. The programme is changed on Thursdays. Details of current programmes are printed in the Evening Post every day or can be obtained directly from the cinema.

2 Don Antonio's Restaurant, 199 Canal Street

This new restaurant is very close to the cinema and serves a good range of traditional Italian food. It has tables outside, and the service is fast and friendly. The menu caters for all tastes, including vegetarians. The average cost of a meal per person is £10. It is open from midday to 2am every day except Mondays.

The best features of the cinema complex are its stereo sound and choice of films. The restaurant is friendly, good value and convenient for cinema-goers.

(178 words)

3 Language study

Formal and informal suggestions

Look at the following sentences.

1 I suggest that you have dinner at Don Antonio's Restaurant.

2 I would recommend having dinner at Don Antonio's.

3 Why don't you have dinner at Don Antonio's?

A **Which two sentences would be more suitable in a formal piece of writing?**

B **Rewrite the following sentences in a more formal way, using the verb in brackets.**

1 Why don't you go to the new cinema complex? (suggest)

....

2 Why don't you go to Don Antonio's? (recommend)

....

3 Why don't you try the vegetarian dish? (suggest)

....

4 Why don't you have some Italian ice-cream for dessert? (recommend)

....

4 Writing task

Reports

Before you begin to write, think carefully who you are writing this report for. This will affect how and what you write.

You will need to include some facts and if appropriate some of your own suggestions.

Keep it simple. The right layout will help you to do this. Using numbered, lettered or bulleted paragraphs would make it clearer as well as simpler.

(Example: 1 ... 2 ... 3 ..., A ... B ... C ... or • ... • ... • ...).

Remember to include a short introduction stating what the report is about and a conclusion making recommendations as appropriate.

Writing a report

Four players from the Under-16 England tennis team are coming to your town for a match. The tour organizer has asked you to write a report suggesting somewhere to have dinner and a suitable evening activity.

Write your **report** (120–180 words).

Notes...

Work through the notes and prepare your report. You could write about real places you know or invent imaginary ones.

Paragraph 1

Write a brief introduction saying what the report is about.

Include a title to introduce the first part of your report.

Paragraph 2

Describe the restaurant, saying what it is called, what sort of food it serves, what the atmosphere is like and why the team would enjoy eating there.

Give some facts about the restaurant. You could include details about:

- exactly where the restaurant is
- how to get there
- what time it opens and closes
- whether it is closed on any day of the week
- how much an average meal costs per head (per person)
- whether there is a set menu
- whether they need to reserve a table.

Paragraph 3

Give a description of the evening activity, e.g. cinema, disco, theatre, you have chosen. When choosing the activity, remember that the members of the team are under 16. Give a reason why you think the team would enjoy this activity.

Give some facts about the activity. You could include details about:

- exactly where the activity takes place
- how to get there
- what time it starts or finishes
- how much it costs to get in
- who to contact (if anyone).

Paragraph 4

You could add a personal touch in your conclusion. Do not be too informal, though.

Remember to check your writing for spelling, punctuation and grammar mistakes.

WORD**POWER**

1 Talking about time

In pairs, ask each other questions to complete the missing information.

1 The time now:

2 The date:

	DAY	
date	month	year

3 Dawn is when the sun ....

4 Dusk is when the sun ....

5 12.01 am is just after ....

6 Monday to Friday are known as .... days.

7 Saturday and Sunday are known as the ....

8 There are .... days in most months of the year but in February there are usually ....

9 There are usually .... days in one year but every .... years is a leap year.

10 The names of the four seasons are ....
....

11 How long is a fortnight? ....

12 Which expression in italic below means:
   - being there at the correct time?
   - sometimes?
   - arriving before something starts?

   a My girlfriend is never *on time*.
   b We arrived just *in time* to catch the train.
   c *At times* I feel very sad.

2 Phrasal verbs with *look*

A In this unit you have come across the verbs *look for* and *look at*. What do these verbs mean? Choose the most suitable word to go with the verb *look* to form a phrasal verb in 1–5 below.

1 If you don't know the meaning of *haunt*, you can look it *round/after/up* in the dictionary.

2 Do look *up/after/in* and see us next time you are in the area.

3 One of the most difficult jobs in the world is looking *into/forward to/after* a new baby.

4 The police are looking *up/after/into* the strange case of the haunted house.

5 John is really looking *into/up/forward* to his holiday in America.

B Now match the verbs with the explanations in a–e.

a feel excited about

b visit (often unexpectedly)

c investigate

d search for information, e.g. in a book

e take care of

3 Describing location

A Match the prepositions with the expressions.

	the top
in	the background
at	the middle
on	the left-hand side
	the bottom right-hand corner
	the corner

B Now draw a box and draw five different objects in it. Do not show anyone your drawing. When you have finished, take it in turns to tell a partner to draw the objects you have chosen in the same place in an empty box. Check that your partner has drawn the objects in the correct place.

4 Words easily confused

Put the words in the correct sentence.

1 **afraid/worried**

   I'm .... about my exams.

   I'm .... of spiders.

2 **boring/bored**

   Bill thinks tennis is ....

   Bill gets .... when he watches tennis.

3 **actually/now**

   Q: What on earth are those children doing .... ?

   A: .... , I think they're helping Jim to tidy up.

4 **with any luck/luckily**

   .... the exam won't be too difficult.

   .... the exam wasn't too difficult.

5 **sleepy/asleep**

   I always feel .... after a big meal.

   I always fall .... when I watch the news on TV.

6 **excited/nervous**

   Most people are a bit .... about going to the dentist.

   Most people get .... before going on holiday.

UNIT 2 ➤ LET'S REFLECT!

1 Open cloze

Read the text and think of one word which best fits each space.

Example: (0) one

THE BIG SLEEP

CAROL suffers from narcolepsy, (0)......*one*...... of the most dangerous sleep problems people can have but fortunately one of (1) .... rarest. According to experts, sufferers suddenly fall into (2) .... deep sleep at any time. Even just laughing at a joke can make them drop off to sleep! Now twenty, and studying geography at university, Carol never thought that (3) .... was much wrong with her.

'(4) .... night I go to sleep straight away but I wake (5) .... at least five or six times – usually when I'm worried (6) .... something.' If cases like Carol's go without treatment, patients can be in real danger. About thirty percent (7) .... the cases of people with unusual sleep habits are not due to medical problems. Perhaps they (8) .... not getting enough sleep because there is too much noise in the place where (9) .... sleep, or the lights are too bright, or they are not sleeping at the right times. Perhaps, as in Carol's case, medical treatment is necessary, since there (10) .... usually a cure available.

(20 marks)

2 Key word transformations

Use the word in bold to complete the second sentence so that it has a similar meaning to the first. Write between two and five words.

1 I'm interested in finding out something about fire-fighting.
   give
   Can you .... fire-fighting?

2 I'd like you to advise me what to do.
   advice
   Could you .... about what to do?

3 I hate to watch late night films on TV.
   stand
   I .... late night films on TV.

4 I never have enough time.
   short
   I .... time.

5 My sister's certain that ghosts don't exist.
   believe
   My sister .... ghosts.

(10 marks)

3 Spot the mistake

Correct each of the following sentences.

1 In some countries, it is a good luck if a black cat walks in front of you.
2 I had some stroke of luck yesterday.
3 The children are watching TV every evening from five to six o'clock.
4 Could you give me an information about trains to the north?
5 Richard studies English at university at the moment.
6 We had a terrible weather on our trip to the seaside.
7 The children are liking to go for walks in a countryside.
8 Some people is very frightened of ghosts.
9 Every night we are hearing the sound of the traffic on the road nearby.
10 It's 9 o'clock – time for a news on the television.

(10 marks)

4 Vocabulary

Write a word from this unit which means:

1 a person who is receiving medical treatment
2 a bad dream
3 not interesting
4 tables, chairs, etc.
5 visited regularly by a ghost.

(10 marks)

Total: 50 marks

3 Getting away

FRAME 1 ▶ READING

LEAD-IN

A Which of these would be your ideal place to live? Number them in order of preference.

B Is there another place you would prefer to live? Give reasons for your choice.

1 Multiple choice

A You are going to read a text about a man called Andrew Martin who has lived alone on a desert island for a long time. Read the text quickly and answer the following questions. Remember it is not necessary to understand every word.

1 What does Andrew Martin feel about the island where he lives?

2 What does the writer think of the island?

B For questions 1–6, choose the best answer from A, B, C or D. The first one has been done as an example.

> Multiple-choice questions focus on understanding specific details of a text, including the meaning of certain words and phrases. You may sometimes be tested on your understanding of the text as a whole.
>
> Always look very carefully at the first part of the question as well as the four options. Underline the part of the text that you think is important in finding the right answer.

1 It was hard to arrange a meeting with Andrew because
   A he rarely answered the phone.
   B he lived a long way away.
   C he did not like visitors.
   D his post was not delivered very often.

D is correct because the text says someone who has no telephone and only gets letters every three months …

Now look for the answers to questions 2–6 in the same way.

2 Andrew first came to Percy Island
   A because he had heard it was for sale.
   B while he was on his way to visit his sister.
   C because he wanted to see a friend.
   D while he was learning to sail.

3 Why was the writer worried?
   A There were spiders in the bedrooms.
   B The house was surrounded by animals.
   C There were lots of snakes on the island.
   D The toilet was outside the house.

4 Life on the island is not very relaxing for Andrew because
   A he knows it is unsafe to swim in the sea.
   B he spends most of his time running the small shop.
   C he has to work very hard to survive.
   D he gets large numbers of visitors.

5 What does the word *it* in line 89 refer to?
   A the hard work
   B living by himself
   C feeling free
   D what happened

6 When the writer left the island,
   A he was glad to leave.
   B he wanted to go back again.
   C he was tired of being alone.
   D he was nervous about the flight.

When you have finished, compare your answers with your partner. If you have different answers, compare the parts of the text that you underlined and try to agree on an answer.

If you lived on a desert island like Percy Island, would you like Andrew Martin's lifestyle? Why? Why not?

UNIT 3

DESERT ISLAND DREAM

Andrew Martin has been living totally alone on a desert island off the coast of Australia for over thirty years. It wasn't easy to set up a meeting with someone who has no telephone and only gets letters every three months, but we finally got in touch and he invited me to visit.

As the helicopter approached, I found myself looking down on the kind of place that people dream of. Percy Island, which is covered in tropical jungle, has golden beaches lined with coconut trees and is set in clear blue sea. When we landed, Andrew Martin was there to greet me, wearing only an old pair of swimming trunks and flip-flops.

As we walked to the house, I found out more about him. After visiting his sister in Japan thirty years ago, he travelled to Australia, where he bought a boat. While a friend was teaching him to sail, they stopped by chance at Percy Island, which was for sale for £16,000. Andrew, whose boat was worth the same amount, immediately decided to buy it. Originally he planned to stay for a few months and sell it at a profit, but he found that he wanted to stay. Now, even though he could probably sell the island for £20 million, he is not interested. 'It's too good to sell to a developer who is going to treat it as some kind of toy. To me it's like the most precious jewel in the world.'

After a forty-five minute walk through the dense jungle, we got to the house, where we were surrounded at once by dogs, chickens, geese and peacocks. The building was not much more than an old wooden hut with a tin roof. He showed me round, and gave me time to unpack. The room which he gave me had a marvellous view, but the first thing I noticed was the largest spider I had ever seen. I tried to stay calm, but I got really nervous when I also learned that the whole island was full of poisonous snakes. Andrew told me not to worry. He said that the only ones I was likely to meet were the boa constrictors that hung in the trees near the outside toilet.

Over the next few days, I began to see what it was really like to live on a desert island. Percy Island is as beautiful as any exotic holiday advertisement, but Andrew does not spend his time sunbathing and swimming; it is much too dangerous to go in the sea, which is full of sharks and stonefish. He has to work more than most people to provide the things he needs, and makes a little money by selling fruit to boats that come to visit from time to time.

He says he never planned to live alone, but 'it just happened that way'. Now he is used to it, and does not miss other people at all. What he enjoys is the feeling of being completely free. Nobody can tell him what to do, and if he does not like anyone who comes to the island, he asks them to leave.

On my last day, as I sat on the beach waiting for the flight back to the mainland, I was desperately looking forward to getting back to the comforts of modern life. It was a great relief when the helicopter landed and took me away. Soon Percy Island was just another green dot in the deep blue sea. To me, it did not feel at all as if I was leaving paradise; it was like being rescued from hell.

2 Vocabulary

A Find a word or phrase in the text that means:

1 made contact
2 what a man wears to swim
3 casual shoes made of rubber or plastic
4 a valuable stone
5 a small wooden building
6 to take things out of a suitcase
7 unusual or interesting because it is foreign
8 a journey by air.

B Now use some of the words and phrases to complete the sentences, making any changes that are necessary.

1 If you take Concorde, the .... from London to New York only takes four hours.

2 Bring your .... in case you want to have a swim.

3 You must .... if you come to Brighton. I'd love to see you.

4 When I get to the hotel, I'd like to .... and get some clean clothes from my case.

5 We'd love to go somewhere .... for our holiday, but we can't really afford it.

WP 1

GRAMMAR ZOOM

LEAD-IN ►

Look at the photograph of the rickshaw and discuss these questions.

1 In which countries would you expect to find this kind of transport?

2 What are the advantages and disadvantages of travelling by rickshaw?

1 Word formation

A Read the text and answer these questions.

1 Where did the doctor get his idea from?

2 What do people like about travelling in rickshaws?

B Use the word given in capitals at the end of each line to form a word that fits in the space in the same line.

Example: (0) enterprising

In this word-building task, always read the whole text first as this will help you to get an idea of what it is about and what kind of words are needed.

You need to spell the word correctly each time.

SEE YORK by rickshaw...

An (0) *enterprising* doctor who works in York has set up a	ENTERPRISE
company which takes (1)............................ round the city in	TOUR
rickshaws. He got the idea after reading an (2)...........................	INTEREST
article about the benefits of cycling (3)............................ ; he	REGULAR
remembered the rickshaws which he had (4)............................	RECENT
seen in Nepal, and thought this might be an (5)............................	ENJOY
way of getting fit.	
The scheme has been (6)............................ ; and the	SUCCESS
passengers who he takes round like visiting places which you can't	
(7)............................ get to by car. He has now recruited two	NORMAL
(8)............................ to help him, and plans to take on some more.	STUDY

C Would you like to do this as a holiday job? Why? Why not?

Defining relative clauses

1 *Who* or *which*?

A Read this relative clause taken from the reading text:

... who works in York ... (line 1)

This is an example of a defining relative clause as it helps to define the word *doctor* and gives us more information about the doctor.

B Read the text again and answer the questions.

1 Underline four more examples of defining relative clauses in the text about rickshaws.

2 Circle the word that each relative clause is defining.

3 What relative pronouns were used (a) to refer to people? (b) to refer to things?

4 Which of these pronouns could we miss out? Why?

5 In which sentence could we use *whom*?

6 There is one word that can always be used instead of *who*, *whom* and *which* in sentences like these. What is it?

C Join these sentences together using *who* or *which*.

1 We went round the city with a guide. I couldn't understand her at all.

2 Last year we stayed in a hotel. A friend of ours had recommended it.

3 I've got a villa. You can use it whenever you like.

4 I'll give you the number of a travel agent. I know him.

5 I've bought a guide book. It has a list of good restaurants.

6 We went on an excursion. It lasted all day.

In which of these sentences could you use *that*?

In which sentences could you omit the relative pronoun?

Remember not to repeat the pronoun after *who*, *which* or *that*.

Let's see the film that Peter recommended.

Not: *Let's see the film that Peter recommended it.*

2 Where

A Read these sentences and answer the question.

The hotel where we stayed was marvellous.

The hotel that we stayed in was marvellous.

Why can't you use the word *where* in the second sentence?

B Tick (✓) the sentences that are right and correct the ones that are incorrect.

Remember that *where* means *in which* or *to which*.

1 The place where we went to last year for our holiday was wonderful.

2 The hotel that we stayed was just next to the beach.

3 The rooms that we slept in were air-conditioned.

4 The place where we spent most of our time was the swimming pool.

5 The restaurant that we usually had dinner had a marvellous view.

3 Whose

A We use *whose* to show possession. Read the sentences and answer these questions.

I gave a lift to a friend. Her car had broken down.

I gave a lift to a friend whose car had broken down.

Which person does *whose* refer to?

Which possession does it also refer to?

B Match the sentences 1–4 with the appropriate endings in the box. Join the sentences together with *whose*.

1 We stayed in Greece with some friends …

2 Our guide was a young man …

3 If you want cheap tickets, I'll talk to a woman I know …

4 My brother stayed with a landlady …

a Their parents owned a house in Athens.

b Her cooking was wonderful.

c His English was very good.

d Her uncle is a travel agent.

4 Practice

In pairs, make up short dialogues using *who, which, that, where* and *whose*. Think of something better than your partner.

Example:

A: I know someone … who has climbed Mount Everest.

B: Oh, really? Well, I know someone who walked to the North Pole all by herself.

1 Last year we went to a hotel …

2 Last night I went to a party …

3 I once went out with someone …

4 I've got a new computer …

5 My parents are going to buy a house …

Non-defining relative clauses

1 Uses

Read these relative clauses from the reading text in Frame 1 and answer the questions.

a *Percy Island, which is covered in tropical jungle, has golden beaches …*

b *The room which he gave me had a marvellous view …*

1 Does the relative clause in *a* tell us which island we are talking about, or does it give us extra information about it?

2 Does the relative clause in *b* tell us which room had a marvellous view or does it provide extra information about the room?

3 What do you notice about the punctuation of the sentences?

4 In which sentence would it be possible to leave out the relative pronoun or use *that*?

2 Defining or non-defining?

Read these sentences. What are the differences in meaning between them?

1 I like going to Greek islands which have wonderful beaches. (defining)

2 I like going to Greek islands, which have wonderful beaches. (non-defining)

3 Molly's sister who lives in the USA has invited her to stay. (defining)

4 Molly's sister, who lives in the USA, has invited her to stay. (non-defining)

5 The hotel rooms which have a sea view are quite expensive. (defining)

6 The hotel rooms, which have a sea view, are quite expensive. (non-defining)

3 Practice

Rewrite the following sentences using defining or non-defining relative clauses and punctuate them correctly.

1 My grandparents are going on a cruise. They are in their sixties.

2 I got a letter from a friend. I met her on holiday.

3 My sister often goes to Paris. She has a flat there.

4 Eleni teaches us English. She is doing a course in Bath.

5 Have you got that guidebook? I lent it to you.

6 Alima is going to Budapest next week. She is one of my best friends.

4 Wordcomb

In pairs, you are going to give each other clues to complete a puzzle.

Student A Turn to page 170 and follow the instructions.

Student B Turn to page 172 and follow the instructions.

What is the missing word in the box?

1 Talking about yourself

In small groups, tell each other about a holiday you remember.
Say why it was good or not. Talk about some of these points.

the place you went to	the weather	the local transport
the people you went with	the entertainment	the shops
the accommodation	the activities you did	the food

> **HELP LINE**
>
> It is useful to practise talking about different aspects of
> your life. You should be prepared to talk about any of the
> following in the exam: education, work, family, hobbies, home
> town, future plans, etc.

2 Taking a long turn

A With a partner, match either a, b or c with one of the pictures
below. In each group of words, there is one word you do not
need.

1 a motoring holiday   b sightseeing trip   c walking tour
2 a on foot   b by coach   c by plane
3 a passengers   b hikers   c tourists
4 a quiet   b empty   c crowded
5 a the desert   b the jungle   c the countryside

📖 P 263

B With the same partner, take it in turns to talk for about 30
seconds about the pictures.

Student A Compare the people in both pictures. Say what they
are doing.

Student B Compare the places in both pictures. Say where the
people are.

3 Discussion

Join with another pair of students and take
it in turns to ask and answer the questions
below. Use the ideas in the Phrase Box to
help to make what you say clear and
interesting.

1 Why do you think people need holidays?

2 How long do you think school holidays
should be?

3 How many weeks' holiday a year should
people have?

> **Giving extra information**   **PHRASE BOX**
>
> *I think people need a break because …*
>
> *Perhaps holidays should not be too long.*
> *What I mean is …*
>
> *We all need a real holiday. The kind of thing*
> *I'm thinking about is …*

FRAME 4 ▶ LISTENING

LEAD-IN

Look at the categories connected with travel and transport. Complete the word map with as many words as possible for each category.

travelling by land
hire car
train

travelling by air

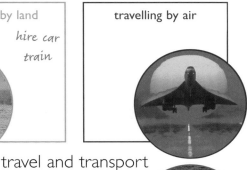

travel and transport

travel agent

jobs in the travel industry

travelling by water

1 Multiple matching A

HELP LINE

There is always a thematic link between the extracts in the Part 3 exercise, unlike the short extracts in Part 1.

Look carefully at the instructions to get an idea of what the extracts will be about. The questions will give you clues about what sort of words to listen for.

A Read the listening task and complete B, C and D before doing the task itself.

You will hear four different people talking about a problem they had while travelling. Decide which of the problems A–E each speaker is talking about. Use the letters only once. There is one extra letter which you do not need to use. There is an example at the beginning (1).

Which speaker:

A	felt seasick ?	Speaker 1	*E* 1
B	had problems on the tube?	Speaker 2	2
C	was involved in a minor accident?	Speaker 3	3
D	had problems at Customs?	Speaker 4	4
E	arrived late at the airport?		

B In the first extract, the speaker talks about arriving late at the airport. Before you listen, think of some words that you may hear, *e.g. check in.*

C Now read and listen to the tapescript below for problem E and underline any words which are related to the topic of airports.

Speaker 1

The only time I had a problem was coming back from Paris last year. I had to wait for ages to get a taxi because there was a bus strike. In the end I got one, but I arrived there when it was meant to take off – so I really thought I was going to miss it. But luckily the plane had been delayed by three hours so I was able to check in without any problems.

D Before you listen to the other extracts, think of words connected with the topics you might hear about on the tape and write them below.

Words connected with

A feeling seasick: .....*ferry, sea, waves, rough*

B the tube: ....

C a minor car accident: ....

D Customs: ....

Listen to the tape twice and decide which problem each speaker is talking about.

 4

2 Multiple matching B

A You will hear four people talking about holidays. Before you listen to the extracts, think of words connected with the topics and write them in the spaces below.

Words connected with

1 cultural activities: ....

2 bad weather: ....

3 spending money: ....

4 a desert island: ....

5 a safari: ....

B You will hear four people talking about holidays they have had. Match the speakers with the statements about their holidays (A–E). Use the letters only once. There is one extra letter which you do not need to use.

Which speaker:

A	was mainly interested in cultural activities?	Speaker 1	1
B	was disappointed by bad weather?	Speaker 2	2
C	spent more money than expected?	Speaker 3	3
D	spent a week on a desert island?	Speaker 4	4
E	went on a safari?		

Listen to the tape again and check your answers.

Writing a transactional letter (1)

Every candidate has to do Part 1 of the writing paper. You will be given several pieces of information, such as adverts, letters or pictures with additional notes to read and will be asked to write a letter based on these in an appropriate style.

1 Sample task

Read the sample task and answer the questions.

You are planning to meet up with an English-speaking friend from another town for a weekend in London. Your friend has asked you to find out about accommodation there. Read the advertisements and the notes you made when you contacted the hotels. Write a **letter** to your friend giving the information about the hotels. Say which one you would prefer and why, and ask your friend to contact you before you make the booking (120–180 words).

Pickwick Hotel

Small family-run hotel in Central London

Close to theatres, major department stores, and tourist sights

10% discount for booking early

All rooms with en-suite bathroom

£50 per person per night including breakfast

Lansdown Hotel

Well-equipped modern hotel in quiet location;

224 rooms

24-hour room service

Frequent buses to central London

35-minute bus ride into centre

£39 per person per night including breakfast

Lansdown Hotel

Task interpretation

1 The sample task asks you to include four main things in your letter. What are they?

2 Do you need to include anything else in your letter?

3 What sort of style would be suitable for a letter like this – formal or informal? How will you make it formal/informal?

2 Sample answer

Read the letter and answer the questions.

Dear Sam,

Thanks for your letter. It was great to hear from you again. Here's some information about where we could stay in London.

The Pickwick Hotel is a small hotel in central London. It sounds great because it's so close to everything we want to visit. It costs £50 for a single room, which is expensive, but we'd get 10% off if we booked early.

The Lansdown Hotel is a lot bigger and costs £39 for a single room. It's further out, but apparently there are lots of buses to the centre and it takes about 35 minutes to get there.

Personally, I think the Pickwick Hotel would be better. It's closer, so we wouldn't have to spend so much time and money travelling. With the discount, it'll be £45, so it's not that much more than the other one.

Could you get in touch and tell me if this is OK? Then I can call to book the rooms. Looking forward to seeing you.

Love

Giovanna

(177 words)

Analysis

1 Read the task again. Is there anything in the letter that has been missed out?

2 Do you think this is a good answer in terms of style? Why? Why not?

3 Find two or three phrases or sentences that help to give the letter an informal style.

3 Language study

Opening and closing letters

In the exam, you do not need to write addresses. However, you must begin and end the letter in a suitable way.

A Match the following openings and closings and discuss briefly when you would use them.

1	Dear Sir / Madam	a	Best wishes
2	Dear Jack	b	Yours faithfully
3	Dear Mum and Dad	c	Yours sincerely
4	Dear Mr Smith	d	Love

B Talk about any other ways you know to open or close a letter and say when you would use them.

Changing styles

Transactional letters may ask you to reproduce some information you have read, but you will often need to say the same thing in a different way.

A Look at this example. In the advertisement you read:

Frequent buses to central London

In a letter to a friend, it would sound strange to say this. Instead, the writer said:

There are lots of buses to the centre.

Look back at the letter again. How did the writer rephrase the following pieces of information?

Close to theatres, major department stores, and tourist sights

10% discount for booking early

B Read the following pieces of information and extracts from advertisements. How would you rephrase these things if you were writing to a friend?

Cambridge Bus Company
Cambridge to London Return £15.⁰⁰
departures every 20 mins

Seaview Restaurant
FULL VEGETARIAN MENU
OPEN 10AM–11.00PM
–groups catered for

KM Kentucky Motorhomes
Model: Denver
• 4 beds • kitchen • toilet • TV

4 Writing task

Transactional letters

Your letter should include an opening and a closing, but <u>not</u> an address.

Make sure you give all the necessary information organized into paragraphs.

Do not copy the information given in the question. Use key words and rephrase.

Learn how to spell words like *faithfully* and *sincerely*. Correct spelling will help you to get a better mark.

Writing a transactional letter

You are studying in England and decide to organize a camping weekend in Wales with an English-speaking friend. Read the information about two campsites and the notes you made when you phoned them. Write a letter to your friend. Describe the two places, say which one you think would be better and why, and ask your friend to contact you before you make a booking.

Write your **letter** (120–180 words).

Three Valleys Campsite
could be quite windy
- Set in stunning scenery in the national park
- Caravans and tents welcome   *no easy way from station*
- Small shop and post office
- Campsite restaurant
- Motorway 11 miles   *one bus per day*

From £5 per night

Woodland Walk

Idyllic position in forest

Village with pub, shops, etc. 2 mins walk   *no shop on campsite*
Convenient for local railway station   *buses every hour*
Tents: £6 per night
Caravans: £14 per night

Notes...

Work through the notes and prepare your letter.

Read the task again carefully and underline the key words. Remember to choose a suitable opening and closing for your letter.

Paragraph 1

Which two of the following would be most suitable for an informal letter to a friend? Choose one or think of your own and continue the paragraph.

I'm sorry I haven't been in touch for so long, but I've been very busy here.

Thanks so much for your letter – it was great to hear from you again.

I am writing in reply to your letter of 23 September.

Paragraph 2

Give information about the first campsite. Use your own words as much as possible.

Paragraph 3

Give information about the second campsite. Use your own words as much as possible.

Paragraph 4

Say which one you prefer and why. Suitable expressions are:

I think I'd rather stay at … , mainly because …

I think the … would probably suit us better because …

Paragraph 5

Ask your friend to get in touch before you book. Your letter will have to have a suitable ending. Which two of the following would be most suitable for an informal letter to a friend?

I look forward to hearing from you soon.

I'm really looking forward to seeing you again.

Anyway, I'd better stop now because I want to catch the post, but I'll be in touch again soon.

WORDPOWER

1 Different uses of *get*

A The word *get* has several different meanings. Look at these extracts from the reading text about Andrew Martin.

1 *... and only gets letters every three months ...*

2 *... I got really nervous when I also learned that the whole island was full of ... snakes.*

3 *After a forty-five minute walk ... we got to the house ...*

In which phrase does *get* mean:

a to change or become?

b to arrive at or go somewhere?

c to receive or obtain?

B Look through the list of phrases below. Put them into three groups according to the meaning of *get*.

to get a new job	to get a phone call
to get angry	to get home
to get old	to get a new car
to get away	to get to London
to get a present	to get on the bus
to get cold	to get better

C Complete the following sentences with some of the phrases from the box, making any changes that are necessary.

1 He's not very well at the moment, but I expect he'll .... soon.

2 When Fatima left college she .... as a tour guide.

3 It was late when I ...., so I went straight to bed.

4 Please don't shout like that. There is no need to ....

5 My brother's car wasn't worth repairing, so he decided to ....

6 I've been working very hard – I need to .... for a few days.

2 Words easily confused

A Match these words with their meanings.

trip	tour	journey
voyage	excursion	travel

1 going to a place for a short time (for pleasure or business)

2 the act of travelling from one place to another

3 a long journey usually by sea or in space

4 to make a journey

5 a visit round a place of interest, often with a guide

6 a visit to a place of interest, often by coach

B Use one of the words to complete these sentences. Use each word only once.

1 The .... to work usually takes me about twenty minutes.

2 My father's gone on a business .... to Paris, but he'll be back tomorrow.

3 We went on an interesting .... of the museum with an excellent guide.

4 My uncle is a salesman, so he has to .... a lot for his work.

5 Do you feel like going on the .... to Brighton on Saturday?

6 The astronauts are training for their .... to the moon.

3 Word grades

A Which six words can be used to describe the weather? Which six words can be used to describe the number of people in a place?

freezing	deserted	cool	warm
hot	busy	crowded	quiet
boiling	packed	empty	cold

B Now arrange the words into two columns.

Hottest:		Most people:	
1	....	1	....
2	....	2	*crowded*
3	....	3	....
4	*cool*	4	....
5	....	5	....
Coldest: 6	....	Fewest people: 6	....

4 Phrasal verbs connected with travel

A Read what one of the ground staff said about people arriving late at airports.

It's surprising how many people miss flights. Occasionally there are people who don't turn up at all, but mostly we have to deal with latecomers. A lot of people set off too late, and they get held up by traffic or their car breaks down. We can usually get them onto the flight if they check in 20 minutes or so before the plane takes off, but anything less than that is almost impossible.

B Look through the text again. Find a phrasal verb that means:

1 to register   4 to appear/arrive

2 to be delayed   5 to leave the ground

3 to start a journey   6 to stop working/have mechanical failure

C Answer the questions using some of the phrasal verbs above.

1 How can you avoid missing a flight?

2 Why is it a good idea to check the car before a journey?

3 When do you have to wear seat belts on a plane?

4 What do you have to do when you get to an airport or hotel?

UNIT 3 ► LET'S REFLECT!

1 Word formation

Use the word given in capitals at the end of each line to form a word that fits in the space in the same line.

Example: (0) different

The PILGRIM
Route to SANTIAGO

If you'd like to do something (0) .... *different* .... | DIFFER
on your holiday, you might be (1) .... in | INTEREST
following the Pilgrim Route to Santiago. The journey starts in
France, and takes you through the (2) .... | MARVEL
scenery of the Pyrenees to Santiago in Spain.

It (3) .... takes about five weeks to | NORMAL
complete the 800-kilometre walk, which gives you more than
enough time to go (4) .... There are | SIGHT
plenty of (5) .... , but you can also get | CAMP
rooms in monasteries, which cost little or nothing. Alternatively,
you can stay in (6) .... hotels, but these | COMFORT
are obviously more (7) .... | EXPENSE

The Pilgrim Route can be quite (8) .... | CROWD
during the summer. Some people find it more
(9) .... to go in October and November, | ENJOY
which are quieter months, but the (10) .... | ADVANTAGE
of travelling then is that some of the hotels are closed.

(10 marks)

2 Key word transformations

Use the word in **bold** to complete the second sentence so that it has a similar meaning to the first. Write between two and five words.

1 Don't forget to contact me if you come to London.
   touch
   Don't forget to .... if you come to London.

2 We took the exam in a very noisy room.
   where
   The .... exam was very noisy.

3 Make sure that you don't arrive late.
   turn
   Make sure that you .... time.

4 The hotel where we stayed was very cheap.
   that
   The .... was very cheap.

5 I hate going to beaches if they are crowded.
   which
   I don't .... are crowded.

6 Your English will improve if you keep practising.
   get
   Your English .... if you keep practising.

7 My sister is going out with someone. He is the son of a film director.
   father
   My sister is going out with someone .... film director.

8 Normally I have a 10-minute journey to school.
   me
   Normally .... to get to school.

9 She is keen on meeting people from other countries.
   who
   She wants .... from other countries.

10 I'll give you the name of a friend of mine. Her son went to that school.
   whose
   I'll give you the name of a friend .... went to that school.

(20 marks)

3 Vocabulary

Look through the groups of words. Which is the odd word out in each group?

1 a take off   b land   c give up   d fly
2 a busy   b crowded   c packed   d deserted
3 a pilot   b travel agent c cabin   d guide
4 a humid   b boiling   c warm   d empty
5 a swimming   b golf   c tennis   d hockey

(10 marks)

4 Spot the mistake

Correct each of the sentences.

1 I'm reading a book which it is very interesting.
2 Do you know who's car this is?
3 My mother, that is nearly 60, is coming to live with us.
4 I don't know why he didn't come to the party – he just didn't turn in.
5 The room where I am staying in is very noisy.
6 I was sorry to hear you are in hospital – I hope you become better soon.
7 I think we should go some sightseeing this afternoon.
8 Look at the pictures that we took them on holiday.
9 Almost everyone, who lives in Holland, speaks Dutch.
10 This is Peter, who his sister works at your school.

(10 marks)

Total: 50 marks

In small groups, decide what age groups these people are.

Example:
A toddler is aged between about 1 and 2 years.

a pensioner	a middle-aged person
a teenager	a child
an adult	a baby
a toddler	an elderly person

1 Gapped text

A Look at these photographs. How old do you think the little boy was when they were taken? Do the photos give you any idea of the little boy's character?

B Read this magazine article about the actor Antonio Banderas and put these stages of his life in the correct order. The first one has been done for you. Take no notice of the gaps in the paragraphs or the underlined sections.

Example: 1 b He started acting.

a   He got divorced.
b   He started acting.
c   He started missing his home and family.
d   His reviews appeared in newspapers.
e   He married Melanie Griffith.

FROM THE HOT STREETS OF MALAGA TO HOLLYWOOD'S HOTTEST PROPERTY: ANTONIO

It was a face only a mother could love. His skin was bad, his teeth were worse and his nose was far too big for his face. 'When I was young I had a lot
05 of spots and one tooth that stuck out. I <u>wasn't a good-looking teenager</u>.'

0	G

It's impossible not to ask him if he realizes just how handsome he is.
10 It's not just the looks, of course. It's the Spanish accent and more importantly <u>the Mediterranean charm</u> which made Antonio a box office attraction that everyone seems to be crazy about. **1** ☐

He was brought up in a lower middle-class family. His father, José, worked for the police; his mother, Ana, was a teacher and
15 he has a younger brother called Francisco. Apparently, everything was perfectly happy and straightforward until, at the age of 14, he took up acting and joined a local theatre group. **2** ☐

In the beginning it was difficult for them to understand. They told him he had to have a normal career and made him feel as if he
20 was doing something terrible. Ana was soon won over, however, and started a scrapbook, carefully pasting his reviews into it.
3 ☐

In between, he married a Spanish girl, the actress Ana Leza. But eight years later, the marriage was over and Antonio fell in love
25 with Melanie Griffith. They married in 1996 and at first it was difficult introducing an American star into the family. **4** ☐

His biggest wish now is to spend more time with his friends and family in Spain. 'You know, something curious happens when you leave your own land,' he says. 'It's like looking at a painting
30 – you have to be at a certain distance to appreciate it. Then you start feeling lonely and missing where you really belong and those who are close to you.' **5** ☐ He hasn't been able to do this lately because of work but he intends to devote more time to doing what he calls all the 'normal things' in life – seeing
35 friends, spending some time alone, having dinner, talking about movies – that's what he likes to do best of all!

C Read the missing sentences A–G below and then read the text again. Choose the sentence which best fits each gap 1–5. There is an extra sentence that you do not need. There is an example at the beginning (0).

The gapped text often makes sense on its own, and the missing sentences are further examples of or comments on what has been said. To choose the correct answer, you may be helped by words like *this, that, it, them* which refer to things or people mentioned in previous or later sentences. If there are no such reference devices, you will have to rely on context.

Look at the words which have been underlined in the main text and the missing sentences.

The answer to (0) depends on the context. In the main text, Antonio himself says he wasn't a good-looking teenager and in G it says, *What a difference time makes ... Banderas now looks even better in real life than he does on the screen.*

The next answer depends on the reference device, *this*, which refers to *the Mediterranean charm.*

Underline the words in the other missing sentences which help you to find the right answer.

A
He says he was the first one to do so in his family and they didn't approve at all.

B
However, after their daughter Estella del Carmen was born his parents were, once again, won over.

C
His parents are old and he needs to take a more active part in their lives now.

D
Banderas was born in 1961 with lots of this, as the family photograph albums, back home in his native Malaga, reveal.

E
All was forgiven until, at the age of 19, he decided to head for the bright lights of Madrid and then, which was far worse, leave Spain to try his luck in Hollywood.

F
He's flattered by the reviews for his work in films like *Philadelphia* and *Evita*.

G
<u>What a difference time makes</u> – for today, sipping tea in the lobby of the elegant Ritz-Carlton hotel in Los Angeles, <u>Banderas now looks even better in real life than he does on the screen</u>.

2 Comprehension

Explain what these parts of the text mean and answer the questions which follow.

1 *Banderas now looks even better in real life than he does on the screen.*

  Why do you think some film stars often look better on the screen than they do in real life?

2 *Ana was soon won over ...*

  Why do you think Antonio's mother began to feel like this?

3 *... started a scrapbook, carefully pasting his reviews into it.*

  Why do you think his mother started doing this?

4 *Then you start ... missing where you really belong ...*

  What other things do people miss if they are away from home?

5 *... he intends to devote more time to doing ...*

  What would you like to devote more time to doing?

3 Speaking

In small groups, tell each other what you can remember about your early childhood. Give one example of:

- a special friend you played with
- an activity you were good at
- a relative you liked or disliked
- a happy or sad time you had
- a special place you used to go to
- a pleasant smell or a sound.

Did anybody in your group have similar memories?

These pictures show different kinds of entertainment. Work in pairs and answer the questions.

1 Read this vocabulary and decide which picture the words could refer to.

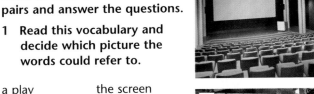

a play	the screen
an act	a performance
a film	a scene
the cast	a star
an interval	the stage
the curtain	scenery

2 Ask each other these questions.

Which do you like best: the cinema, the theatre or a different kind of entertainment? Why?

What is the most popular form of entertainment for young people in your country?

THE GLOBE THEATRE

Going to the theatre has been a popular pastime for centuries. One of the most famous theatres in history was the Globe Theatre in London, opened during the reign of Elizabeth I.

Wealthy people sat in the 'two-penny' galleries. These were not really the best places to be because (0)......*A*........ those days people wore hats, often with huge feathers, which blocked the (1)...................... of those sitting behind them.

Members of the royal court sat in the best 12 pence (2)...................... showing off their expensive clothes and smoking tobacco.

Before (3)...................... the theatre, people used to pay to get in by putting money into a box, which was held by one of the theatre staff.

With no lighting, early theatres were (4)...................... open in the middle to let in daylight – and the rain! Getting soaked was a risk you (5)...................... if you paid the cheap entrance fee.

As the actors were coming onto the stage, a trumpet sounded. A flag was raised in the tower to show that the performance was starting and it remained in position (6)...................... the performance ended.

1 Multiple-choice cloze

About 30 years ago, the American actor and director Sam Wanamaker began a project to rebuild Shakespeare's Globe Theatre in the same place as it used to be in the early 1600s. The theatre is now finished.

Look at what the theatre was like all those years ago. Read the text and decide which answer A, B, C or D best fits each space.

Example: (0) A

> Think about what the missing words might mean and what parts of speech they might be before you look at the suggestions below. Could they be prepositions, adverbs, nouns, adjectives or verbs?

0	A	in	B	by	C	for	D	during
1	A	sight	B	picture	C	scene	D	view
2	A	seats	B	chairs	C	benches	D	stools
3	A	going	B	entering	C	arriving	D	passing
4	A	held	B	forced	C	left	D	stopped
5	A	took	B	had	C	put	D	made
6	A	before	B	while	C	until	D	since
7	A	among	B	in	C	around	D	between
8	A	doing	B	making	C	playing	D	being
9	A	all	B	whole	C	both	D	full
10	A	spectators	B	audience	C	viewers	D	group

There were no intervals (7)...................... acts, so food was sold during the performance. Apples and nuts were popular. If the audience did not like the play or the cast, they used to throw the cores and shells at the actors on the stage.

Actors (8)...................... the parts of ghosts and witches crouched inside the area beneath the stage. When needed, they used to jump out onto the stage through a trapdoor.

The poorest theatre-goers paid one penny to get in. They watched the (9)...................... play standing up in the yard. Often 1,000 people squeezed in to see a popular play.

The high stage was in the middle of the yard. There was no curtain, which meant that at the end of violent plays the actors' bodies were carried off in full view of the (10)...................... .

GRAMMAR ZOOM

The past

1 Simple past or past continuous?

A In the text it says, *As the actors were coming onto the stage, a trumpet sounded.*

When do we use the simple past and when the past continuous?

B Put the verbs in brackets into the simple past or the past continuous.

The other day I (1)...................... (stand) in a queue to buy some theatre tickets when a small group of musicians suddenly (2)..................... (appear) on the pavement. They (3)..................... (wear) brightly-coloured clothes and (4)..................... (play) jazz. After a while, one member of the group (5)..................... (begin) to walk up and down the queue. I (6)..................... (notice) that he (7)..................... (collect) money in a hat. It (8)..................... (be) a cold, windy day and, just as he (9)..................... (reach) my part of the queue, a sudden gust of wind (10)..................... (blow) the hat out of the musician's hand. The money (11)..................... (fall) out all over the pavement. Can you guess what (12)..................... (happen) next?

2 Talking about a particular time in the past

A Write the times under the correct headings.

at	on	in	no preposition
12.40 pm	my birthday	1997	last week

12.40 pm	a few weeks ago	Monday morning
last week	my birthday	the day before yesterday
winter	the weekend	the end of the week
1997	the morning	the beginning of the term
night	September	

B Choose an example from each list and tell a partner about something that happened to you at these times.

C Correct each of these sentences.

1 My friend and I celebrated our birthdays at the day before yesterday.

2 Our neighbours went to the beach on last week.

3 The temperature often drops to –10°C at winter.

4 We moved into our new house in a few weeks ago.

5 When the children were babies, they often used to wake up in night.

3 *Used, used to do* and *be / get used to doing*

A Match the underlined words in these sentences with the meanings below.

1 The actors <u>used</u> the area beneath the stage to hide in.

2 The actors <u>used to</u> jump out through a trapdoor.

3 The actors <u>were used to</u> crouching beneath the stage.

4 The audience <u>got used to</u> stánding in the open air.

a *did this regularly but do(es) not do it any longer*

b *was (were) accustomed to*

c *made use of*

d *became accustomed to*

B Answer these questions in pairs.

Why is *used to* followed by *jump* in 2, but by *crouching* and *standing* in 3 and 4?

When is *used* pronounced / ju:st / and when is it pronounced / ju:zd /?

4 *Used to do*

A Look at these pictures and say what life used to be like in the past.

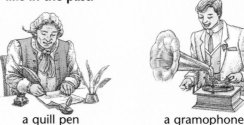

a quill pen   a gramophone

a stagecoach

candles

an open fire   a penny-farthing

B In pairs, take it in turns to tell each other how life has changed. Say what people usually do now.

Example: Nowadays, people usually write with a biro, pen or pencil, or on a computer.

5 *Got used to, got used to doing*

Imagine that you were a time traveller and you found yourself living a hundred years ago. Tell a partner what you didn't like about life at first but what you *got used to* or *didn't get used to*. Think about:

the food   houses

the transport   ways of heating and lighting

1 Talking together

A Here are some ways in which people entertained themselves at home before the arrival of television and radio. With a partner, describe what people used to do.

Can you think of some other things people used to do before the arrival of television?

B In the same pairs, explain what the different kinds of programmes are in 1–9 below. Give an example of each kind on television at the moment.

1 drama
2 comedy
3 nature programme
4 current affairs
5 documentary
6 game show
7 soap opera
8 chat show
9 cartoons

What other kinds of programmes are shown on television?

2 Talking about yourself

In pairs, ask and answer these questions.

1 Which do you prefer: listening to the radio or watching TV? Why?
2 How often do you watch TV or listen to the radio?
3 Do you ever have any family arguments about what to watch on TV? Who usually wins?
4 What is your favourite TV programme? Why do you like it?
5 What kind of TV programmes do you not enjoy?

3 Talking together

Your class is taking part in a project to encourage young people to watch less television. You are going to design a poster to advertise what there is for young people to do where you live. Work in small groups. Try to use the expressions in the Phrase Box.

1 Choose which three activities shown in the pictures in the next column you think young people will find the most interesting.
2 Decide how to present these ideas on the poster, e.g. words, pictures. (You can make a sketch of the poster if you want to.)
3 Decide where to put the posters so young people will see them.

When you are talking together it is useful and natural to use certain expressions to give yourself time to think.

Giving yourself time to think
Now, let's see ...
Well, I suppose we could ...
Let's think about this for a moment ...

Which poster do you think would be the most successful at persuading young people not to watch so much TV?

In small groups, think of three good things and three bad things about television.

1 Note taking A

A Read the listening task and try to work out what the missing information might be, e.g. a time, a place, before doing the task itself.

> In the exam, you need to write a word or a short phrase. This word or phrase will be on the tape – you do not need to use different words.

Example: In Question 1 the speaker says, <u>St Helena switched on to TV at 9 am on a Friday morning in March 1995</u>. The prompt for Question 1 is: TV arrived on St Helena in ... so you write <u>March 1995</u>.

B You will hear a presenter of a radio programme talking about the effects of being without TV. Listen to the presenter and write in your answers.

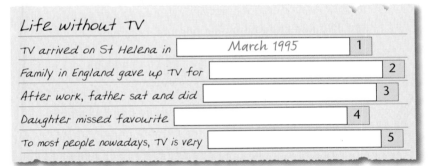

Life without TV

TV arrived on St Helena in	March 1995	1
Family in England gave up TV for		2
After work, father sat and did		3
Daughter missed favourite		4
To most people nowadays, TV is very		5

Listen again and check your answers.

2 Note taking B

A Read the listening task and try to work out what the missing information might be.

B You will now hear the presenter talking about St Helena and life there before the arrival of TV. Listen to the presenter and write in your answers.

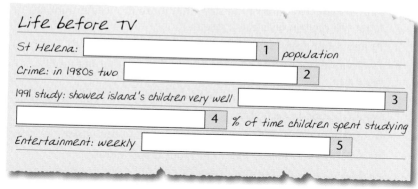

Life before TV

St Helena:	1	population
Crime: in 1980s two	2	
1991 study: showed island's children very well	3	
	4	% of time children spent studying
Entertainment: weekly	5	

Listen again and check your answers.

3 Note taking C

A Read the listening task and try to work out what the missing information might be.

B You will now hear the presenter talking about life on St Helena after the arrival of TV. Listen to the presenter and write in your answers.

Life after TV

TV meant that islanders were at last in the	1
Arrival caused a big change in islanders'	2
Islanders became more interested in the	3
TV cost 12% of islanders'	4
Islanders hoped for more	5

Listen again and check your answers.

WB 4

4 Time expressions

These expressions with time appear on the tape. Match the definitions with the expressions.

1 try to be modern
2 at an unspecified time in the past
3 a particular time in the past
4 not modern or fashionable
5 just for the present but maybe not for long

a some time ago
b for the time being
c keep up with the times
d at the time
e behind the times

Writing a story (1)

In Part 2 of the writing paper, you may be asked to write a story. You will be given either the first or last line to base your story on.

1 Sample task

Read the sample task and answer the questions.

You have been asked to write a story for a student magazine. It must begin with these words:

When he returned home, the house was unusually quiet.

Write your **story** (120–180 words).

Task interpretation

The words you are given in the task will suggest what you have to write about. For example, the reader will need to know:

1 who the person in the story is

2 why the house is so unusually quiet

3 whether there is anyone else there, etc.

2 Sample answer

Read the story and answer the questions.

When he returned home, the house was unusually quiet. Bill was surprised when he walked into the sitting room to find his parents waiting in silence. His mother was standing by the window, and his father was sitting on the sofa holding a letter. They both looked nervous, but everyone in the family seemed to be nervous at the moment. They were expecting Bill's exam results any time.

'A letter arrived for you today,' said Bill's father, holding it out. 'Here.'

'Thank you,' Bill replied. He took the letter quickly and tore it open. His mother held her breath.

'What a pity,' said Bill, looking at the letter. Bill's mother gasped and his father ran over to comfort her. Bill was shocked by his parents' reaction.

'But I've passed!' he exclaimed. 'Seven grade A's.' What a pity I only got a 'B' in Chemistry.'

His parents looked amazed. Bill quickly hid the letter – an invitation to a party. If his parents found out his real results, which had arrived yesterday, they would never let him go to the party.

(179 words)

Analysis

1 What does the reader think the letter is going to be about?

2 Find at least two parts of the story that make the reader think the letter will contain Bill's exam results.

3 At first, what does the reader think the letter actually said?

4 Find two reactions that give the reader the idea that the results were bad.

5 Read the following sample opening lines. Discuss in pairs what you would include in each story.

   a *As I approached the house, my heart began to beat faster.*

   b *I realized very quickly that I had made a bad mistake.*

   c *I sat up in bed, looked around and found myself in a large white room with no windows.*

3 Language study

Focus on tenses

Answer the questions.

1 What tense does the writer use to describe what was happening when Bill went into the sitting room? Find two examples. Why is this tense used here?

2 What actions take place after Bill's father mentions the letter? What tense does the writer use for these? Find two examples. Why is this tense used here?

Punctuation

A Match the following punctuation signs with the words below.

comma	exclamation mark	full stop
question mark	inverted commas	dash
apostrophe		

B When you are writing a story, you may want to include the things people say. Look back at the story and answer the questions.

1 Which punctuation marks do we use to show that someone is speaking?

2 What happens to the paragraphs every time there is a new speaker?

3 At the end of a piece of direct speech where does the punctuation mark go – before or after the inverted comma?

C Punctuate the following text.

I was sitting alone at home one evening when the phone rang hello I said Jack here hello said the voice at the other end of the phone it was a womans voice a voice that sounded familiar in a way although I could not work out who it was then suddenly I realized who I was talking to Susan I said is that really you yes she said its me Im very impressed that you can remember after all its been a long time yes I know I replied its been more than ten years

4 Writing task

Writing a story

Read the task carefully.

Don't try to adapt a story you have used before. This will probably be obvious to the examiner because it won't fit in naturally with the words you are given and you will lose marks.

Do not include more than two or three exchanges of direct speech.

Remember to write in paragraphs and to keep to the word limit.

Writing a story

You have entered a short story competition for a local radio station. Your story must begin with the following words:

I'll never forget the time ...

Write your **story** (120–180 words).

The story begins with the phrase *I'll never forget the time ...* which means that your story must be about something memorable that happened to you in the past, perhaps when you were a child. Writing about a real experience is quite often simpler than inventing a story and has good results.

In pairs, think of some possible ideas to write about.

Notes...

Work through the notes and prepare your story.

Paragraph 1

Start your story using exactly the same words, and continue the paragraph.

Paragraph 2

You may want to describe a scene at the beginning of your story or to talk about other things, such as where you were living and what you were doing when this event took place. You may need to use the past continuous in this section.

Paragraphs 3–4

Give details of the events that took place. You will probably use mainly the simple past in this section. You may want to include two or three exchanges of direct speech.

Paragraph 5

Think of an interesting way to finish your story. It could be a comment about how you felt then and how you feel now.

Check your writing for spelling, punctuation and grammar mistakes.

WORD POWER

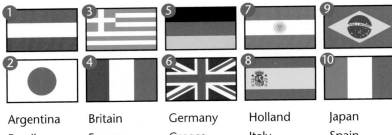

1 Countries, people and languages

A Match the flags with the countries.

Argentina   Britain   Germany   Holland   Japan
Brazil   France   Greece   Italy   Spain

B Can you name the people and the languages of the countries above?

Example: Britain (flag 6) – the British (the English, the Welsh and the Scots who speak English, Welsh and Gaelic)

2 Words easily confused

> Keep a vocabulary notebook and include an example of new words in a phrase or sentence. This will help you to remember how to use them.

A Read the sentences below and match the words (1–3) with the meanings (a–c).

Antonio and his wife *both knew the marriage was over*. He wanted to spend some time with *the whole family*, and he liked doing *all the boring things in life*.

1 *whole*   2 *all*   3 *both*
a the two   b the total number of   c with no part left out

Which of the words above:

can be followed by *the*?   is used after *the*?   can be followed by *of*?

B Read the examples from the reading text and match the words with the meanings.

Antonio says *you start feeling lonely* and he wants to spend some time *alone*.

1 *alone*   a unhappy to be on your own
2 *lonely*   b being on your own

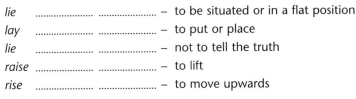

C Fill in the other parts of the verbs.

lie	....	....	– to be situated or in a flat position
lay	....	....	– to put or place
lie	....	....	– not to tell the truth
raise	....	....	– to lift
rise	....	....	– to move upwards

D Use one of the words from A, B or C in its correct form to complete these sentences.

1 Not .... the writer's childhood memories are happy ones.

2 The writer spent a .... term at the local school for acting.

3 .... the writer's parents were Spanish.

4 .... the children in the school were studying English.

5 Don't just .... around on the sofa. Please .... the table for dinner.

6 .... your hand if you want information about the recent .... in school fees.

7 I can never believe a word he says. He has .... to me so many times before.

8 During her illness, the child .... in bed all day and read books and magazines.

9 The island of Crete .... in the Mediterranean.

10 The cost of producing plays for TV has .... over the last year.

3 Phrasal verbs with *take*

A Choose the most suitable word to go with the verb *take* to form a phrasal verb in 1–7 below.

1 I must take this book *off/back* to the library tomorrow.

2 The children have taken *up/after* tennis and they are really enjoying it.

3 I take *in/after* my father but my brother is more like my mother.

4 The announcement was made so quickly that most people couldn't take it *up/in*.

5 The plane took *over/off* two hours late because of the fog yesterday.

6 Please take your jacket *up/off* if you find the room too warm.

7 The Worldwide Travel Group is going to take *off/over* a much smaller company.

B In which sentences can the object come before or after the second part of the verb?

4 Numbers

There are many numbers and dates in this unit. Write these numbers in words.

1 15% = ... p................... c...................

2 Longer numbers: 3,450,102 = ...

3 Temperatures: 19°C = ...

4 Decimals: 6.5 = ...

5 Fractions: $2\frac{1}{2}$ = ... $\frac{3}{4}$ = ...

6 Dates: 1/3/99 = ...

UNIT 4 ▶ LET'S REFLECT!

1 Multiple-choice cloze

Read the text below and decide which word or phrase A, B, C or D best fits each space.

Example: (0) B

▶ Greek Theatres

The word *theatre* comes from Greek and literally means *seeing place*. The theatre has been popular (0)........B........ ancient times. People did not go to the theatre simply to see an interesting (1)..................... , for the plays formed part of religious festivals. (2)..................... early Greek theatres consisted of no more than a flat space with an altar at the foot of a hillside. (3)..................... that time, there were no (4)..................... as there are in modern theatres, so the (5)..................... stood or sat on the slopes of the hillside. Gradually, special theatres were made by building large stone or wooden steps one (6)..................... another up the hillside. In later times, a hut was built at the far side of the acting area where it formed a background for the actors (7)..................... the parts of the different characters. Eventually, a (8)..................... platform was built so that the actors could be seen more clearly. This was the first appearance of anything (9)..................... our modern stage. As well as these permanent theatres, there were simple wooden stages (10)..................... around by actors wandering from one place to another. There was also a hut with curtains that served both as background scenery and as a dressing room.

0 A for	B since	C in	D at
1 A scene	B performance	C scenery	D stage
2 A Whole	B Complete	C Full	D All
3 A In	B For	C At	D On
4 A chairs	B benches	C seats	D stools
5 A watchers	B players	C viewers	D audiences
6 A among	B between	C around	D behind
7 A playing	B making	C doing	D being
8 A lifted	B raised	C moved	D pulled
9 A as	B like	C equal	D similar
10 A carried	B held	C brought	D fetched

(10 marks)

2 Key word transformations

Use the word in bold to complete the second sentence so that it has a similar meaning to the first. Write between two and five words.

1 Ripe tomatoes were often thrown at actors in Shakespeare's time.

used

People .... ripe tomatoes at actors in Shakespeare's time.

2 After a while, I could speak English easily.

used

I eventually .... English.

3 This dictionary must be returned to the teacher.

back

We must .... to the teacher.

4 William had done very little acting and he was terrified.

used

William .... and he was terrified.

5 Giovanni's father likes to try to be as modern as he can.

keep

Giovanni's father likes to try to .... if he can.

(10 marks)

3 Right or wrong?

Choose the correct answer, (a) or (b), to complete these sentences.

1 The sun (a) *rises* (b) *raises* in the east.
2 The island of Sicily (a) *lays* (b) *lies* next to mainland Italy.
3 Antonio wanted to spend time (a) *lonely* (b) *alone*.
4 Rashid has taken (a) *up* (b) *in* climbing as a hobby.
5 The windows are (a) *left* (b) *remained* open to let in air.
6 I went to see that new film (a) *at* (b) *in* the weekend.
7 The TV's broken so we'll have to try to manage without it (a) *at the time* (b) *for the time being*.
8 Life (a) *was used to being* (b) *used to be* more difficult than it is today.
9 The flight to America took (a) *over* (b) *off* late.
10 Your sister's son is your (a) *nephew* (b) *niece*.

(10 marks)

4 Vocabulary

Answer these questions using words which appear in this unit.

1 In what kind of book can you stick photographs?
2 What is the word for a person over 60 or 65 who no longer works?
3 What word is used for a group of actors performing a play?
4 What word can you use to describe people standing in a line waiting for something?
5 Which phrasal verb with *take* means *understand something*?
6 Write this number in words: 4,850,209
7 What do you call someone who lives on an island?
8 Which expression with *times* means *not modern or fashionable*?
9 What do you call a regular TV or radio programme about the lives of a group of people?
10 What do you call people who come from Holland?

(20 marks)

Total: 50 marks

In pairs, explain the difference between the pairs of words below. They are all connected with working.

1 salary / wages
2 staff / bosses
3 employers / employees
4 job / work

WP 1

MEGABUCKS & MEGABYTES

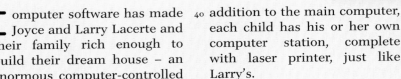

Computer software has made Joyce and Larry Lacerte and their family rich enough to build their dream house – an enormous computer-controlled mansion complete with swimming pool, baseball pitch, miniature estate cars for racing round the grounds, and tennis court, in a leafy Dallas suburb. There are so many rooms in the house itself that to send messages to family members they need intercoms, absolutely essential in a house where it could take half an hour to find somebody.

It is morning in the kitchen. Sitting in line at the huge breakfast bar in order of age from two to eleven are their seven children. The daily printout from the master computer in the attic with its five gigabytes of memory has already told them what the day holds for them by producing a list of activities for each member of the family. The computer has also recorded the outside temperature, the air pressure, the wind direction and speed. Inside the house it controls the lights, the room temperatures, each child's computer, the back-up generator, the TV sets and the massive security system which protects the property. In addition to the main computer, each child has his or her own computer station, complete with laser printer, just like Larry's.

It takes an army of helpers, dozens of machines and clockwork precision to make it all work. But then precision is something the family knows all about, for this is a house that computers have designed. Larry is the founder of a company which has built up its business providing computer software for small firms. Larry talks as he takes us on a four-hour tour of the mansion.

'I've always been fascinated by computers. In fact, I was brought up with them – worked with them since the age of fourteen! I've been lucky, though, because I've always had good people to work for me. But I think my real strength is that I've done every single job in the company myself, so I know just what's involved in each one. We've got three hundred and fifteen employees at the moment and we're still taking people on. That's not to say that we haven't had some scary moments, of course. Like when we had to borrow money to pay the bills. I really hated being in debt but it's actually worked

out well for us. We've also bought four or five other small companies along the way. I suppose we came to Dallas mainly for the children's sake, because the schools here are wonderful … and I've also worked out that I get a couple of hours a day more with the children – you see, the office is so close to home!'

The children are very important to Larry and Joyce. Particularly when Larry thought that he might not live to see them grow up. Three years ago the doctors thought that he had a brain tumour and the future looked grim. 'It's changed the way I think about my family, the way I look at life, even though everything seems to be all right now,' says Larry. 'I don't want to give up my job but I don't work as hard as I did before!'

1 Multiple choice

A **Look at the photos and title of the magazine article and say what you think it will be about. Read the article and answer these questions.**

1 How big is Larry's family?

2 What professional problem has Larry had?

B **Read the article again and choose the correct answer A, B, C or D for questions 1–7.**

> Even if you think you know the answer, read all the other options to see if they could be correct before choosing the best one.
>
> Underline the information in the text which helped you to choose your answer.

1 What disadvantage is mentioned about living in a big house like Larry's?

   A It is very expensive to provide lighting and heating.

   B It is easy for someone to try and break in.

   C It can be difficult to communicate with family members.

   D It takes too long to walk from one room to another.

2 What does *what the day holds for them* in lines 26–27 mean?

   A what problems might arise during the day

   B what arrangements have been made for that day

   C what they must achieve during the day

   D what they have been advised to do that day

3 What does Larry do for a living?

   A He works for several small companies.

   B He makes electrical goods.

   C He designs dream houses.

   D He has his own computer business.

4 What does Larry think is the secret behind his successful career?

   A his educational background

   B his knowledge of the business

   C his friends and family

   D his strong financial position

5 What does *one* refer to in line 69?

   A each member of staff

   B each company

   C each type of job

   D each computer

6 Larry said that he moved to Dallas

   A to manage some smaller companies.

   B to be nearer the office he works in.

   C to build a dream house for the family.

   D to give the children a good education.

7 What changed Larry's outlook on life?

   A having children

   B being ill

   C working away from home

   D moving to Dallas

2 Vocabulary

Can you explain what these words and phrases in the text mean?

1 *essential* (line 15)

2 *controls* (line 34)

3 *precision* (line 47)

4 *the founder* (line 52)

5 *taking people on* (line 72)

6 *scary* (line 74)

7 *in debt* (lines 77–78)

8 *grim* (line 97)

3 Phrasal verbs with *up*

A **Put the verbs in brackets into their correct form, then match the phrasal verbs in sentences 1–6 with the meanings in a–f below.**

1 Larry says he was (bring) .... up with computers.

2 Larry has (build) .... up his business over the years.

3 Larry doesn't want to (give) .... up his work.

4 The generator always (back) .... up the main electricity supply in an emergency.

5 Could you (pick) .... up some computer paper on your way home?

6 The children have (take) .... up baseball.

a *give support to*

b *make larger*

c *to be raised as a child*

d *go and buy or collect something or someone*

e *start a new hobby*

f *stop doing*

B **Use one of the phrasal verbs in A in its correct form to complete these sentences.**

1 Ted has tried to .... smoking but it's impossible.

2 It sometimes takes years to .... a company and make it successful.

3 I think it would be a good idea to .... a sport and get some physical exercise.

4 Could you .... me .... about 6 o'clock tonight?

5 As children, we were .... in the centre of a large city.

6 If I tell the boss what I really think, will you .... me .... ?

WP 2

1 Look at the pictures and describe the homes the people are living in.

2 Choose a caption for each photo. There is an extra one you do not need.

Temperatures underground remain a pleasant 19°C to 24°C.

Extend your house by blowing a hole in the wall.

A dry climate means endless dust.

1 Error correction

A Read the text quickly to find out what kind of place Sarah and Chris live in and why they have moved there.

THE opal ★ MINERS of Coober Pedy

S arah and Chris Orloff have decided to risk everything and try their luck in Australia after losing their jobs in England. They now run Coober Pedy's only dentist's surgery.

0	The Orloffs have exchanged their extremely comfortable life in <u>the</u>
00 ✓	England for life in one of the remotest places in the world. They have
1	been in Coober Pedy, a hot, dry place in the desert in Australia, for
2	several months now. The most people in the town have built their
3	homes underground to shelter from temperatures that can reach the
4	50°C. At the first Sarah and Chris could not get used to these strange
5	homes with their stone walls and almost total lack of natural light.
6	'We used to sleep for the hours on end because it was so dark and
7	quiet,' says Sarah. Almost everyone who lives there works the
8	underground, too, either in the opal mines, or in the town's
9	restaurants, hotels, shops and cafés. This strange the lifestyle is very
10	practical. Residents wanting to make their homes the bigger have
11	simply used the dynamite to blow a hole in existing walls! Sarah and
12	Chris now feel they have got used to their lifestyle and are thinking
	about staying on there.

B Read the helpline below and then read the text again. Some of the lines are correct, and some have a word which should not be there. Tick (✓) the lines which are correct and underline the unnecessary words. There are two examples at the beginning (0 and 00).

Read the whole sentence rather than just a line to help you understand the meaning fully.

Look out in particular for auxiliary verbs, prepositions, pronouns or articles.

No more than five lines will be correct, excluding the example.

2 Articles

A Make these sentences plural. Check your answers with a partner.

1 A dictionary is a useful reference book.

2 The dictionary is the most useful book I have ever bought.

B Why is *a* used in the first sentence and *the* in the second sentence below?

Coober Pedy is *a* hot, dry place. *The* town looks like something from another planet.

C Why is an article used in sentences 1a and 2a, but not in 1b and 2b below?

1 a The advice you have given me has been very useful.
  b Students have always come to me to ask for advice.

2 a I have never liked the furniture in my house.
  b I have always liked old-fashioned furniture.

D Read the sentences and put the article *the* in the space if necessary.

1 a If I drink .... coffee at night, I find it hard to sleep.

  b I love .... coffee they make in Greece.

2 a Many tourists walk round .... university to admire the beautiful buildings.

  b Most students go to .... university when they are eighteen.

E In pairs divide the words below into two categories.

Words used with articles	Words used without articles
the biggest	Sicily

biggest	Sicily	United States of America
Atlantic	Lake Victoria	tea / milk / sugar / butter
Japan	knife and fork	happiness / anger
Madrid	Eiffel Tower	(play) guitar / piano

GRAMMAR ZOOM

The present perfect simple

1 Puzzling pairs

What's the difference between these pairs of sentences?

1 a Susan's been to Sydney.
   b Susan's gone to Sydney.

2 a Adrian is here for a month.
   b Adrian has been here for a month.

3 a The mine hasn't made a profit for ten years.
   b The mine hasn't made a profit since 1995.

4 a I've drawn a plan of the town on the board.
   b I drew a plan of the town on the board.

5 a The students have already learned these verbs.
   b The students have just learned these verbs.

6 a Ben hasn't seen that new Australian film yet.
   b Ben still hasn't seen that new Australian film.

2 *For* and *since*

A Which of these words and phrases connected with time are used with *for* and which are used with *since*?

three years	at least ten years
yesterday morning	the end of last year
a week	ages
Wednesday	I came to live here
a few minutes	ten past two
the second of April	midday

B Use words and phrases like the ones above to tell a partner how long it is since you did these things.

Example:

I haven't bought any new clothes since last year / for a year.

buy new clothes	go abroad on holiday
go to a concert	go to a party
buy a CD	take an exam

3 How many so far ...?

Use a suitable verb and the suggestions in the list below to ask a partner questions.

Example: films this month

How many films have you seen this month?

books this term

phone calls to friends this week

hot drinks today

new friends in the last few years

good programmes on TV over the last week

pairs of shoes this year

4 What's just happened?

Look at these pictures and, with a partner, decide what the people have just done.

Example:

1 The children have just painted some pictures.

5 *Yet* and *still*

In pairs, make questions using the prompts in 1–6 and answers using an appropriate prompt in a–f. Use *yet* and *still*.

Example:

1 Have you finished your homework yet?
*   No, I still haven't done my composition.*

1 finish / homework   a lay / table
2 tidy / room   b buy / new tyre
3 telephone / cinema   c leave / the old one
4 mend / bicycle   d find / the number
5 have / your dinner   e finish / putting everything away
6 start / new school   f do / my composition

6 *Have you ever ...? Yes, I have. / No, I haven't.*

In pairs, ask each other questions to find out if your partner has ever done these things. If the answer is *Yes, I have*, ask for more information.

Example: ride a motorbike

A: Have you ever ridden a motorbike?
B: Yes, I have.
A: What was it like? / Did you enjoy it?

stay in an expensive hotel

have an embarrassing moment

have a really bad argument with someone

do really well in an exam

win a competition

do something really stupid

feel really nervous

1 Talking about yourself

A You need special physical and mental qualities to do some jobs. Match the words with the meanings.

Example: patient = staying calm and not becoming angry

patient   strong   kind   confident
co-operative   sympathetic   dedicated   courageous

showing that you understand people's feelings   feeling sure of yourself
staying calm and not becoming angry   brave
able to work with others   powerful
giving time and energy to something   friendly and thoughtful

B Now write the qualities in their noun form.

Example: patient – patience

strong ....   kind ....

confident ....   co-operative ....

sympathetic ....   dedicated ....

courageous ....

C What kind of a person are you? Tell each other about your good and bad qualities. You could use the adjective or noun form.

Example:

I think I have quite a lot of patience although I'm not very courageous.

2 Talking together

A In small groups, name the jobs the people are doing.

WP 3&4

B Choose two or three of the jobs and take it in turns to tell your partners what qualities you think you need to do these jobs well.

C In the same groups, decide which of the people above you think:

have had the most training for their job.   earn the most money.
will stay in their jobs the longest.   enjoy their jobs most.
have the most difficult jobs.

WP 5

D You are going to be interviewed for one of the jobs below. Choose the job that interests you most and decide what you might have to do and what qualities you would need to do it well.

Looking for an interesting job?
Do you want to
• work in a safari park?
• join a research trip to the Antarctic?
• help find buried treasure on the seabed?
• be a racing driver?
• be a chocolate taster?

Phone the _____
fASCINATING fIELDS JOB AGENCY
now on 0500 377623 _____

E In pairs, prepare a list of questions together for the interview.

1 full name and address
  What .... ?
2 age
  How .... ?
3 qualifications
  What .... ?
4 previous experience (if any)
  Have .... ?
5 able to work long hours
  Would .... ?
6 reasons for wanting the job
  Why / interested .... ?
7 the right person for the job
  Why / suitable .... ?
8 expected wages / salary
  How / earn .... ?
9 starting date
  When .... ?

When you have finished your list of questions, take it in turns to interview each other.

It is important to show your partner you are listening when he / she is talking. See the Phrase Box below, but remember that such expressions should be used to encourage the speaker, not to interrupt!

Showing that you are listening

Right. / I see! (I understand.)
Oh, really!
That's interesting!

LEAD-IN

1 Describe the five people in the photographs below.

2 You will hear the five people in the photographs talking about themselves in turn. Listen and write the age of each person and choose the best answer for each question A, B or C.

1 How old is Amanda Green ?
   What is she training to do?

   ....
   A to read the weather forecast
   B to tell people's fortune
   C to help people with problems

2 How old is Nigel Byrne ?
   What does he do for a living ?

   ....
   A interviews lottery winners
   B sells lottery tickets
   C works for the national lottery

3 How old is Claudia Wells?
   Who does she work for?

   ....
   A the Police Force
   B the Air Force
   C the Army

4 How old is Tim Monroe?
   What does he do in his job?

   ....
   A takes pictures
   B makes films for TV
   C works as a news reporter

5 How old is Valerie Bennett?
   What does she do in her job?

   ....
   A records CDs and tapes
   B looks after musical groups
   C writes songs for famous singers

Listen again and check your answers.

Which of these people's jobs would you enjoy doing?

1 Multiple matching

You will hear the same five people talking about their jobs. For questions 1–5, choose which of the opinions on the list A–F they express. Use the letters only once. There is one extra letter which you do not need to use.

A feels they have achieved a lot   Speaker 1 [1]

B enjoys doing something different all the time   Speaker 2 [2]

C spends most of the day on the phone   Speaker 3 [3]

D wants to change jobs   Speaker 4 [4]

E has very little time for themselves   Speaker 5 [5]

F meets a lot of very contented people

Listen again and check your answers.

2 Everyday expressions

The expressions in italic appear on the tape.

1 *To tell the truth*, I spend about 70% of my time on the phone to clients.

2 But, *to be honest*, the best bit's always presenting them with the cheque.

3 But I *have to admit* that I really love the job …

4 I *can honestly say*, at first, I had no intention of making a living out of my interest in photography.

These expressions are used when we are emphasizing something important or what we really feel. In small groups, use the expressions to tell a partner how you feel about:

doing homework   having arguments
going to parties   being on time
meeting new people   getting up early

Example: To tell the truth, I quite enjoy/hate doing homework.

Writing an application letter

In addition to Part 1 of the writing paper, you may be asked to read a job advertisement and write an application letter in Part 2. The advertisement will tell you what the employers are looking for, and it is important to mention all these points in the letter.

1 Sample task

Read the sample task and in pairs discuss how you would answer it.

including cv and letter of application
closing date: 10 May

We are an equal opportunities employer

WANTED –
JUNIOR CLUB ORGANIZERS
FOR AN INTERNATIONAL SUMMER CAMP

We are looking for keen and enthusiastic people to arrange activities for members of our Junior Club who are between 8 and 11 years old and of various nationalities.

Do you have:
• an interest in children?
• a good command of English?

If so, then write to Mrs Koralek enclosing your CV, and informing us of your availability for interview.

Previous experience of working with young children would be advantageous, but not essential, as full training will be given.

CONNECTIONS
employment agency

Opportunities in Australia

Write a **letter of application** (120–180 words).

2 Sample answer

Read the letter and then answer the questions below.

Dear Mrs Koralek

I am writing in response to your advertisement and would like to apply for a position as a Junior Club Organizer.

I am a 19 year-old student and have one older brother who is at university. I am currently doing a Teacher Training Course at college and am looking for work during the summer holidays. I feel I would be well qualified to work as a Junior Club Organizer.

As you will see from my CV, I have some experience of working with young children. Last year I worked in France in a similar position, and my responsibilities included arranging children's parties and excursions to local places of interest. I really enjoyed the work and would like to have another opportunity of working in a summer camp. In addition, my hobbies include playing chess and reading.

I look forward to hearing from you.

Yours sincerely,

Steve Jones

(151 words)

Analysis

In many ways this is a good answer, but the content is not quite right because the writer has not done exactly what the task requires. Read the advertisement and the letter again. Can you find:

a   two things that should be mentioned in the letter but which are missing?

b   two things that are mentioned in the letter but which are not required by the task?

3 Language study

Set phrases

Look back at the sample answer and write down five set phrases which can always be used in a letter of application.

....
....
....
....
....
....
....
....
....
....
....

4 Writing skills

How to plan your writing

Read the points and number them in the correct order.

Example: 1c

a   Highlight the key words in the task and base your answer around these.

b   Read your writing again and check carefully for spelling, punctuation and grammar mistakes.

c   Read the task carefully and make sure you fully understand everything.

d   Write your letter, constantly referring to your notes.

e   Think about the task as a whole and decide what you will write about.

f   Write notes for each paragraph, putting closely related ideas together.

g   Read through your notes, making sure you have included everything you underlined in the task.

5 Writing task

Application letters

Remember, it is not necessary to include an address on your letters in the exam.

You may need to make up relevant information about your skills and experience.

Use some of the set phrases you have learned.

Writing an application letter

You have seen the following advertisement in a local newspaper. Write a **letter of application** (120–180 words).

Patton Publishing House
112 Longacre Road • London • WC2 1XN

Wanted – Film Reviewers

We publish a newspaper for English language learners and are looking for part-time reporters to write reviews of the latest English language films. Previous experience is an advantage but is not essential.

Do you have:
– **good English skills?**
– **an interest in the cinema?**

If so, write to Bill Long at the above address, enclosing your CV and letting us know when you would be available for interview.

Notes...

Work through the notes and prepare your letter.

• As this is a formal letter, do not use the first name of the person you are writing to.

• Plan and write your answer. Make sure you include all the necessary information.

Remember to check your writing for spelling, punctuation and grammar mistakes.

WORD POWER

1 Words connected with work

job   ?   work
housework   ?   homework

Which word can be used in the plural with the same meaning?

Which verb can be used with all these words?

Which word can be used as a verb?

Use one of the words above to complete these sentences.

1 I can't stand ironing or any other kind of .... , to be honest.

2 My brother has had the same .... for over ten years now.

3 I actually enjoy doing writing tasks for ....

4 Looking after small children is hard ....

5 There are hundreds of people out of .... in this area.

2 Computer technology

Write these words connected with computer technology in the correct places.

mouse mat	monitor
keyboard	CD-ROM
mouse	computer operator

3 Different jobs

Find words for someone who does these jobs. Mark the main stress in words of more than one syllable.

Example: (0) travels into space   àstronaut

1 looks after animals   v ....

2 tries to find a murderer   d ....

3 discovers new places   e ....

4 performs medical operations   s ....

5 writes newspaper articles   j ....

4 Job search

A Divide the words below into three groups.

1 looking for a job, 2 doing a job, 3 not having a job

retire, promote, redundant, interview, contract, reference, pensioner, applicant, career, training, unemployment

B Use one of these words in its correct form to complete the text.

Example: (0) unemployment

ADVICE TO YOUNG PEOPLE ABOUT TO START WORK

In these days of high (0) *unemployment* , it is often difficult for young people to find a job. If they are lucky enough to be asked to go for a(n) (1)................................... , they may find that there are at least 20 other (2)................................... for the job. If a company is thinking of offering you a job, they will ask you for at least one (3)........................... , from either your previous employer or someone who knows you well. Before taking up your job, you may have to sign a (4)............................... . You will probably have to do some (5)................................... , which will help you to do the job more successfully. Once you have decided that this is your chosen (6)................................... , you will then have to work hard to try and get (7)................................... , which usually brings more responsibility and more money! If you are unlucky, you may be made (8)................................... , and not be able to find another job. It is also a good idea to pay some money into a (9)................................... scheme, which will help you to look after yourself and your family when you are (10)................................... . Finally, good luck!

5 Word formation

Negative prefixes: *un-*, *in-* and *im-*

These words all appear in the unit. Choose the correct prefix for each one.

a co-operative   f usual

b patient   g successful

c interesting   h lucky

d friendly   i ambitious

e employed   j expensive

UNIT 5 ➤ LET'S REFLECT!

1 Error correction

**Read the text and look carefully at each line.
Tick (✓) the lines which are correct and underline
the unnecessary words. There are two examples at
the beginning (0 and 00).**

> ### ➤ Life in a cold climate
>
> | 0 | ✓ | The Inuit people live in some of the remotest places in the world, |
> |---|---|---|
> | 00 | | e.g. Greenland, northern Canada and <u>the</u> Alaska. They speak more |
> | 1 | | or less the same as language and, for hundreds of years, they |
> | 2 | | have been lived by hunting, fishing and gathering plants during the |
> | 3 | | summer. The Inuit people have skilfully adapted their way of the life |
> | 4 | | to cope with the cold climate of the northern lands in which they |
> | 5 | | live. Many of people think that all the Inuit live in igloos, which are |
> | 6 | | homes made out of ice and a snow. This is not the case. In fact, |
> | 7 | | *igloo* is the Inuit word for all kinds of houses, whether they |
> | 8 | | are made of ice, stone, wood, skins or no other kinds of material. |
> | 9 | | Inuit snowhouses were actually only be built in winter to shelter |
> | 10 | | from temperatures which drop to the minus 40°C. Nowadays, most |
> | 11 | | Inuit have given up to their traditional homes and instead live in |
> | 12 | | modern huts and houses – just one of the many ways in which the Inuit lifestyle has changed over the years. |

(12 marks)

2 Key word transformations

**Use the word in bold to complete the second sentence
so that it has a similar meaning to the first. Write
between two and five words.**

1 Please give me your support at the meeting this
afternoon.

   up

   I'd like you .... at the meeting
   this afternoon.

2 Gavin has lent Frank some money.

   from

   Frank has .... Gavin.

3 Children who spend their childhood in the countryside
have a lot of freedom.

   up

   Children who .... in the
   countryside have a lot of freedom.

4 The shop opened a year ago.

   since

   The shop has been open .... year.

5 Molly came here a year ago.

   for

   Molly ....a year.

6 The students haven't done their homework yet.

   still

   The students ....their
   homework.

7 I'd like you to go and get some milk from the
supermarket.

   up

   Could you go and .... from the
   supermarket?

8 This is Richard's first day in his new job.

   just

   Richard ....his new job.

9 I can't see you tomorrow.

   impossible

   It ....see you tomorrow.

10 I hate visitors arriving unexpectedly.

   up

   I don't like it when ....
   unexpectedly.

(20 marks)

3 Spot the mistake

Correct each of these sentences.

1 Andrew's been a teacher of English since a very long
time.

2 It is not easy to grow up children in a modern world.

3 We have been to Spain last year.

4 It can be difficult for young people to find a work
nowadays.

5 You were wrong to mention the accident – I told you
not to bring up it.

(10 marks)

4 Words connected with work

**Match the words on the left with the meanings on the
right.**

1	*retirement*	a	being given more money and/or responsibility at work
2	*redundancy*	b	being taught how to do a job
3	*interview*	c	the end of your working life
4	*training*	d	another person's opinion about you and your work
5	*reference*	e	losing the job you have
6	*promotion*	f	being asked questions about your suitability for a job
7	*application*	g	money paid to you after you retire
8	*pension*	h	a formal request to be considered for a job

(8 marks)

Total: 50 marks

6 Get moving!

FRAME 1 ▶ READING

LEAD-IN

Discuss these questions in pairs.

1   Can you guess what the objects are and name the sports?

2   What are the most popular sports in your country?

3   What are the sports you like most / least?

4   In what ways can sport be good for you / bad for you?

1 Multiple matching

A   Read the magazine article opposite about some unusual sports and answer these questions.

1   Which of these sports seems the most dangerous to you? Why?

2   Which of these sports would you like to try? Why?

3   Do you think any of these sports could become popular in your country? Why? Why not?

B   Read the article again and answer questions 1–12 by choosing from the sports A, B, C or D. There is an example at the beginning (0).

> **HELPLINE**
>
> Look in the text for words that are similar in meaning to those in the questions.
>
> Read all the different sections of the text before you look at the questions. This will help you to see the similarities and differences between the various sections.

Which statement refers to which sport (A–D)?

You do not need great athletic skills to do this.	0	*B*
Some people have been killed doing this.	1	
You need to have very fast reactions.	2	
This sport involves going downhill very fast.	3	
This sport is forbidden in some countries.	4	
You require special clothing.	5	
This can be enjoyed by a wide age range.	6	
Only do this if you have had experience of a similar sport.	7	
This sport was in a film a long time ago.	8	
This sport should only be done at organized events.	9	
This sport will soon become more popular.	10	
This sport becomes more exciting as you get more experienced.	11	
Better technology is still being developed for this sport.	12	

2 Vocabulary

A   When you have finished the multiple matching task find a word or phrase from the text that means:

Section A	1	in a film	....
	2	a great success	....
Section B	3	no good at	....
	4	a difficult task	....
Section C	5	afraid	....
	6	organized	....
Section D	7	very quick reactions	....
	8	forbidden	....

B   Complete each of these sentences with one of the words or phrases you found in the text.

1   Getting to the top of any profession is a huge ....

2   You need very quick .... to be a goalkeeper in ice hockey.

3   I am .... at tennis. I can never seem to hit the ball.

4   It is .... for Olympic athletes to take drugs to improve their performance.

5   I always hated cricket because I was .... of being hit in the face by the ball.

WP 1

If you thought that sport had anything to do with health, then think again. Here are some of the latest sports people have invented to scare themselves to death. Any of these sports will give you a thrill, but we've awarded them 1 to 5 broken legs to show just how dangerous they are.

THRILLS AND SPILLS

B.A.S.E. jumping

A JET BELTING

If para-gliding seems to be a bit safe to you, why not do what James Bond did on screen 20 years ago and take to the skies in a jet belt? They were originally
05 invented in the 1960s, but new materials and fuels have now made the jet belt much more practical. You may remember seeing one at the Los Angeles Olympics. The Texan Flying
10 Belt Company have made the latest version that uses a jet of super-heated air to give lift-off. Take-off and flying are fairly safe, but it's probably worth mentioning that you might have a few
15 problems when you get round to landing. You can't afford to make a mistake.

At the moment, flight times are short, but the makers are thinking of
20 selling a version that can fly for well over an hour, so jet-belting is bound to become a big hit in the near future. Prepare yourself for the thrill of a lifetime.

DANGER RATING: ♿ ♿ ♿

jet belting

street luge

B AIR CHAIR

air chair

25 We'd suggest taking up the air chair if you're either lazy or useless at sport. Basically the equipment is a water ski with a seat on top, and the whole thing lifts out of the water. You are strapped
30 to the seat.

The air chair can give so much lift in one jump that the results are spectacular – when you've learned to do it, jumping out of the water,
35 twisting the chair and trying to land again is a real challenge and a real thrill.

If you ever feel like giving up because it's too hard, then just
40 remember this. The air chair was designed by Mike Murphy, whose 77 year-old mum loves doing it. You don't intend to be beaten by a pensioner, do you?

DANGER RATING: ♿ ♿

C STREET LUGE

45 You're up in the hills above Hollywood, and you're about to race, feet first, down a steep road. You can't help feeling scared. That's OK. Street luge has that effect.

50 It's a version of the skateboard, but is longer and more stable. This is a good thing when you realize that you can expect to go over 150 km an hour.

Street luge appears to be a great
55 way to hurt yourself unless you do it at official meetings that are properly run and supervised – don't even consider doing it on an ordinary road. You'll need a decent race suit and special
60 shoes, because your boots are your brakes. What does it feel like? Well, just imagine being in a bed that someone has turned into a powerful motorbike!

DANGER RATING: ♿ ♿ ♿ ♿

D B.A.S.E. JUMPING

65 There's one thing you need above all else when you go B.A.S.E. jumping – nerves of steel. B.A.S.E. stands for Buildings, Antennae, Span, Earth, which is another way of saying
70 jumping off high objects. If you aren't used to skydiving, then forget it – you need to have incredibly fast reflexes because you have to open the parachute at exactly the right moment.
75 It's easy to see why B.A.S.E. jumping is so exciting – you really do risk being seriously injured.

B.A.S.E. jumping is against the law in the UK and America, so you'll have
80 to go to France or Norway if you want to try it where you're allowed to jump. And think very carefully before you decide to have a go – more than 20 people have already died looking for
85 this kind of thrill.

DANGER RATING: ♿ ♿ ♿ ♿ ♿

LEAD-IN ▶

Which of the Olympic sports do you like watching?

Are there any Olympic athletes you remember in particular? Why?

1 Multiple-choice cloze

Read the text about an Olympic athlete who became famous in the 1980s. Decide which answer A, B C or D best fits each space.

Example: (0)B

EDDIE 'THE EAGLE'

Few people know who (0).......*B*........ the ski jump at the Calgary Olympics, but many people remember Eddie 'the Eagle' Edwards, who (1)..................... last.

A builder from Cheltenham, England, he amazed everyone by deciding to (2)..................... the Olympics after just a few practice sessions on a dry ski slope where a (3)..................... instructor had taught him to ski. A number of Olympic officials asked him to stay away, but his friends wanted him to go and the media encouraged him to take part. A (4)..................... crowd met him at the airport, where things began to go wrong. First of all, his plane arrived late and then, while he was collecting his luggage, his bag (5)..................... open. The next morning he found that some of his (6)..................... had been broken, which prevented him from having his first two practice runs.

(7)..................... as the 'Barmy Brit'*, he soon became (8)..................... throughout the world. Millions (9)..................... his final jump, and when he finished, the cheering crowd stood up to congratulate him on landing safely.

A true (10)..................... in the amateur Olympic spirit, he said that he did not like training in the gym because it made him (11)..................... . After the Games, Burt Reynolds invited him to appear on his TV chat show, and when he returned home, he was driven round town in an open-top bus while he thanked the crowds for (12)..................... him in his great challenge. ■

*mad British person

0	A	gained	B	won	C	achieved	D	beat
1	A	arrived	B	failed	C	lost	D	came
2	A	enter	B	join	C	compete	D	go
3	A	neighbouring	B	nearby	C	local	D	common
4	A	tall	B	high	C	huge	D	wide
5	A	split	B	smashed	C	broke	D	cracked
6	A	apparatus	B	machinery	C	devices	D	equipment
7	A	Called	B	Known	C	Named	D	Said
8	A	popular	B	common	C	typical	D	usual
9	A	looked	B	glanced	C	watched	D	noticed
10	A	believer	B	supporter	C	member	D	follower
11	A	wound	B	hurt	C	pain	D	ache
12	A	relying	B	supporting	C	carrying	D	holding

-ing form and infinitive

1 Verbs + -ing or infinitive

A **Look at these sentences and answer the questions.**

If you can't afford to buy / buying an air chair, you can hire one.

Don't even think about to try / trying street luge on a normal road.

1 Which of the options is correct in each sentence?

2 What form does the verb usually take after phrasal verbs and prepositions?

B **Look through the reading text in Frame 1 again. Find at least five verbs or expressions that are followed by the -ing form and five verbs that are followed by the infinitive. Add them to the lists below.**

Verbs + -ing	Verbs + infinitive
consider	*afford*
....	....
....	....
....	....
....	....
....	....

C **Read the following texts. Put the verbs in brackets into the -ing form or infinitive.**

FASCINATING FACTS *you never knew!*

☞ At the 1972 Northern Counties athletics championship, only one team managed (1) *(turn up)* .... for the 4 x 100m relay race. They therefore expected (2) *(win)* .... and were looking forward to (3) *(go)* .... home with their medals. However, they dropped the baton at the first change-over, and the judges decided (4) *(disqualify)* .... them.

☞ In the 1956 FA Cup Final, Manchester City's goalkeeper Bert Trautmann broke his neck saving a ball. The captain offered (5) *(bring)* .... on a substitute, but the goalkeeper refused (6) *(leave)* .... the pitch, and he carried on (7) *(play)* .... until the end of the match.

WP-2

D Complete the sentences using your own ideas and a verb in the *-ing* form or infinitive.

I'd like to get fit, but it's not worth missing TV for.

PIZZA PIZZA

1 Martin wants to get fit, so he has decided …
2 I know my tennis racket isn't very good, but I can't afford …
3 Could we have our squash game tomorrow? I don't really feel like …
4 He's 50 now, so he's had to give up …
5 The final is on Friday. I'm really looking forward to …
6 The player was sent off because he threatened …

2 *-ing* form and infinitive: changes of meaning

A **Some verbs can be followed by the *-ing* form or infinitive, but the meaning changes. Look through these pairs of sentences and discuss the difference in meaning.**

1 He remembered to buy the tickets.
2 He remembered buying the tickets.
3 The referee stopped to talk to the linesman.
4 The referee stopped talking to the linesman.
5 I regret to say that we have no chance of winning.
6 I regret saying that we have no chance of winning.

B **Complete the sentences by putting the verb into the *-ing* form or infinitive.**

1 You will remember .... (get) the tickets this afternoon, won't you?
2 I can clearly remember .... (watch) a race when Schumacher didn't manage to finish.
3 Halfway through the Marathon, he stopped .... (have) a rest and a drink of water.
4 I regret .... (say) that your team has been disqualified.
5 He had to stop .... (play) because of a knee injury.
6 He always regretted .... (be) left out of the team that played in the World Cup Final.

3 Verbs + objects

A **Look at these sentences from the text about Eddie 'the Eagle'.**

Some verbs are followed by an object and an infinitive.

Example: Burt Reynolds invited him to appear on his TV chat show …

Some verbs are followed by an object and a preposition + *-ing* form.

Example: … he thanked the crowds for supporting him …

B **Look at the following list of verbs that appeared in the text about Eddie. Say whether they are followed by:**

a an object + *-ing* form
or
b an object + infinitive.

ask	teach
prevent … from	want
encourage	congratulate … on

Can you think of any other verbs that follow one of these patterns?

4 Key word transformations

Use the word in bold to complete the second sentence so that it has a similar meaning to the first. Write between two and five words.

1 Our coach would be pleased if we practised more.

wants

Our coach .... more.

2 He gave them his congratulations when they won the race.

congratulated

He .... the race.

3 She couldn't finish the race because she was injured.

prevented

Her injury .... the race.

4 The players did their best, so the manager thanked them.

for

The manager .... their best.

5 Jack wants my help this afternoon.

asked

Jack has .... him this afternoon.

5 Speaking

In pairs or small groups, talk about:

1 a sports event you'd like to go to.
2 a sport you would never consider trying.
3 something you'd like to learn to do.
4 something that happened during a sports event that you'll never forget.
5 something that you're looking forward to seeing.
6 any activity that you have arranged to do next week.

1 Talking together

A In groups of three, match these words with the six pictures below. Some words may match more than one picture.

people	place	activity	reason
wrestlers	rink	dancing	to win a competition
jockeys	ring	fighting	to win the match
figure skaters	course	galloping	to win the race
football teams	countryside	playing	to win the contest
bullfighters	pitch	hunting	to entertain the crowd
riders	bullring		to kill a wild animal
			to beat an opponent

B Now decide which of the activities above you think are:

a dangerous to humans. c interesting to watch.

b unkind to animals. d exciting to do.

C Choose two of the pictures above and take it in turns to compare them. Say how you feel about such activities. Use the words in the Phrase Box to help you.

Saying that you approve

I think ice-dancing is wonderful.
I'm all in favour of women playing football.

Saying that you disapprove

I think it's wrong to kill animals for sport.
In my opinion, hunting is wrong.

NB: We do not say *According to me …* or *According to my opinion …*

Saying that you don't disapprove

I can't see anything wrong with wrestling.
I'm certainly not against horse-racing.

2 Talking about yourself

A Have you ever suffered from any sports injuries? Tick the things below which have happened to you.

Have you ever …

… twisted your ankle? … sprained your wrist?

… pulled a muscle? … been knocked out?

… cut yourself? … broken your arm or leg?

Tell a partner what you were doing when these things happened.

B Decide which of the following might be suitable for the injuries above.

Example:
A bandage might be useful for a sprained wrist.

some pills / medicine

an operation

a sticking plaster

a sling

a bandage

a plaster cast

an X-ray

stitches

a splint

1 Multiple matching

A Read the listening task and think about the different topics and words you might hear.

B You will hear five people talking about sports personalities who they believe were the greatest in their field. Listen and match the speakers 1–5 with the sportsmen A–F. Use the letters only once. There is one extra letter which you do not need to use.

A	Ayrton Senna, Formula 1 racing driver	Speaker 1	1
B	Michael Jordan, basketball player	Speaker 2	2
C	Pete Sampras, tennis player	Speaker 3	3
D	Johnny Weissmuller, swimmer	Speaker 4	4
E	Muhammed Ali, boxer	Speaker 5	5
F	Ferenc Puskas, footballer		

C Listen to the tape again. In each section, write down two key words or phrases that helped you identify the correct answer.

Speaker 1 ....

Speaker 2 ....

Speaker 3 ....

Speaker 4 ....

Speaker 5 ....

WP 3

2 True or false?

In the exam, there are different types of Part 4 questions. You may have to answer true/false or yes/no questions, matching (who said what?) or multiple-choice questions.

You will be given sufficient time to read the questions before you hear the extract.

As always, you will hear the tape twice, so don't worry if you can't answer all the questions the first time.

A You will hear a couple talking about getting fit. Listen to the tape and say whether the following statements are true or false.

1 Susan says that Harry needs to lead a more active life. ☐ 1

2 Harry is enthusiastic about the idea of jogging. ☐ 2

3 Harry appears to be keen on the idea of swimming. ☐ 3

4 They can't go swimming straight away because the pool is shut. ☐ 4

5 Susan believes Harry is disappointed. ☐ 5

6 They cannot join the tennis club immediately. ☐ 6

7 Harry decides to go for a walk with Susan instead. ☐ 7

Listen again and check your answers.

B Look at these extracts from the tape:

Joggers are difficult to see ...
The pool is lovely to swim in ...
The club is expensive to join ...

How could you rephrase these sentences beginning with *It*?

C Look at these sentences. How could you rephrase them beginning with the word in italic?

1 It's exciting to watch *Sampras*.

2 It's difficult to climb *Everest*.

3 It's hard to play *chess* well.

4 It has always been dangerous to take part in *motor racing*.

5 It's easy to learn *volleyball*.

6 It will be impossible to beat *Barcelona*.

WP 4

Writing an article (2)

When you answer a task in Paper 2, it is very important to read the task carefully and answer it fully.

1 Sample tasks

Read the four sample tasks.

A A local tourist magazine has asked you to write an article about sporting events that are taking place in your area in the next few weeks and which will be of interest to international visitors.
Write your **article** (120–180 words).

B Your teacher has asked you to write a composition on the following subject: 'Team sports are more competitive than individual sports. Do you agree?'
Write your **composition** (120–180 words).

C An international magazine for schools has asked you to write an article telling their readers about an interesting or unusual sport that you know about.
Write your **article** (120–180 words).

D Your headteacher has asked you to look into new sports that could be played at the school. She would like you to write a report, explaining why the sports you have chosen would be suitable.
Write your **report** (120–180 words).

2 Sample answer

Read the sample answer and answer the questions.

> ## Lacrosse – a great game!
>
> It's fast, it's fun, it's dangerous – it's lacrosse, one of the most exciting team games that you can play.
>
> Lacrosse is played in some schools and universities in England and in the USA, but it's also an Olympic sport and it's an exciting game to watch either live or on TV.
>
> Modern lacrosse looks like a combination of football and hockey. Like football, it's played on a pitch with goals at each end. There are ten members in each team, and the aim is to get the ball into your opponents' goal using a lacrosse stick. This is a cross between a tennis racket and a fishing net, and it means you can catch the ball or throw it at great speed from one end of the pitch to the other.
>
> So if you ever get the chance to see or play it, have a go. It's been called the fastest game on two feet and is a great game.

(171 words)

Analysis

1 Which of the four questions does this article answer?

2 In what ways would the answers to the other three questions be different from this one?

3 Think of a suitable heading for each paragraph of the sample answer, summarizing its contents.
Example: Paragraph 1: Introduction

Paragraph 2 ....

Paragraph 3 ....

Paragraph 4 ....

4 Why do you think the writer has used contractions, e.g. *it's*?

5 Why does the writer use the words *you* and *your*? What effect does this have on the reader?

6 Would you describe the vocabulary as formal or informal? Give examples of words that help you come to this decision.

Talking about similarities and differences

A Read the sentences and answer the questions.

Modern lacrosse looks like *a combination of* football and hockey.

The aim of the game is *more or less the same as* in hockey.

The modern game is *very different to / from* the game the American Indians invented.

A lacrosse stick is *a cross between* a tennis racket and a fishing net.

Like basketball, there are attacking and defending players.

Unlike football, you are allowed to use your hands.

Which words or phrases in italic are used to point out similarities?

....

....

....

....

Which words or phrases in italic are used to point out differences?

....

....

B Rewrite these sentences using the word in bold and the structures above.

1 American football is a team game. Rugby is a team game.
like

....

2 Volleyball is nothing like basketball.
different

....

3 'Australian Rules' football is a mixture of soccer and rugby.
cross

....

4 Paragliding has elements of parachuting and gliding.
combination

....

5 Basketball is widely played in schools in England. Baseball is not.
unlike

....

6 Is judo very similar to karate?
more

....

7 American football is nothing like soccer.
to

....

Writing an article

Your teacher has asked you to write an article for the school magazine about a sport or game that you are interested in. Write your **article** (120–180 words).

Notes...

Work through the notes and prepare your article.

- As this is a magazine article, it needs a title to catch the readers' attention.

- Divide the article up into four main paragraphs:

1 Introduction

Write an interesting first sentence to interest the reader and encourage them to read on.

2 History

Give a few details about the history of the game or sport. You can probably find this information in a library or from an encyclopaedia. If not, your teacher may be able to help you.

3 The aim of the game

Give a brief idea of the game, the rules, etc.

4 Conclusion

Write one or two short sentences saying what your feelings are about the sport, and why you think it is interesting.

Remember to check your writing carefully for spelling, punctuation and grammar mistakes.

WORD POWER

adjectives expressions
Phrasal verbs nouns

1 Adjective and preposition combinations

A In small groups, discuss which prepositions are used with the words below. Remember that verbs that follow prepositions are usually in the *–ing* form.

about	of	with	at	on	in	for

capable ......*of*......	interested	frightened ....
keen	enthusiastic	responsible ....
excited	serious	fed up ....
sick	good	tired ....

B Complete the following sentences with an adjective or preposition from the list.

1 If you are really .... about becoming a professional tennis player, we'll get you some proper coaching.

2 I'm going to give up playing for the team. I'm fed up .... having to go to the gym three nights a week.

3 Satellite TV is great if you are interested .... football.

4 As the captain, you will be .... for making sure that everyone plays to the best of their ability.

5 What would be a good present for someone who's very .... on playing basketball?

6 I am beginning to wish he had lost the match. I'm sick .... hearing how wonderful he is.

2 Words easily confused

A Match the question openings with the endings.

Example: Did you win a prize?

	a prize?	the other team?
Did you win ...	a gold medal?	him?
Did you beat ...	easily?	the match?
Did you gain ...	weight?	the European Cup?
	any experience?	Manchester United?
	three nil?	

B Match the sentence openings with the endings.

Example: I lost the game.

	the game.	the last bus home.
I lost ...	my driving test.	a very easy shot.
I missed ...	the penalty.	my French exam badly.
I failed ...	my ticket.	concentration.
	to qualify.	

C Complete the sentences using the correct form of *beat, win, gain, lose, miss* or *fail*.

1 Anderson .... the last two matches of the season because he was injured.

2 When you have .... some more experience, you will be able to play in the team.

3 The runner was disqualified after .... a drugs test.

4 Our team played well all season, but unfortunately we were .... in the final.

5 She played very badly and as a result she .... the match.

6 I'm sure Oxford will .... the boat race this year – they're much better than Cambridge.

3 Phrasal verbs connected with health

A Read the information and answer the questions.

 I know I've put on a lot of weight, but I can't stand the thought of dieting. I can't live on lettuce leaves. Any suggestions?

 Yes, eat healthy food and do more. Remember that you don't have to give up anything – all you have to do is cut down on things like butter and cheese. The other important thing to do is to take up some kind of exercise. If you do, you'll lose weight very quickly.

B Which phrasal verbs or idioms mean:

1 to stop doing something?

2 to gain weight?

3 to start a new hobby or pastime?

4 to have less of something?

C In pairs or small groups, discuss these questions.

1 What sorts of food make people put on weight? What should they eat if they want to lose weight?

2 Is there anything you feel you should cut down on or give up to lead a healthier life?

3 Is there any kind of exercise you would like to take up to get fitter?

UNIT 6 ► LET'S REFLECT!

1 Word formation

Use the word given in capitals at the end of each line to form a word that fits in the space in the same line.

Example: (0) inventor

BASKETBALL

James Naismith, the (0)......*inventor*...... of	INVENT
basketball, was a teacher who worked with	
(1)............................. at the YMCA*. In 1891, he was	TEEN
asked by the (2)............................. to think of a new	ORGANIZE
kind of ball game that would be (3).............................	SUIT
for playing indoors in the winter. He put up two	
peach baskets on the wall of the gym, and the	
(4)............................. had to try to throw a soccer	PLAY
ball into them. The game was very (5).............................	SUCCESS
and soon schools and colleges all over the country	
became very (6)............................. about the new game.	ENTHUSE
In 1892, Naismith made some (7)............................. to	MODIFY
the rules, (8)............................. the introduction of a	INCLUDE
lightweight ball that was easier to throw, and a	
(9)............................. in the numbers in each team.	REDUCE
Since then the game has remained more or less	
(10)............................. .	CHANGE

*YMCA = Young Men's Christian Association

(10 marks)

2 Key word transformations

Use the word in **bold** to complete the second sentence so that it has a similar meaning to the first. Write between two and five words.

1 Joining a gym is too expensive for me.

   afford

   I .... a gym.

2 I haven't had the time to do my homework yet.

   round

   I haven't .... my homework yet.

3 I don't really want to go out this evening.

   like

   I don't .... out this evening.

4 Joan couldn't come with us because she was ill.

   prevented

   Joan's illness .... us.

5 It seems that he has injured himself quite seriously.

   appear

   His .... quite serious.

(10 marks)

3 Spot the mistake

Correct each of these sentences.

1 I like playing tennis, but I'm not very interested in to watch it on TV.

2 Jason says he wants that you pick him up this afternoon.

3 I'm just writing to congratulate you about winning the competition.

4 I hate it when tennis players start arguing with the judge.

5 There's no point to argue with the referee.

6 I can't afford me to go away this weekend.

7 I've really got to cut up smoking.

8 I'm very excited about to see the final.

9 Who learned you to ski like that?

10 Have you ever considered to become a professional footballer?

(10 marks)

4 Wordcomb

Complete the sentences and write the answers in the puzzle to find the missing word.

1 Villeneuve .... to finish the race, so he didn't get any points. (6)

2 My parents are having a tennis .... built. (5)

3 I love .... football on TV, but I rarely play it. (8)

4 We didn't score any goals, so the final result was three .... (3)

5 At the moment my son's very .... on Kung Fu. (4)

6 I'm much better at squash than Harry – I .... him all the time. (4)

7 Our team is much stronger. I'm sure we'll .... the match easily. (3)

8 You ought to give up smoking or at least .... down a bit. (3)

9 I .... the last practice session because I was ill. (6)

(20 marks)

Total: 50 marks

7 Times to come

LEAD-IN

Look into the crystal ball to see some predictions for the 21st century.

2005 Cures will be found for some of today's serious illnesses.

2007 Wood like teak and mahogany will be as expensive as gold and silver.

2020 People will be put into hibernation for long-distance space travel.

2008 A comet will hit our planet.

2023 Computers will be able to read your mind.

2015 The average life expectancy will be over 100 years.

In small groups, decide which prediction you think is:

the most likely   the most interesting   the most worrying.

1 Multiple matching

A The title of the text is *What won't be around in 50 years' time*. Think of five things that might be mentioned. Read the text quickly to see whether you were right. Take no notice of gaps 0–6.

B Read the list of headings and then read the text again. Choose the most suitable heading from the list A–H for each part (1–6) of the article. There is one extra heading you do not need. There is an example at the beginning (0).

> **HELPLINE**
> Look for similar ideas and words in the text to those in the headings, e.g. *H* is the answer to (0) because the paragraph talks about water shortages in the future and new washing methods to save water.

A   Convenient health care

B   Don't rely on others to look after you

C   Say goodbye to traffic jams

D   Forget the annual seaside holiday

E   A return to traditional values

F   Until we get fed up with each other

G   No more purses and wallets

H   New ways of cleaning things

What won't be around in 50 YEARS' time

0   *H*

A combination of a larger population and greater demands on resources will result in water becoming scarcer and all households will have water meters. There will, however, be a number of water-saving ideas, such as low-water washing
05   methods. Dirty crockery and cutlery will be put in an ultrasound machine – from which they will come out spotless. Newly developed materials will not only be dirt-shedding but will also be crease-resistant and self-pressing.

1

In some countries, only one in two marriages lasts, so marriage
10   will almost certainly become less popular in the future. Instead of marrying for life, the majority of people will enter into voluntary partnerships and sign an agreement for a specific period of time. At the end of that time, it will be possible to renew the agreement if both partners want to. The rise in single-
15   parent families will continue and, as the population increases, we may even introduce a tax system which encourages people to have no more than one child.

2

The sea may still be fashionable but the sun will be a definite no-no. The ozone hole is now an accepted fact and is expected
20   to get worse – even if we stop producing all the CFCs* which are thought to be causing it, there are already enough in the atmosphere to continue their deadly work for another 75 years. A suntanned skin will be a sign of ill-health and no-one will lie on beaches risking their lives for that important suntan.

3

25   As the average age of the population increases, medical costs will also go up. In future, we won't visit doctors. Family doctors will no longer exist, and, in their place will come self-examination by computer. You'll be able to carry out most of your own medical tests and check-ups at home and you'll be
30   able to transmit the results, with a description of any symptoms, to a medical centre. Any medicines needed will be sent by post or special delivery.

4	

With fewer jobs and many people available for work, job-sharing will be common. The working week could be only 15
35 hours, and most of those who are in full-time jobs will have short-term contracts. Welfare benefits will disappear as governments cut back on spending. State pensions and unemployment benefit will no longer exist. So start saving for your private pension and redundancy insurance now.

5	

40 People in the next century won't have to deal with the congested roads of today. Cities and town centres will increasingly be car-free with hundreds of moving walkways to assist an ageing population. Public
45 transport will become more popular and, within 10 years from now, most electric cars will offer the
50 same performance as petrol and diesel vehicles.

6	

Enjoy the feeling of coins jingling in your pocket while you can, as one day they'll be nothing but a distant memory. Notes and
55 coins will gradually disappear and be replaced by a central computer system. The local high street bank will vanish, and all our personal banking will be done on special telephone lines.

*Chloro-fluorocarbons – gases considered harmful to the earth's atmosphere

C Which of the predictions in the text above do you think:

• is the least likely to happen?
• is the most depressing?
• would be the greatest improvement on life nowadays?

WP 1

2 Vocabulary

In pairs, find words and expressions in the text which mean the same as those below. The words are listed according to the paragraphs in which they appear.

• in shorter supply / plates, cups, etc. / knives, forks, etc. / very clean
• done willingly / put your name to something
• something not advised / fatal
• send / signs of illness
• usual / having lost your job
• blocked / getting older / cars, lorries, etc.
• little by little / become impossible to see (2 words)

3 Phrasal verbs with *cut*

A In the text it says *as governments cut back on spending.* **What does** *cut back on* **mean?** Underline **the phrasal verbs with** *cut* **in these pairs of sentences. Which of the phrasal verbs with objects can be separated?**

1 If we cut down on the amount of paper we use, we'll help to save the rainforests.

   If we cut down any more trees, the rainforests will disappear.

2 The whole area was cut off by the floods.

   Peter phoned to tell his mother the good news but they were cut off.

3 It's rude to cut in when someone is speaking.

   It's dangerous to cut in when you're overtaking another car.

4 The doctors have advised Susan to cut all fatty foods out of her diet.

   He cut the picture out of the newspaper.

B What's the difference in meaning between the verbs in each pair of sentences?

C Complete these sentences using one of the verbs above.

Example: It is considered impolite to cut in.

1 We can reduce the danger of heart disease by .... certain foods.

2 If you don't pay the electricity bill, you'll get ....

3 We should try not to .... too many trees and forests in the future.

4 Occasionally when you're on the phone you're .... while talking.

5 Motorists sometimes cause accidents by .... when overtaking.

6 If you want to keep an article from a newspaper, you can ....

7 After a heavy fall of snow, some places can be ....

WP 2&3

LEAD-IN ▶

Telecommuting means working from home while communicating with the office and elsewhere via computer links. In small groups, discuss these questions.

1 What do you think some advantages of telecommuting will be?

2 What might some of the disadvantages of telecommuting be?

1 Open cloze

Read the text about what life will be like for young people growing up in the future and think of one word which best fits each space. *Example: (0) or*

> The open cloze concentrates on grammar, so the words you need will mainly be prepositions, pronouns, articles and auxiliary verbs. Contractions may not be used since they count as two words.

> You are having a geography lesson on screen four later this morning. The lesson begins at 10.30.......

When telecommuting becomes universal, a marvellous thing will happen. We won't have to live near our jobs (0).....*or*..... travel to work. At present, most companies just haven't realized that telecommuting is going to change the lives (1)..................... each generation. One big change is that parents will be (2)..................... to buy their children's education from competitive telecommuting programs. From (3)..................... early age, probably about two, tomorrow's children will telecommute from home into databases. From the child's input, (4)..................... computer will decide what questions it is going to ask the child next. The (5)..................... serious loss to children is that they won't make friends of their (6)..................... age. To combat this, competitive leisure groups will be created (7)..................... that children can meet new companions and form friendships. As many new telecommuting jobs will involve operating computers which are constantly changing, it is probable (8)..................... many 11 to 15 year olds will prove better (9)..................... handling these than their parents. For (10)..................... reason, a lot of children will be allowed (11)..................... give up school early and work in the 'family commuting firm'. A possible future pattern (12)..................... that young people (13)..................... the age of 11 to about 23 will do more paid work; people aged between 25 (14)..................... 35 will learn to play more, and this includes playing (15)..................... their young children; and people over 35 will go back to learning more through telecommuting into the database.

GRAMMAR ZOOM

The future

1 Which future is which?

A Look at these sentences and say which form of the future is being used.

1 I'm going to do computer studies next year.

2 My brother will be sixteen next year.

3 Computers are going to take over our lives.

4 The university term begins in October.

5 We're getting together to discuss the computer course tomorrow.

B Which form of the future in A is used to talk about:

a information about the future which is definite?

b a future event, e.g. on a timetable?

c an intention or a decision to do something?

d a probability based on evidence now?

e a definite future arrangement?

2 What does *will* mean?

A Look at the sentences 1–7 and match them with the functions in a–f saying what meaning *will / will not* expresses in each sentence. More than one answer may be correct.

1 I haven't a clue what I'm going to do this weekend. I know! I'll go for a long bike ride.

2 I will pass the exam, even if I have to take it three times!

3 Will you wait for me while I make a quick phone call?

4 I'll help you unpack the shopping.

5 I won't take no for an answer!

6 I'll take you to the cinema – but not today!

7 This cooker just will not light.

a *a willingness or an offer to do something*

b *a snap decision (made just now)*

c *a promise*

d *a request*

e *an inability or a refusal to do something*

f *a determination to do something*

B **In small groups, take it in turns to:**

ask someone to post a letter for you.

say you are determined to learn how to drive.

tell someone the computer isn't working.

make a quick decision about what you want to
have for lunch.

promise to lend someone a video at the weekend.

offer to help someone clean their car.

C **People often make resolutions to improve
their lives when a new year starts. Think
of three resolutions that you will make.**

Example:

*I'll try to work harder. I won't argue with my elder
brother. I'll stop slamming doors.*

D **We often use *Shall I/we … ?* when we
make a suggestion or offer. Make
suggestions about the ideas below.**

Examples:

Shall I help you with your suitcase?
Shall we go for a coffee?

that you open a window in the classroom
going to the cinema
that you clean the board
having a game of tennis

3   Present continuous, *will* or *going to*?

**Put the verb in brackets into the appropriate
form of the future. More than one form may
be correct.**

Example: (1) Are you doing

Sophie: (1).*Are you doing*. (you do) anything
        special tonight?

Maria: Actually, I (2)........................... (have)
        dinner with a friend. We
        (3)........................... (go) to that
        cheap restaurant in the High Street.
        Do you want to come?

Sophie: Thanks very much. I'd love to, but I
        (4)........................... (have) to phone
        home first. I know, I (5)...........................
        (phone) after the lesson. But what
        about that homework we're supposed
        to hand in tomorrow?

Maria: Oh, I forgot the homework! When
        (6)........................... (we do) it?

Sophie: Well, our teacher (7)...........................
        (not/be) here tomorrow, so Mr
        Williams (8)........................... (take) the
        lesson. I think we (9)...........................
        (be) able to hand it in the day after
        tomorrow.

Maria: We (10)........................... (do) the
        homework tomorrow night, instead!

4   So what are the chances of … ?

A **Number the phrases in the Phrase Box 1–6 so that the one
expressing the greatest probability comes first and the one
expressing the least comes last.**

Expressing probability/improbability	
There definitely won't be …	*I'm absolutely convinced that … will …*
I don't think … will …	*I don't think it's very likely that …*
I think … will …	*I think … is/are (probably) going to …*

B **Use the phrases to discuss the probability of these things
happening in the next 50 years.**

1   There will be a single world currency.

2   Almost everybody will have false teeth.

3   We will be invaded by a race from outer space.

4   All machines will be operated by remote control.

5   All fresh water will be sold in bottles.

6   Diseases like cancer will disappear.

5   Personal Filofax

**You are going to arrange to meet a friend one night next week.
Work in pairs.**

Student A   Look at the information in the Filofax on page 170.

Student B   Look at the information in the Filofax on page 172.

**Use the information in your Filofax to find a possible night to
meet. Student A, begin by suggesting you meet one night when
you are free.**

Example:
A: Shall we meet next Friday evening?
B: No, I'm sorry but I'm going to a concert next Friday.
A: What about … ?

6   Tricky situations

A **Match the pictures with the tricky situations.**

a   forgotten to do homework for today's lesson

b   locked out of your house – no one at home

c   see someone breaking into the house opposite

B **Say what you think the people decide to do. Use either *will* or
going to.**

1 Talking about yourself

**What kinds of things worry or excite you about your future?
In pairs, talk about how you feel about some of these things.
Use the expressions in italic below.**

school work	job interviews	earning money
getting married	taking your driving test	celebrations

I'm dreading my exams.

I'm nervous about going to the dentist's.

I'm excited about our trip to the USA.

I can't wait until I leave school!

> **HELP LINE**
> Even if you are asked to talk about things you have never really considered, always try to answer the examiner's questions as fully as possible.

2 Talking together

A In pairs, match the words on the left with those on the right to find some problems the world is facing today.

Example: acid rain

acid / global / skin /
wasting / traffic /
natural / oil / air

spills / natural resources /
congestion / disasters / cancer /
pollution / rain / warming

Now match the problems with the pictures below.

B With the same partner, decide which of the problems in A you think will be the most serious for the world in the years to come. Do you have any of these problems in your country?

> **HELP LINE**
> In the exam, you may need to be able to express some opinions about what is happening in the world around you.

C Below is a list of possible solutions to present-day problems. Decide with your partner which solutions would be the most helpful in your country and why.

Use the expressions in the Phrase Box.

a encouraging the recycling of glass, paper and plastic

b using smokeless fuels

c controlling waste from factories

d using unleaded petrol

e planting more trees

f using electric cars

g making greater use of wind, wave and solar energy

h creating a better system of public transport

> **PHRASE BOX**
> **Expressing uncertainty**
> *I'm not really sure but I think … would be … because …*
> *I can't say for certain but … is going to be …*
> *It's difficult to say exactly but perhaps … would be …*

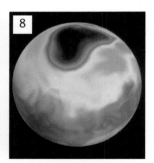

LEAD-IN

In pairs, take it in turns to describe one of the pictures below.

1 Note taking A

You will hear a recorded message giving information about the Earth Gallery. Listen to the message and write in the answers.

NATURAL HISTORY MUSEUM

EARTH GALLERY

Open from 11 am to 6 pm on

| | 1 |

Admission: £16 for a

| | 2 |

To enter gallery, use

| | 3 |

See a volcano from

| | 4 |

See model of Japanese

| | 5 |

Advance booking available for

| | 6 |

Information pack advises how to

| | 7 |

Remember your answer should fit into the box.
Write only the most important information.

Listen again and check your answers.

2 Note taking B

You will now hear a guide taking some younger visitors on a guided tour of the museum. Listen to the conversation and write in the answers.

Tour takes about

| | 1 |

Museum opened in

| | 2 |

Cost of the development project is

| | 3 |

Tour does not include

| | 4 |

Guide will take visitors inside

| | 5 |

Visitors will see what earth was like

| | 6 |

Toilets are next to the

| | 7 |

Listen again and check your answers.

3 Everyday expressions

A These underlined expressions are used on the tape.

1 … to see what it's like, you mean?
2 You see, it's called restless because …
3 There's always something going on, you know – even inside – right at the centre of the earth.

Which expression:

a is sometimes used to give you time to think what to say next?

b checks you have understood correctly?

c introduces an explanation?

B Use one of these expressions to complete this conversation.

Jill: We're going to that museum next weekend.
        (1) .... , the one that's only just opened.

Sam: (2) .... the one with all those fantastic science exhibitions?

Jill: That's right. (3) .... I told my parents all about it and they thought it sounded great, so they've arranged to take me on Saturday. Do you want to come too?

Sam: Yes. What time are you going?

WP 5

Writing a transactional letter (2)

In Part 1 of the writing paper, you may be asked to write a transactional letter to a company or someone you do not know well. In this case, you need to make sure that the letter is written in a suitably formal style and that details are not directly copied from the given information.

1 Sample task

Read the sample task and, in pairs, make notes to summarize the key points you would need to include if answering this question.

You are at a language school in England. Your class is planning an excursion, and is going to invite the host families as well. Read the advertisement and the note from your teacher asking you to write a letter to one of the host families. Write your **letter** (120–180 words).

Open-air theatre:
ROMEO & JULIET
AUGUST 17 & 18

✳ Shakespeare as never seen before
✳ internationally-renowned theatre group
✳ incredible special effects
✳ a beautiful open-air setting beside the lake

Make sure you don't miss out on one of the most popular events of the summer calendar.

This year Shakespeare leaps to the year 2050 where his sixteenth century Romeo and Juliet are radically changed. The music will be played by one of Britain's best orchestras. Bring your own picnic to enjoy beside the lake. Book early to avoid disappointment.

Admission: £15 per ticket (no reductions)
Free Parking

Write to Mr and Mrs Smith to invite them on the 18 August (depart: 6.30 pm).

They pay for the tickets but we'll provide the transport and picnic (should be great!).

They must contact us immediately if they want to come.

---

2 Sample answer

Read the letter and answer the questions.

Dear Mr and Mrs Smith

I am writing to tell you that we are arranging an excursion to the open-air theatre on 18 August at 6.30 pm which is one of the most popular events of the summer calendar. We wondered whether you would like to join us.

The evening will consist of an internationally-renowned theatre group performing Shakespeare with incredible special effects as never seen before beside the lake. The music will be played by one of Britain's best orchestras and I am sure it will be a very enjoyable evening. During the play we will enjoy a picnic beside the lake.

We are going on August 18 and tickets for the concert cost £15.00 per person. I am afraid that there are no discounts for children. You'll have to pay for the tickets but we'll provide the transport and picnic for free. Contact us immediately, if you want to come. Remember to book early to avoid disappointment.

I look forward to hearing from you,

Yours faithfully

Juanita Martinez

(168 words)

Analysis

The key points were all included in the letter. However, the writer has copied a lot of the information instead of rephrasing it. It is important to remember that you have to use the information you are given but should not just copy phrases straight from the task or you may be penalized in the exam.

1   Underline all the phrases the writer has copied.
2   In pairs rewrite four of your underlined phrases in a more suitable way.

Writing a transactional letter

You have volunteered to help your language school in England organize a trip to London to visit the special exhibition at the Science Museum called 'Earth 2100'. You have been asked to write to the social organizer of a nearby language school to tell him about the excursion and to invite his students to join you. He'll need to know a little about the exhibition, transport arrangements and costs. The final date for booking and payment (in full) is the 18 June.

Write your **letter** (120–180 words).

Notes...

Work through the notes and prepare your letter.

In pairs, underline the key words in the question and discuss what points you need to make in your letter. Organize the points into three topic areas.

A   General information

....

....

B   Transport arrangements

....

....

C   Payment

....

....

These topic areas will form the basis of your three main paragraphs.

Paragraph 1

Say why you are writing, what exhibition you are planning to visit, and what it will be about.

Paragraph 2

Give details of *when* the excursion will take place, *when* and *where* the coach is picking you up, and *what time* you will probably get back in the evening, etc.

Paragraph 3

Give details of ticket prices and say when bookings need to be made.

Paragraph 4

Finish your letter in a suitable way.

THE SCIENCE MUSEUM
SPECIAL EXHIBITION

THE WORLD IN 2100
18–24 July

Fascinating exhibits and talks on:

✳ developments in technology

✳ transport in the year 2100

✳ the environment

✳ future medical advances

Admission:
ADULTS £15.00
STUDENTS £10.00
CHILDREN UNDER 5 £2.00

GEORGE'S COACHES
BOOKING CONFIRMATION

CLIENT: Lawson Language School
             21 High Street

OUTWARD JOURNEY

DATE: 21 July
PICK-UP POINT: Lawson Language School
                     21 High Street
TIME: 8.45 am
DESTINATION: Science Museum, London
ARRIVAL TIME (estimated):   10.30 am

RETURN JOURNEY

DATE: 21 July
PICK-UP POINT: Science Museum, London

TIME: 4.15 pm
DESTINATION: Lawson Language School
ARRIVAL TIME (estimated):   6.00 pm

COST PER PASSENGER: £8.50

WORDPOWER

1 Words easily confused

Use these words to complete sentences 1–8. More than one answer may be possible.

no	no one	none
neither … nor	nobody	nothing

1 .... can tell if there is life on other planets or not.

2 The new buildings will be .... spacious .... attractive.

3 The top floor offices will have plenty of windows but those on the ground floor will have ....

4 In 50 years' time there will be .... cars allowed in city centres at all.

5 .... knows what private housing will be like in the future.

6 .... has been decided about the future of the city centre.

7 There are .... lifts in this building.

8 I know .... about the new fire regulations.

2 Phrasal verbs with *back*

A Match the phrasal verbs in questions 1–8 with the meanings in a–h.

1 Do you usually pay people back if they are unkind to you?

2 What time will you get back home tonight?

3 When might you ring somebody back?

4 When would you turn back on a journey?

5 What can we fall back on if the electricity is cut off?

6 How do you feel if people don't give back things they borrow from you?

7 When you talk to friends, what kinds of things do you keep back?

8 Do you want to go back over this unit?

a *revise / explain again*

b *rely on sth or sb when in difficulty*

c *reverse the direction*

d *get revenge on sb*

e *refuse to tell / not tell sb sth*

f *return a phone call*

g *return*

h *return to its owner*

B In pairs, take it in turns to ask and answer questions 1–8.

3 Extreme weather conditions

Match the extreme weather conditions with the explanations.

1	*drought*	a	a large amount of water in an area that should be dry
2	*blizzard*	b	a serious shortage of water
3	*gale*	c	a very bad snowstorm
4	*flood*	d	a very strong wind
5	*hurricane*	e	a storm with very strong winds

4 Word formation

Use the word given in capitals at the end of each line to form a word that fits in the space in the same line.

Example: (0) traditional

•● LIFE IN THE FUTURE ●●

(0).....*Traditional*..... holidays by the sea will no	TRADITION
longer be (1)..................... . In the future, people	FASHION
will take cheap VR (virtual reality) holidays, or watch	
three (2)..................... TVs in their free time. Real	DIMENSION
holidays will become (3)..................... for the	EXCLUSIVE
(4)..................... . Although we will have more	WEALTH
leisure time, spending power will be greatly	
(5)..................... .	RESTRICT
(6)..................... will be a problem. It may lead	EMPLOY
to a rise in crime which could be (7).....................	DISASTER
and the world may become a much more	
(8)..................... place in which to live. However,	DANGER
criminals will be given (9)..................... to return	ENCOURAGE
to a crime-free life and become (10).....................	USE
members of the community.	

5 The same or different?

A Write S beside the words which are pronounced the same, and D beside those which are different.

1	cheap / chip	3	life / live	5	their / there
2	rise / rice	4	plays / place		

B Read these sentences and complete the spaces with an appropriate word from the pairs in 1–5 above.

1 He lives in a really nice .... with a sea view.

2 .... mother has been in the news a lot recently.

3 I think the price of petrol is going to .... again.

4 She's writing a book about her father's ....

UNIT 7 ▶ LET'S REFLECT!

1 Word formation

Use the word given in capitals at the end of each line to form a word that fits in the space in the same line. *Example: (0) natural*

crystal ball gazing

Look into the crystal ball to see some problems facing the (0) ...*natural*... world which could be (1)............................ for the human race. Most people are in (2)............................ that it is time to make some important decisions about how to deal with these (3)............................ problems. Natural resources are (4)............................ than ever before. Food production is falling and, if there is no (5)............................ by the beginning of the next millennium, the world will be (6)............................ near to running out of supplies. It is now time to put (7)............................ differences to one side and concentrate on giving all countries of the world real (8)............................ to work together in an understanding and (9)............................ way to ensure that they do all they can to find a (10)............................ to our planet's problems.

NATURE

DISASTER

AGREE

DIFFER
SCARCE
IMPROVE
DANGER
TRADITION

ENCOURAGE
FRIEND
SOLVE

(10 marks)

2 Talking about the future

A **Complete these sentences with a suitable form of the future using the given verbs. More than one answer may be possible.**

1 The next computer course .... (start) on September 17.

2 They turned down David's job application so he has no idea what he .... (do) now.

3 I .... (fly) to Greece at 10.30 on Monday morning.

4 I don't know how I .... (tell) your mother what you've done.

5 There's something wrong with this torch. The light just .... (not/come) on.

(5 marks)

B **Match the meanings of *will* with the sentences below.**

a *a promise*   c *a sudden decision*   e *determination*
b *a request*   d *willingness/offer*

1 I'll carry that bag for you.

2 I will learn to use this computer, even if it takes me a whole year.

3 Don't worry! I won't tell anyone what you said.

4 Will you wait here, please?

5 I don't feel like staying in tonight. I know! I'll go to the cinema.

(5 marks)

3 Key word transformations

Use the word in **bold** to complete the second sentence so that it has a similar meaning to the first. Write between two and five words.

1 The numbers of cars on the roads must be reduced.
   down
   We must .... the numbers of cars on the roads.

2 Interrupting when someone is speaking is rude.
   cut
   It's rude .... when someone is speaking.

3 We have an emergency electricity supply in case we are cut off.
   back
   If we are cut off, we can ....
   .... our emergency electricity supply.

4 We've decided to leave early tomorrow morning.
   set
   We are .... early tomorrow morning.

5 I know you are hiding something from me.
   back
   What .... from me?

(10 marks)

4 Vocabulary

These nouns and adjectives all appear in the unit. Complete them and use them in a sentence of your own.

1 expens.................... (adjective)
2 predict.................... (noun)
3 appoint.................... (noun)
4 populat.................... (noun)
5 harm.................... (adjective)
6 popul.................... (adjective)
7 congest.................... (noun)
8 competit.................... (adjective)
9 develop.................... (noun)
10 glob.................... (adjective)

(20 marks)

Total: 50 marks

8 Money matters

LEAD-IN ▶

In pairs or small groups, discuss these questions.

1 Do you think people with money should do more to help those without money? How?

2 Have you ever given any money to a charity or to someone who really needed it? Why? Why not?

1 Gapped text

A Read the text about a man called Charles Gray. As you read, look out for the answers to these questions. Take no notice of the gaps.

1 In what way is Charles Gray different from most people?

2 How does he feel about his way of life now?

3 What do you think of what he did?

Who wants to be a millionaire?

Sixteen years ago, Charles Gray was a millionaire. He worked as a university professor and had a huge six-bedroomed mansion in the centre of
05 Eugene, Oregon. Today he has nothing. But this is no sob story – there have been no Stock Market crashes or terrible illnesses or gambling debts. Charles Gray is poor on purpose. | 0 | *H* | And this,
10 he says, has brought him happiness.

Charles Gray was born into a poor family where he developed, as he puts it, 'a kind of working-class dislike of the rich'. However, he became very successful, in
15 the traditional American dream fashion. | 1 | | He married for love but later inherited both a large mansion and a small fortune – a little over $2 million.

| 2 | | The enormous amount of
20 money that he had inherited began to make him feel guilty and uncomfortable. 'It bothered me that I lived this way when I knew that people all over the world were starving and didn't have a
25 fair chance.'

The solution came when his wife Leslie announced over breakfast one morning that she thought they should give away half of their money. Instead of choking
30 on his cornflakes, Charles' reaction was 'What an excellent idea!' | 3 | | Soon afterwards, they moved out of their big house into a smaller apartment.

But in spite of giving away more money
35 than most people make in their lifetime, Charles still wasn't happy. Although he was a lot poorer than he had been the year before, he wasn't poor enough. Then he thought up the idea of dividing
40 the world's wealth by its total population, and working out how much each person should have. | 4 | | So he gave away everything he still owned, and decided to try and live on his fair share. At this
45 point his wife decided to leave.

Now, sixteen years later, he lives in a small rented caravan in the backyard of someone else's house. He does not need to buy much, so he only has to work for
50 a few hours a week. He grows his own

vegetables and in the summer he collects the fruit that most people can't be bothered to pick. Charles believes that working too hard and being
55 over-ambitious is a major cause of unhappiness, a view which many people would agree with. 'We have lost our traditional values as we have grown richer, because the consumer goods
60 that are put before us are so appealing. | 5 | | It doesn't contribute to happiness – in fact many people are more miserable. They would be much happier if they wanted less and
65 worked less.'

He believes that most people try to escape from the rat race by earning so much money that they will be free from everyday worries, but most people never
70 succeed. | 6 | | He is no longer guilty about his undeserved wealth, and says 'I'm much happier now – I wouldn't go back to being rich for anything – no way.'

B Seven sentences have been removed from the text. Choose from the sentences A–H the one which fits each gap (1–6). There is one extra sentence that you do not need. There is an example at the beginning (0) H

Remember to look for contextual clues and reference devices. You also need to look at what comes before *and* after the gap to choose the best sentence.

A   He has found an easier way of getting out of it, and has discovered that choosing to be poor makes you free.

B   Most people would be very happy with this, but Charles Gray was different.

C   He worked out that this came to about $100 a month.

D   She always used to say that Charles was the most unselfish person in the world.

E   So the Grays set up a small charity and gave away half of their money to their favourite causes.

F   But in order to pay for a bigger house or better car you have to put in an enormous amount of work.

G   He passed his exams, got a car, credit cards and a good job as a university professor.

H   Tired of being a 'have' in a world of 'have-nots', he made the deliberate choice to get rid of his wealth.

C Now answer these questions.

1   Which answers depend mainly on reference devices?
2   Which answers depend mainly on the context?

2 Vocabulary

Match the words and phrases from the article 1–5 with their meanings in a–e.

1	*sob story*	a	products bought and used by customers
2	*over-ambitious*	b	competitive society
3	*consumer goods*	c	sad tale to make you cry
4	*the rat race*	d	wealthy and poor people
5	*the 'haves' and 'have-nots'*	e	wanting to succeed too much

W·1

3 Language study

too and *not … enough*

A Look at these sentences from the text. What do you notice about the position of the adjectives / adverbs?

Although he was a lot poorer than he had been the year before, he was <u>not poor enough</u>.

Charles believes that working <u>too hard</u> … is a major cause of unhappiness …

B Read through the following sentences. Which ones are correct and which ones are incorrect?

1   I thought the film was too good.

2   The sea isn't enough warm to swim in at this time of year.

3   I haven't got enough time to finish my homework.

4   The car was too expensive for me to buy it.

5   My brother was too ill to go to the party.

C Complete the following sentences with *too* or *not … enough* and a suitable adjective / adverb.

Example: I can't afford that new dress; it is too expensive.

1   A friend of mine had a nervous breakdown because she worked .... and never had any time off.

2   The doctor said I was .... nervous and that I should try to relax more.

3   My sister is only fifteen, so she is .... to vote.

4   My grandmother enjoys the weather in spring and autumn, but she finds it much .... in the summer.

5   We've got to move; we have six children and our house is .... for us any more.

1 Open cloze

A Read the text below and answer these questions.

1 Which way of making money appeals to you the most?

2 Can you think of any other ways of getting rich?

MONEYMONEYMONEY

You could win the lottery or inherit a fortune at (0).....*the*..... age of 50. But most of us dream about getting rich as soon as (1)..................... can. So, if you want to find out how to make a fortune, read on.

BE A SUPERMODEL

Follow the example of Linda Evangelista, (2)................... won't consider getting out of bed for less (3)................. £10,000. That's the minimum fee the supermodel (4)................... Canada charges for a day's work, and she (5)................... thought to earn $2 million a year. But even if you can't be a model, don't give (6) .... hope. There are other ways (7)................... getting the money.

WRITE A BRILLIANT BOOK

If you wrote a best seller, you probably wouldn't have to work again. The author Peter Mayle, who had previously (8)..................... in advertising, wrote two amusing books about his home (9)..................... the South of France. The books were very successful, (10)..................... he also made a fortune from the TV series. If he makes a film, he will no doubt make even more money.

HAVE A BRIGHT IDEA

Bette Nesmith invented something (11)..................... make every secretary's life a little easier – she invented Liquid Paper, the original typewriter correction fluid. She came up with the idea (12)..................... day while she was working (13)..................... a typist. By (14)..................... so, she changed office life forever and earned herself a fortune (15)..................... the same time.

B Read the text again and think of one word which best fits each space.

Example: (0) the

WP 2&3

GRAMMAR ZOOM

Conditionals

1 Zero conditional

We can use the zero conditional to give instructions.

A Look at the following example from the text:

if + present tense, imperative

… if you want to find out how to make a fortune, read on.

B Complete the sentences below using the verbs in the box. Some spaces may have more than one option.

call	come	give	reply
need	help	want	take

1 If you .... any food, ... yourself.

2 .... now if you want to .... advantage of this special offer.

3 If you .... to Thessaloniki, ... me a ring.

4 .... me if you .... any help.

2 First conditional

We can use the first conditional to refer to real possibilities.

A Look at the example below. What other words can we use instead of *will*?

If + present tense, will future.

If he makes a film, he will make even more money.

B Put the verbs in these sentences into the correct tense.

1 Where .... (you / live) if your parents .... (move) to America?

2 If the plane .... (arrive) on time, I .... (get) home at about 8.15.

3 I .... (not / buy) the book if it .... (cost) more than £5.

4 If you .... (get) a new computer, you .... (have to) spend a few weeks learning how to use it.

5 If I .... (see) Peter tomorrow, I .... (invite) him to the party.

6 Jane's father says he .... (buy) her a car if she .... (pass) her driving test next week.

C Complete these sentences with your own ideas.

He'll be disappointed if he doesn't see any lions.

1   I will be very happy if …
2   My mother will be furious with me if …
3   He will be disappointed if …
4   If they have the time this weekend, …

3 *If, unless, in case*

A Look at these pairs of sentences. What is the difference in meaning?

1   I'll stay here if your sister phones.
    I'll stay here unless your sister phones.
2   I'll take a coat if the weather is bad.
    I'll take a coat in case the weather is bad.

B Rewrite the following sentences using *unless* or *in case*.

Example:
Only phone me at work if it's a real emergency.
Don't phone me at work unless it's a real emergency.

1   We can't go out tonight if we can't find a babysitter.

    ....

2   We need to insure the car because something might go wrong.

    ....

3   If she doesn't apologize, I won't talk to her again.

    ....

4   We'll leave you a contact number because you might want to phone us.

    ....

5   I'll take some cash because I might want to buy something.

    ....

6   Michael will do well in the exam if the questions aren't too difficult.

    ....

4 Practice

For this exercise, imagine that you have a pessimistic outlook on life. Make suitable responses to the following statements, using questions or statements in the first conditional.

Examples:
A: I'm having a barbecue next Saturday.
B: It won't be much fun unless the weather improves.
A: We're going to have a big party at the end of term.
B: Yes, but what will you do if nobody wants to come?

1   I'm taking my driving test next Friday, and my instructor says he's sure that I'll pass.
2   I'm really excited. My father's got a job in Australia and we're moving there next month.
3   My brother's really pleased. He's got an interview for a job with a film company next week.
4   I've had some great news. I'm going on a sailing holiday this autumn.
5   I've found a second-hand car to buy and it's really cheap, too.

5 Second conditional

We can use the second conditional to talk about imaginary or unreal situations.

A Compare the following sentences.

First conditional
If you write a best seller, Peter, you probably won't have to work again.

Second conditional
If you wrote a best seller, Peter, you probably wouldn't have to work again.

1   What is the difference in meaning between the two sentences?
2   What tenses do we use when we are talking about imaginary or unlikely situations?

NB: Remember that in the *if* clause, we usually use *were* instead of *was*.

If I were you, I would complain.

If my brother were here, he would be able to help us.

B Complete the following sentences using the verbs in the box. You may need to change the form of the verb.

apply	can	change	give
have	spend	be	

1   I'm sorry I can't help. Of course, if I
    .... her number, I ....it
    to you.
2   I .... the laws about cruel sports if
    I .... the prime minister.
3   You .... a lot more money left if you
    .... so much on clothes.
4   I .... for that job if I ....
    speak Italian.

6 Practice

Think of four different ways of finishing these sentences.

Example:
If Charles Gray were my father …

… I would be angry with him for giving all the family's money away.
… I would try to make him see a psychiatrist.
… I would feel proud of him.
… I would be worried about his health.

1   If my parents gave all their money away, …
2   If I were a millionaire, …
3   If I lived a long way from my family, …
4   If I had a year's holiday, …

1 Talking about yourself

In pairs, tell your partner which of these statements about shopping applies to you.
Explain why.

a *I love shopping. If I had more time, I'd go shopping every day.*

b *Shopping bores me stiff. I always get out of going shopping if I can.*

c *I don't get enough pocket money to go shopping.*

d *I can't say I'm mad about shopping but I don't mind it if I need something special.*

2 Taking a long turn

A With the same partner, match the words on the left with those on the right, then talk about what the people are doing in the pictures below.

Example: The people in the picture on the right are discussing the price of something.

discussing   cash
queuing up   the price
paying in   credit card
paying by   at a market stall
looking for   at the till
                      a bargain in the sales

B Now take it in turns to talk for about one minute about the pictures. Use the phrases above. When your partner has finished, briefly say if you agree with what he/she has said.

Student A   Compare and contrast the shopping places in both pictures. Say which of these places you would prefer to shop in.

Student B   Compare and contrast the people in both pictures. Say which people you think are enjoying shopping and which are not.

3 Talking together

A In small groups, imagine that the town where you live is planning to build a new shopping centre to attract families to shop together. Talk about how popular the facilities below would be and decide which three would appeal most to families.

HELPLINE

Remember you have to discuss all the facilities first, then choose the three most popular. It is not necessary to agree with each other.

B In the same groups, imagine that you have all won a competition and the prize is £50 each to spend on one thing of your choice. Each make a list of four possible things to buy. Show each other your lists and take it in turns to ask for advice and make suggestions about what to spend the money on. Give reasons for your suggestions. Use the questions and answers in the Phrase Box to help you.

PHRASE BOX

Asking for advice

If you were me, what would you buy (on this list) … ?

What would you advise me to buy (on this list) … ?

Giving advice

If I were you, I'd buy … , because …

I certainly wouldn't spend my money on … if I were you, because …

How about buying … ?

1 Multiple choice

In the exam, the eight short extracts are not linked in any way.

Read through the questions carefully to find out what sort of information you need to listen for.

For example, you may be asked to do any of the following:

- work out where people are
- identify someone's feelings
- answer a question about detail.

You will hear people talking in eight different situations. For questions 1–8, choose the best answers A, B or C.

1 You will hear two people talking. Where are they?

A in a bank
B in a post office
C in a supermarket

`1`

2 You hear someone talking to a small group of people. What is the speaker trying to persuade them to do?

A to go to a department store
B to buy what he is selling
C to save money

`2`

3 You are at a hotel reception desk when you overhear this conversation. Why has the hotel guest received less money than he expected?

A He has had to pay a charge to change the money.
B The cashier has made a mistake.
C The exchange rate has changed.

`3`

4 You hear part of a TV programme. What sort of programme is it?

A a game show
B a travel programme
C a comedy show

`4`

5 You hear someone talking about an experience she had at a restaurant. How did she feel?

A embarrassed
B shocked
C angry

`5`

6 You hear someone being interviewed on a radio programme. Where did his money come from?

A the lottery
B his business
C an inheritance

`6`

7 You hear two people in a record shop. What does the customer want?

A a refund
B a replacement
C a different CD

`7`

8 You are in the street when you hear this conversation. The people come from

A the local area.
B a different part of the country.
C a foreign country.

`8`

Listen again and check your answers.

2 Talking about numbers

You heard several figures and numbers on the tape. How you would say the following pairs of numbers.

a You can call me at home on 581 6745.
b The population of the city is 5,816,745.
c 12.8742 divided by 2.58 = 4.99
d I can't believe it only cost £4.99.
e In some parts of the country it will reach 23°C.
f The latest survey says sales have risen by 23%.
g I'll meet you there at 6.45.
h 1.12 plus 5.33 equals 6.45.
i A square inch is 6.452 square centimetres.
j We have exactly 6,452 books in the library.

3 Multiple matching

You will hear five different people talking about the charities they work for. Match each speaker with one of the options A–F. Use the letters only once. There is one extra letter which you do not need to use.

Which speaker works for a charity that is mainly concerned with:

A education?   Speaker 1   `1`

B animals?   Speaker 2   `2`

C the needs of   Speaker 3   `3`
old people?

D the environment?   Speaker 4   `4`

E providing   Speaker 5   `5`
emergency relief?

F providing medical
services?

Listen again and check your answers.

Writing a composition (1)

In Part 2 of the writing paper, you may be given a composition to write, such as agreeing or disagreeing with a given statement.

1 Sample task

Read the sample task and answer the questions.

The following comment was printed in an article in a student magazine:

'Lotteries do more harm than good.'

Your teacher has asked you to write a **composition** on this subject, saying if you agree or disagree (120–180 words).

Task interpretation

1   The best way to write a composition like this is to look at two main points. What do you think these will be?

2   What else do you need to include?

3   What sort of language would be suitable for this composition – informal and chatty, or more formal?

2 Sample answer

Read the composition and complete the task.

Analysis

1   Look at the notes that were used to write the sample composition. Complete them with other information and ideas from the composition.

NATIONAL LOTTERY	
good points	*bad points*
provide excitement	make people spend too much money
....	....
....	....
....	....
....	....
....	....

Add some more ideas of your own to these lists.

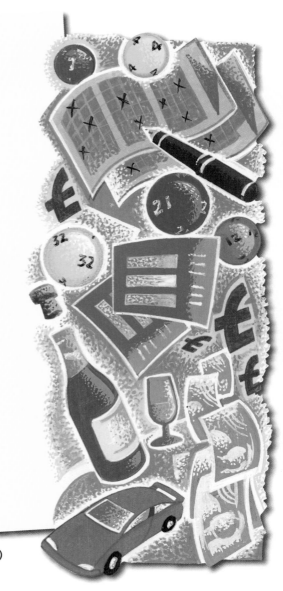

Lotteries are popular in many countries, and people enjoy taking part in them every week. Some people, however, think they can do more harm than good.

In my opinion, there are certainly a lot of good things about lotteries. Firstly, they can be fun to take part in as they provide a little excitement. They can also be enjoyed by everyone, and winning even a small prize can be very satisfying. What's more, some lotteries give away part of their profits to charities.

On the other hand, buying lottery tickets does have some potential dangers. For example, people could be tempted to spend much more than they can afford. In addition, they can attract people to other forms of gambling. Finally, winning as well as losing can bring unhappiness and some of the people who have won large amounts of money have lost some of their friends.

So, in my opinion, despite there being some positive aspects to lotteries, I think it is important not to spend too much on them or to take them too seriously.

(177 words)

Using linking words

Compositions are much clearer if you use link words and phrases to join your ideas together. Look back at the way the underlined words were used in the sample answer. Then complete the sentences using the words and phrases in the box.

also	what is more	on the other hand	firstly
however	in my opinion	in addition	finally

1 There are three reasons why I decided to get a new job. .... , I wasn't getting paid enough. Secondly, the office was miles from home and .... , I couldn't stand my boss.

2 I was rather angry with my sister because she lost one of my tapes and she .... damaged two of my books.

3 If I lose my job, I will have to give the company car back. .... , I may not be able to afford to stay in my flat.

4 Travellers' cheques are easy and convenient. .... , you can get your money back if you lose them.

5 The meal in the Dolce Vita was excellent. .... , the service was a little slow.

6 .... , smoking should be completely prohibited. .... , we do live in a democracy.

4 Writing task

Compositions

You may be asked to write a balanced argument about a given topic, statement or question. This may take the form of one of the following: advantages and disadvantages, for and against, agree and disagree.

You should always give your opinion when asked to do so. In tasks where it is not requested, you may choose to give your opinion in the final paragraph.

Use appropriate link words and do not repeat structures such as *think* too often, as it will sound very repetitive.

Writing a composition

The following comment was printed in an international magazine.

Winning a fortune doesn't always make people happy.

Your teacher has asked you to write a composition on this subject, saying if you agree or disagree.

Write your **composition** (120–180 words).

Notes...

Work through the notes and prepare your composition.

Before writing the composition, note down a few ideas in the table below. These notes will form the basis of your writing.

WINNING A FORTUNE	
good points	*bad points*
....	....
....	....
....	....
....	....
....	....
....	....

When you are writing the composition, organize your paragraphs as follows.

Paragraph 1

Explain quickly and clearly the theme of your composition.

Paragraph 2

Write about what a person could do if they won a great deal of money. Use the ideas from your notes above. The following structures may be useful for you:

If someone won a fortune, they could...

Maybe they would... and...

They might also...

Paragraph 3

Discuss some of the bad things that could happen to them. Use your ideas from the notes above.

Paragraph 4

Finish by giving a brief summary of your own opinion as to whether you agree or disagree with the statement.

Check your writing for spelling, punctuation and grammar mistakes.

WORD POWER

adjectives phrasal verbs expressions nouns

1 Words connected with money

A Match the phrases in the box with the verbs below. The phrases can be used more than once. The first one has been done for you.

a good salary	the bill	money
someone back	a new car	a fortune
someone £5	£5 from someone	

win: *money, a fortune, a new car*

make: ....

earn: ....

lend: ....

pay: ....

afford: ....

owe: ....

spend: ....

borrow: ....

cost: ....

B Complete these sentences using one of the verbs above.

1 If you don't .... that electricity bill soon, we'll get cut off.

2 I gave you £50 last week; you've given me back £35, so you still .... me £15.

3 My brother had to .... a lot of money from the bank to go to university.

4 I bought the car for £3,000 and sold it for £5,000, so I managed to .... a lot of money out of it.

5 Anna always wears designer dresses. She must .... a fortune on clothes.

6 When are you going to give me back the money I .... you?

C Choose three of the verbs and use them in sentences of your own.

1 ....

2 ....

3 ....

2 *Make* and *do*

A The verbs *make* and *do* are very common in a lot of everyday expressions. Which of the following words or phrases are used with *make*? Which are used with *do*?

.... a profit .... your homework

.... a noise .... progress

.... a living .... a phone call

.... sb a favour .... military service

.... a decision .... a difference

.... sense .... the washing up

.... a course .... a mistake

.... well .... sth/anything/nothing

B Which of the following sentences are correct and which are incorrect?

1 I don't want to make military service at all.

2 I did a number of silly mistakes in the test.

3 I find it very difficult to make decisions.

4 I usually do well in my exams.

5 Please try not to do any noise or you'll wake the children.

6 Listen, you have got to make your homework before you go out.

3 Forming words

A How many words can you make using the base word and a prefix, a suffix or both?

prefix	base	suffix	new words
in-	expense	-less	*expensive, inexpensive*
	price	-ive	....
	value	-able	....
	worth		....

B Now put the words under the correct headings below.

high price/of great worth		low price/of little worth	
expensive	....	*inexpensive*	....
....	....	....	

C Complete the following sentences. Use a word based on *cost, expense, price, value, worth*, making any changes that are necessary.

1 The .... of living in Tokyo is very high.

2 I'm so glad I spoke to you. Your advice was absolutely ....

3 Please let me pay. I can put the bill on my .... account.

4 Because of a bad harvest in South America, the .... of coffee in the supermarkets is going up.

5 The diamonds were fakes, so the ring was practically ....

UNIT 8 ➤ LET'S REFLECT!

1 Open cloze

Read the text and think of one word which best fits each space. *Example: (0) ever*

Have you (0).....*ever*..... dreamed of finding hidden treasure and wondered what you (1)..................... do if you were lucky enough (2)..................... find a fortune? Well, for Martin James, a professional treasure hunter, it (3)..................... all in a day's work, because that is how he (4)..................... a living. During his highly successful career, he (5)..................... discovered over 80 different shipwrecks, including one of the biggest cargoes of gold that has ever (6)..................... found. However, Martin would be the first to point (7)..................... that not all of his discoveries are as dramatic (8)..................... that. (9)..................... you are prepared to put in a great deal of hard work and careful research, treasure hunting is much less romantic (10)..................... it sounds. Just sailing around in the hope of finding something would (11)..................... a waste of time. Martin (12)..................... a great deal of time in museums and libraries looking at old maps and shipping records. (13)..................... this way, he can work out (14)..................... ships have sunk and where, and it is only then that he can begin to look (15)..................... them.

(15 marks)

2 Key word transformations

Use the word in **bold** to complete the second sentence so that it has a similar meaning to the first. Write between two and five words.

1 I think that house would be too small for us.
   enough
   I don't think that house .... for us.

2 Take the mobile phone because I might need to contact you.
   case
   Take the mobile phone .... to contact you.

3 Come on Thursday or Friday. It's all the same to me.
   difference
   Come on Thursday or Friday. It .... me.

4 I will only go if you come with me.
   unless
   I .... come with me.

5 Amanda has improved a lot this term.
   progress
   Amanda has .... this term.

(10 marks)

3 Spot the mistake

Correct each of the following sentences.

1 I'll give Tania your letter if she will come to school tomorrow.

2 Please don't disturb me without it's something really urgent.

3 You couldn't borrow me your bike, could you?

4 I'd be much happier if you made your homework before you went out.

5 If I would choose to learn another language, I'd probably do Italian.

(5 marks)

4 Vocabulary

Complete the spaces using the words in the box. Make any changes to the tense that are necessary.

make	spend	earn	borrow
afford	owe	pay	be (not) worth
buy	cost	lend	

My brother has (0).....*made*..... a lot of money because his business has been very successful. Of course, when he started, he had to (1)..................... a lot from the bank, but it didn't take him long to (2)..................... back what he (3)....................., and now he can (4)..................... to do almost anything he wants. He (5)..................... a very good salary, but he (6)..................... it carefully and he is never wasteful. If he ever wanted to (7)..................... something that (8)..................... a great deal of money, he would save up until he had enough money – he would never ask for a loan for something like a car. Similarly, he has a rule that he will never (9)..................... money to a friend – he says that this can create problems, and it (10)..................... taking the risk.

(20 marks)

Total: 50 marks

LEAD-IN ▶

In pairs or small groups, name the animals and discuss the questions below.

Which of these animals:

1 could be kept as pets?
2 are endangered species?

WOOLLY WILMA

*W*ilma the sheep, star of our wool commercial,
was bored. She sat
motionless in front of the
05 cameras and refused to
perform. *It had been like
this for over an hour and
no amount of coaxing
would make her do it. We
10 were getting desperate.
Finally the director had an
idea. Wilma's job was to
end the commercial by
jumping into a small box
15 full of soft woollen
clothes. It was going to be
my job to tempt her into *it*
with some of her favourite
food.

20 *Wilma's eyes lit up* when
she saw the bunch of
carrots. She stood up and
sniffed encouragingly. I
was sitting on the other
25 side of the box dangling

the carrots just out of
reach. Suddenly Wilma
whirled round and leapt at
the box. 'Action!' yelled
30 the director, but Wilma
in her eagerness had
misjudged the distance,
and the crew watched in
amazement as she sailed
35 into the air and carried on
right over the top of
it. No one was more
horrified than I was to see
two pairs of neat hooves
40 coming directly at me
from the studio ceiling. I
leapt out of my chair just
in time as Wilma crashed
into it and landed in
45 a heap of fleece and
chairlegs. The director
began to bite his nails
anxiously. It seemed very
likely that this part of the
50 commercial would have to
be axed.

We were thinking that
we may as well give
up for the day, but
55 Wilma had other ideas.
After her Oscar-winning
performance she felt she
deserved her carrots, and
after shaking herself to
60 dislodge the bits of chair
from her coat she began
to walk determinedly
towards me, her yellow
eyes fixed on the prize in
65 my hand. Then she began
to trot ... then broke into
an awkward kind of
canter which gathered
speed. The director
70 grabbed my arm. 'Run!' he
cried in desperation,
seeing our last chance of a
shot. And so I scrambled
through the ring of studio
75 lights and cameras with
Wilma hot on my heels.
I tore round the back of

the crew and galloped
towards the box. I must
80 have looked ridiculous: an
out of breath cameraman
running for his life from a
hungry sheep. I wasn't
laughing, though – she
85 was gaining on me! With
just inches to spare, I
tossed the carrots into the
box and dodged to the
side. 'Action!' the director
90 yelled again.

With wonder and relief we
watched as Wilma leapt
into the air and landed
perfectly on the springy
95 pile of clothes. As though
nothing at all had
happened, she came to a
halt, turned to the camera
and paused beautifully. *It*
100 made a brilliant shot that
could not be improved.
Then she settled herself
down and began to nibble
her carrots, ignoring us
105 completely as we were
celebrating. At that
moment it was as clear as
day that Wilma had what
it takes to be a real star.
110 There was an unmistakable
glint of mischief in her
yellow eyes.

1 Multiple choice

A You are going to read a text about an animal. Read the text quickly and find out:

1 who wrote the article.

2 what the people were doing.

B Read the text again. For questions 1–7, choose the answer A, B, C or D which you think fits best according to the text.

1 What problem did the camera crew have?

  A The cameraman refused to work with the sheep.
  B The box was too small to hold the sheep.
  C The sheep wouldn't do what they wanted.
  D They couldn't find any food for the sheep.

2 What happened when Wilma took her first jump?

  A She landed on top of the box.
  B She hit the studio ceiling.
  C She crashed into the director.
  D She nearly flattened the author.

3 How did the director seem to be feeling?

  A hungry
  B worried
  C angry
  D afraid

4 After her first jump, Wilma decided to

  A give up trying to land in the box.
  B claim the reward she'd been offered.
  C run away from the film set.
  D chase the director from his chair.

5 Why did the writer think he looked comical?

  A He was trying to escape from a sheep.
  B He was losing a race with a sheep.
  C He was being attacked by a sheep.
  D He was hiding from a sheep in a box.

6 What happened the second time the crew tried filming?

  A They were disappointed with the shot.
  B The sheep would not look into the camera.
  C They managed to film the sheep eating carrots.
  D The scene they filmed was just what they wanted.

7 What point is the writer trying to make?

  A You should never do a commercial with animals.
  B Animals can be trained to perform.
  C Working with animals can be unpredictable.
  D Animal stars get more attention than humans.

2 Reference devices

What do these words in the text refer to?

1 *It* (line 6)

2 *it* (line 17)

3 *it* (line 37)

4 *It* (line 99)

3 Vocabulary

A Find words in the text which mean the same as the words below.

Paragraph 1

1 persuading

2 without hope

Paragraph 2

3 shouted loudly

4 cut because of the costs involved

Paragraph 3

5 caught hold of suddenly and firmly

6 climbed over quickly

Paragraph 4

7 astonishment

8 freedom from anxiety

9 doing something special because of an important event

B Explain what these phrases from the text mean.

1 *had other ideas* (lines 54–55)

2 *came to a halt* (lines 97–98)

3 *as clear as day* (lines 107–108)

In small groups, find out if your partners:

have any pets.

would like to have a pet. Why? Why not?

know anyone who has an unusual pet.
What is it?

1 Multiple-choice cloze

A Look at the picture below and answer the questions.

1 What is the woman doing?

2 Why do you think she is doing this?

B Read the story and find out what happened. Take no notice of the missing words.

Night of the iguana

Ashley Wales hurried breathlessly through the door, (0)........*B*........ a bag to his chest. (1)................ puzzled, his wife Tina gazed in amazement (2)................ he pulled a green reptile out of the bag. Ashley proudly (3)................: 'It's an iguana.' He heaved the creature onto the kitchen table. 'Don't touch it,' Tina told her daughter nervously.

Ashley had almost fallen (4)................ his bike in surprise when he'd first spotted the creature clinging to a wall. Slowly creeping up on it, he (5)................ the iguana. It was a frosty night and the creature was ice-cold. Nothing (6)................ . Its tail was gradually (7)................ grey. Ashley realized that the iguana wouldn't survive much longer (8)................ those temperatures. Suddenly, the creature opened one eye and stared at him. He grabbed the lizard, bundled it into a carrier bag and (9)................ home with it on his bike. When Ashley arrived home, the iguana was hardly moving. After her initial surprise, Tina disappeared – and came (10)................ with her hair-dryer. She aimed it at the reptile and switched it on. A few minutes later, the creature took a (11)................ breath and smacked its lips. Ashley ran to the phone and (12)................ the RSPCA*. By the time they arrived, the family had named the creature 'Iggy'. That night, the family (13)................ Iggy a new home with a local policeman who (14)................ exotic animals. 'Unfortunately, his (15)................ owner never came forward,' says Tina.

*RSPCA = Royal Society for the Prevention of Cruelty to Animals.

C Read the text again and decide which answer A, B, C or D best fits each space.

Example: (0) B

0 A	grabbing	B	clutching	C	catching	D	seizing
1 A	Watching	B	Staring	C	Looking	D	Glancing
2 A	since	B	as	C	before	D	although
3 A	spoke	B	told	C	announced	D	suggested
4 A	out	B	down	C	off	D	by
5 A	looked	B	saw	C	spoke	D	touched
6 A	appeared	B	happened	C	passed	D	resulted
7 A	changing	B	turning	C	moving	D	returning
8 A	in	B	by	C	for	D	to
9 A	set up	B	set off	C	set back	D	set down
10 A	back	B	to	C	from	D	out
11 A	low	B	high	C	wide	D	deep
12 A	named	B	called	C	shouted	D	ordered
13 A	took	B	discovered	C	found	D	created
14 A	maintains	B	holds	C	runs	D	keeps
15 A	primary	B	original	C	beginning	D	leading

WP 2

GRAMMAR ZOOM

The past

1 What happened when?

Put these events in the story about the iguana in the correct order.

Example: 1c

a The iguana was hardly moving.
b They called the creature 'Iggy'.
c Ashley was cycling home one night.
d Ashley saw a strange green creature.
e Ashley phoned the RSPCA.
f Ashley almost fell off his bike.
g Tina revived the creature with a hair-dryer.
h Ashley bundled the creature into a carrier bag.
i The iguana was taken to a new owner.

2 What happened first?

A Look at this sentence. Which of the underlined actions happened first? How do you know this?

Ashley <u>cycled</u> home after he <u>had bundled</u> the reptile into a carrier bag.

B Here are some other things which took place that night. Put the verbs into the simple past or the past perfect.

1 Ashley .... (be) to a party the night he .... (spot) the iguana.

2 The creature .... (probably / escape) from its original owner some time before Ashley .... (find) it.

3 Ashley .... (know) it .... (be) an iguana because he .... (see) one on TV the week before.

4 He .... (run) to a nearby house and .... (tell) the owner he .... (find) an iguana.

5 Ashley .... (wrap) the creature up in a towel the woman .... (give) him.

6 The RSPCA man .... (say) that what Ashley and his family .... (do) .... (save) the creature's life.

3 Unusual experiences

Read this newspaper article and put the verbs in brackets into the correct past tense (simple past, past continuous, past perfect).

Example: (0) invited

When zoo-keeper Melanie Gage (0) *invited* (invite) Kwa Kwa, a baby gorilla, into her home, she (1)..................... (know) that manners (2)..................... (be) not his strong point. The nine-month-old mountain gorilla, unable to feed from his mother, (3)..................... (be) close to death before Melanie (4)..................... (come) to his rescue. She (5)..................... (agree) to act as his 'surrogate' mother, taking him home each night to her house not far from the zoo. Looking after him (6)..................... (prove) far from easy, however. After he (7) .... (spend) a few weeks at Melanie's, he (8)..................... (begin) to be more curious about his surroundings. One night, after Melanie (9)..................... (go) to bed, she (10)..................... (hear) a strange sound coming from the living room. She (11)..................... (tiptoe) quietly down the stairs. As she (12)..................... (creep) into the living room, she (13)..................... (see) that the baby gorilla (14)..................... (eat) her precious plants! One night she (15)..................... (have) a feeling that someone (16)..................... (enter) her bedroom and (17)..................... (sit) on the end of the bed. When she (18)..................... (switch) on the light, the baby gorilla (19)..................... (sleep) quietly with its arm around her foot. After a few months, the gorilla (20)..................... (grow) strong enough to return to the zoo.

1 Talking together

A In pairs, name the animals opposite and say what they are doing.

WP 3

B These pictures show some ways in which humans use animals. In pairs, talk about how useful these animals are to us, then decide which ones we could not easily manage without.

> **HELP LINE**
>
> Try to use different words and phrases. Don't just repeat the same ones over and over again.

Use the expressions in the Phrase Box below to help you.

> **PHRASE BOX**
>
> **Asking if someone agrees**
> *Do you agree?*
> *Don't you think that … ?*
> *Do you think so too?*
>
> **Agreeing**
> *I quite agree.*
> *I agree with you.*
> *I think you're right.*
>
> **Disagreeing**
> *Actually, I don't agree.*
> *I don't think that's (true, right, correct).*
> *Well, I'm not sure if that's (true, right, correct).*

2 Discussion

Use the expressions in the Phrase Box above to talk about the following statements.

Some animals are more intelligent than human beings.

Animals have feelings.

LEAD-IN

Look at these words which are all connected with diving.

1	life jacket	3	flippers	5	wetsuit
2	aqualung	4	snorkel	6	mask

In pairs, use the expressions in the Phrase Box to try to explain to a partner what three of the objects are used for or what they look like.

Student A   You will find three objects on page 170.

Student B   You will find three objects on page 172.

> **Paraphrasing**
>
> *Example: a weight belt*
> *It's something that helps you to sink into the water.*
> *What I mean is, you put it on and it helps you to dive.*
> *It's a kind of/sort of special nylon belt to make diving easier.*

PHRASE BOX

1 Who said what?

A **You will hear a conversation between an interviewer Tom Dougal, the Olympic swimmer Sharron Davies and her husband, Olympic sprinter Derek Redmond. Answer questions 1–7 by writing T (for the interviewer Tom), S (for Sharron) or D (for Derek) in the boxes provided.**

1 Who thinks people have the wrong opinion about sharks?   [1]

2 Who brings up the subject of competitive swimming?   [2]

3 Who is planning a new television programme?   [3]

4 Who believes in taking young children out with them?   [4] [5]

5 Who first mentions music as a way of relaxing?   [6]

6 Who will always remember the Bahamas?   [7]

7 Who is looking forward to visiting the Bahamas again?   [8]

Listen again and check your answers.

B **Here are some sentences which appeared in the listening. In pairs, talk about the meanings of the underlined words, using the phrases you came across in the lead-in where appropriate.**

1 *There's no <u>thrill</u> quite like meeting a shark or dolphin face to face …*

2 *They both <u>took the plunge</u> with the killer fish …*

3 *… I'm <u>scared stiff</u> of them!*

4 *When did you first <u>get hooked on</u> sharks and dolphins?*

5 *We both got <u>the diving bug</u> and decided to become qualified divers.*

6 *He's an <u>easygoing</u> little boy…*

WP 4

2 Multiple choice

A **Describe what is happening in the picture.**

B **You will hear a couple talking to a reporter about their work looking after wild animals in Namibia. As you listen, choose the best answer A, B or C.**

1 Lise and Wayne had always been interested in
  A studying photography.
  B raising cattle.   [1]
  C observing animals in their own habitats.

2 They raise money for their centre by
  A taking in visitors as paying guests.
  B asking international organizations for help.   [2]
  C farming the surrounding countryside.

3 What eventually happens to the animals they look after?
  A They are sent to safari parks.
  B They are released into the wild.   [3]
  C They become part of the family.

4 The family try to train the animals to
  A avoid electric fences.
  B be more independent.   [4]
  C stay away from cattle.

5 What kinds of animals do they have at the centre?
  A babies without mothers
  B all different types of creatures   [5]
  C mainly cheetahs

6 What do Lise and Wayne think about their way of life?
  A Lise misses her town life.
  B They are both very happy there.   [6]
  C Wayne would like more free time.

Listen again and check your answers.

Writing a story (2)

If you choose to write a story, it is important to make correct use of the tenses you have practised in this unit.

1 Sample task

Read the sample task and write a brief outline of what you would include in your answer.

You have been asked to write a story for the school magazine ending in these words:

If anyone had seen me at that moment, they would have thought I was mad.

Write your **story** (120–180 words).

2 Sample answer

Read the story and answer the questions.

I was swimming slowly across the bay; the waves were sparkling in the sunshine, and everything seemed calm and peaceful.

I took a deep breath, dived under water and suddenly I saw an enormous black shape. It came towards me and then swam right past at great speed. I was filled with terror as I thought of the stories I had heard about shark attacks. I realized with horror that I had come to the beach alone. There was nobody to help me.

I came up to the surface and took a deep breath. I looked round and saw that the shark had turned round and was coming back towards me. I tried to stay still, in the hope that it might not see me.

As my attacker approached at great speed, it suddenly burst above the water, and I could not believe my eyes. It was only a dolphin, and it swam off into the distance. I was so relieved and began to laugh really loudly. If anyone had seen me at that moment, they would have thought I was mad.

(180 words)

Analysis

1 How similar was your outline to the sample answer?

2 What tense does the writer use to describe the scene at the beginning of the story? Find two examples.

3 Why is the verb *seemed* in the simple past in the first paragraph? Can you think of any other verbs that you would put in the simple past rather than the past continuous?

4 What tense does the writer use to talk about things that happened before the writer went into the sea? Find two examples.

5 What tense does the writer use to talk about the series of actions that began after the fish appeared? Find three examples.

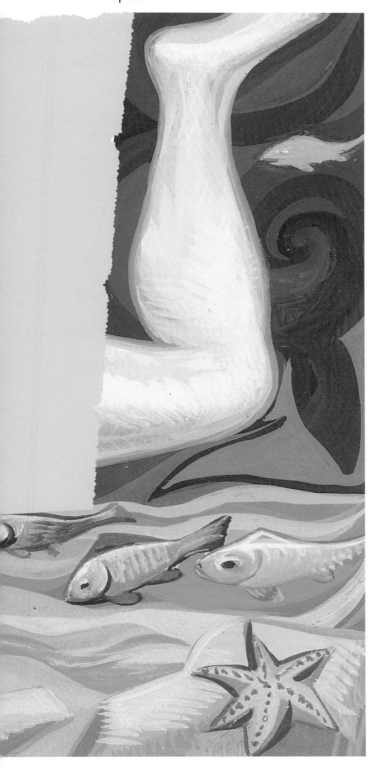

Paragraph writing

Read the following sentences and then develop them into a paragraph using your own ideas. Think carefully about which tenses you should use. Read the example to help you.

1 As soon as I saw the snake, I froze.

It was an enormous stripy one, lying on my bed. It was horrible. I was so terrified I didn't know what to do. With my heart beating madly, I decided to go and get some help.

2 As we sat down to have our picnic by the lake, I looked around.

....

....

....

....

3 When the photographs had been developed, he realized he had made a terrible mistake.

....

....

....

....

4 The beach was full of happy holidaymakers sunbathing and having fun.

....

....

....

....

Writing a story

You have decided to enter a short story competition for a student magazine. It must begin with these words.

I had been walking through the forest for several hours, when suddenly I heard something behind me.

Write your **story** (120–180 words).

Notes...

Work through the notes and prepare your story.

* Think about what will happen in your story from beginning to end.
* Write notes for each paragraph.
* Write your story, thinking carefully about your choice of tenses.

Check your writing carefully looking out for mistakes you often make.

WORDPOWER

1 Words connected with talking

A Match the words with their meanings.

> gossip   mumble   whisper   yell   argue   discuss

1 speak to someone softly so that no one else can hear you
2 give a loud cry of pain or excitement
3 talk about other people and their private lives
4 talk about something seriously or formally
5 disagree with somebody about something
6 speak in an unclear way without opening your mouth properly

B Use one of the words above to complete the sentences below.

a It's rude to .... when there are other people in the room.

b Stop .... ! What's the matter? Have you hurt yourself?

c The two boys don't get on well at all, I'm afraid. They are always ....

d Could we .... the matter of the missing money tomorrow?

e If you .... like that, nobody will be able to understand a word you are saying.

f The couple next door spend most of their time .... about their neighbours.

2 Words easily confused

Choose two appropriate words from each group and use them in their correct form to complete the sentences.

1 harm	damage	injure	hurt
2 near	close	nearby	next
3 country	countryside	nature	wildlife
4 extinct	dead	died	endangered
5 asleep	sleepy	tired	exhausted

1 Most house spiders are not dangerous – in fact they are .... and cause no .... at all.

2 The family who live .... door to the Browns have always had a .... relationship with their neighbours.

3 I love escaping from the city and getting back to .... for a while when we go walking in the beautiful .... in Scotland.

4 I knew the dodo was .... but I didn't know that the cheetah was a(n) .... species.

5 I was so utterly .... after our long journey that I fell .... while I was eating my dinner.

3 Irregular plurals

Make the following plural.

1 sheep	....		5 goose	....
2 wolf	....		6 calf	....
3 deer	....		7 mouse	....
4 fish	....		8 butterfly	....

4 Expressions with *get*

A Underline the expressions with *get* in these sentences, then match them with the meanings in a–g.

1 We should get together one weekend and go to the theatre.

2 We are getting nowhere with this new plan for nature conservation.

3 If you want to get ahead in this company you have to be prepared to work long hours.

4 The conservationists will have to try much harder to get their message across to young people.

5 You can try to lie about your age but you'll never get away with it.

6 My younger brother always tries to get out of doing any housework.

7 I really must get down to doing that composition.

a *be successful*

b *succeed in making people understand sth*

c *make the time to do/start doing sth*

d *avoid doing sth you should do*

e *make no progress*

f *do sth bad and not be punished for it*

g *meet socially*

B Take it in turns to ask and answer these questions.

1 Who do you often get together with when you go out?

2 Do you think you are getting anywhere with your English?

3 Besides working hard, what other things do you have to do to get ahead in this world?

4 Why is it sometimes difficult to get your point of view across to someone?

5 What kinds of things should people not be allowed to get away with?

6 What do you sometimes try to get out of doing?

7 Can you think of anything you should get down to doing this weekend?

UNIT 9 ► LET'S REFLECT!

1 Multiple-choice cloze

Read the text and decide which answer A, B, C or D best fits each space.

Example: (0) C

a strange encounter

Policeman Alan Godfrey had almost finished work one November evening when his boss (0).........C......... him to investigate reports that some cows had escaped from a (1).................... farm and were getting onto private land. Alan drove towards the area and, (2).................... he rounded the bend, he noticed to his surprise that what looked like a bus (3).................... to be parked across the middle of the road. A closer inspection (4).................... that it was a diamond-shaped object hovering above the ground. Alan (5).................... his radio and hurriedly tried to (6).................... his headquarters. Unfortunately, his radio would not work (7).................... . He decided to draw the object in his notebook but, after having (8).................... so, he found himself suddenly and mysteriously about 50 metres (9).................... along the road. The object had vanished. He returned to the police station, (10).................... a colleague and went back to the site of the encounter. They noticed that the ground was (11).................... drier where the object had been. Under hypnosis, Alan's story emerged. In his excitement, he had (12).................... to get a better look at the object and could now (13).................... being inside the craft. He had seen a tall, bearded figure, together with some smaller creatures which the bearded figure (14).................... were robots. However, (15).................... he could recall these facts, he was unfortunately unable to remember anything else.

0	A suggested	B reported	C ordered	D announced
1	A near	B nearby	C next	D close
2	A since	B as	C for	D because
3	A arose	B resulted	C happened	D occurred
4	A revealed	B discovered	C invented	D created
5	A clutched	B grabbed	C caught	D hugged
6	A call	B speak	C shout	D talk
7	A rightly	B justly	C properly	D nicely
8	A made	B done	C acted	D finished
9	A far	B remote	C further	D distant
10	A picked up	B set up	C turned up	D made up
11	A very	B more	C too	D much
12	A seen	B begun	C come	D gone
13	A remind	B remember	C recognize	D realize
14	A named	B called	C said	D told
15	A although	B moreover	C when	D therefore

(15 marks)

2 Which past tense?

Put the verbs in brackets into either the simple past, the past perfect or the past continuous to complete the sentences below.

1 After the cameraman .... (spend) several hours shooting the scene, he .... (realize) that there .... (be) no film in the camera.

2 While Sharron and her husband .... (swim) with dolphins, a noisy jet plane suddenly .... (fly) by overhead.

3 Sharron .... (develop) the dolphin photographs she .... (take) underwater the previous day.

4 I .... (walk) down a street I .... (walk) down many times before, when I suddenly .... (see) a strange creature at the side of the road.

(10 marks)

3 Vocabulary

A Write another word which sounds the same as those below but has a different spelling and meaning.

1 right   3 shore   5 I

2 sea   4 guessed

B Make the following plural.

1 sheep   3 mouse   5 goose

2 wolf   4 butterfly

C Mark the main stressed syllable on the pairs of words below.

	VERBS	NOUNS
1	inspect	inspection
2	investigate	investigation
3	conserve	conservationist
4	celebrate	celebration
5	perform	performance

D Choose one of the words from each pair and use it in a sentence of your own.

(25 marks)

Total: 50 marks

Have you ever had a favourite teacher? Who?

In pairs or small groups, tell each other why this person was your favourite teacher.

WP 1

1 Multiple matching

A You are going to read an article about how important certain teachers were in the lives of four people who have become very successful. Read the text quickly and find out which subjects the teachers taught.

INSPIRATION

Have you ever had a teacher who inspired you? We asked four successful people to tell us about a teacher who had a great influence on them.

A Benedict Allen
EXPLORER

I was so quiet at school. I was a dreamer and I had the romantic idea that I wanted to be an explorer. The trouble was that I thought all the
05 exploring had been done.

Sam Hunt taught me French at school and he inspired me by accepting me. He was also my class teacher and he allowed me to be myself. I think he realized that
10 my dreams weren't complete nonsense. He gave me space to develop in my own way. By my final year I was much more confident. I was even given an award for my collection of plants.

Sam was noble and free-thinking. He was also quiet and reserved. He was, I think, concerned about how quiet I was – I
15 remember him mentioning it on school reports – and worried that my dreams wouldn't come to anything. However, he always made me feel that making a dream come true is special. I discovered he was right, when I became the first person to walk the whole Skeleton Coast in Africa.

B Siobhan Redmond
ACTRESS WITH THE ROYAL SHAKESPEARE COMPANY

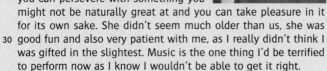

20 I went to The Park School from the age of five to eighteen. I've avoided any school reunions mainly because I was such a monster at school.

My music teacher, Irene Di Ciacca,
25 went some way to teaching me to calm down a little. She also taught me that you can persevere with something you might not be naturally great at and you can take pleasure in it for its own sake. She didn't seem much older than us, she was
30 good fun and also very patient with me, as I really didn't think I was gifted in the slightest. Music is the one thing I'd be terrified to perform now as I know I wouldn't be able to get it right.

Irene also encouraged me to sing. I loved it – I didn't have a wonderful voice but I could sing with feeling. In my last year I
35 was presented with a prize for music. I've benefited from the advice of a lot of wise people. But under Irene's instruction I learned some of the most important lessons of my life.

C Rory Bremner
COMEDIAN AND IMPERSONATOR

My best teacher was my French teacher Derek Swift. What stuck out
40 instantly was that he was unconventional – the type of teacher you didn't expect to see in a school like ours in the south. He was a Northerner with a strong northern accent.
45 One of his responsibilities was looking after the school library. I read such things as Pushkin's love poems and it was inspiring stuff. We were mad keen on Russia and he said he would teach us Russian in our spare time, which he did brilliantly. He was a genius at languages – he spoke about
50 10 or 12. Mr Swift was also different from every other teacher. There was always a twinkle in his eye and he had a sense of humour. He used to put his feet on the desk and cover the blackboard with words during his lessons. You can tell how good he was because there were 24 in our class and in the French
55 exam 21 got top grades.

Even at school, if I was inspired by someone, I would imitate them. He was the first person I did an impression of in public. We met again, years later, when he turned up at one of my shows. I was thrilled to bits.

D Darcus Howe
JOURNALIST

60 I went to school in Trinidad. I was in the top stream of the school in my first year and I was more or less average in terms of achievement, but I used to be very rebellious. I was often kept behind after class. At the end of the year they had decided to expel me. However, one teacher, Ralph Laltoo, said,
65 'Howe can come into my class. I'll take responsibility for him.' I only learned that long afterwards.

He was a Trinidadian Indian. He used to wear a white linen suit, white shirt and black
70 tie. On the first day I was set to continue in my old ways but he made me come and sit at the front of the class and then began to teach us English literature. From then on, it was wonderful. I was good at writing
75 essays and he inspired me to do even better. To this day I am mad about English literature.

Later, when I was 21, I was back in Trinidad on holiday and found
80 Laltoo had become principal of the school. He told me what he had done to defend me. He was a remarkable man.

B For questions 1–7, choose from the students A–D. Some of the students may be chosen more than once. There is an example at the beginning (0).

A   Benedict Allen
B   Siobhan Redmond
C   Rory Bremner
D   Darcus Howe

Which statement refers to which student?

I was pleased to see my teacher again.	0	C
I still love the teacher's subject.	1	
I had no talent for the teacher's subject.	2	
I won something at school.	3	4
I behaved badly at school.	5	6
I was not a talkative child at school.	7	

Which parts of the text helped you find the right answer?

Example: In C, Rory Bremner says 'I was thrilled to bits'.

C For questions 8–15, choose from the teachers A–D. Some of the teachers may be chosen more than once.

A   Sam Hunt
B   Irene Di Ciacca
C   Derek Swift
D   Ralph Laltoo

Which of the teachers:

looked a similar age to the students?	8		
used to make the students laugh?	9		10
was worried about one of the students?	11		
believed you can enjoy things you aren't good at?	12		
was prepared to give a student an opportunity?	13		
encouraged a student to achieve an ambition?	14		
came from a different part of the country?	15		

Which parts of the text helped you find the right answer?

Which of the four students do you think was the most difficult to teach?

Which of the four teachers do you think was the most inspiring?

Explain the meaning of the following phrases in the article.

Paragraph A
1 *The trouble was ...*
2 *... in my own way.*

Paragraph B
3 *... a monster at school.*
4 *... to calm down a little.*
5 *... for its own sake.*

Paragraph C
6 *What stuck out instantly ...*
7 *We were mad keen on Russia ...*
8 *... a genius at languages ...*

Paragraph D
9 *... to expel me.*
10 *I was set to continue in my old ways ...*

So and *such*

In paragraph A, Benedict says he was *so quiet at school*, and in B, Siobhan says she was *such a monster at school*.

What kinds of words follow *such* and *so*?

Complete these sentences using either *such* or *so*.

1   Carl was .... a fantastic sportsman that he won the school cup.

2   Fatima was .... confident about passing the exam that she did no revision.

3   Barry was .... proud of becoming an explorer.

4   Isobel had .... a good sense of humour.

5   The pupils were lucky because they had .... excellent teachers at the school.

6   Dennis always looked .... smart.

Tell a partner about somebody who has inspired you to do something. Talk about:

who the person was.

what the person was like.

how they inspired you.

what effect this had on you.

In small groups, discuss these questions.

1 Why do you think relationships between teenagers and parents can sometimes be difficult?

2 What could teenagers do to keep their parents happy?

3 What could parents do to keep their teenagers happy?

1 Word formation

A **Read the following advice about how parents should treat teenagers. Which piece of advice do you think is the most useful?**

★ Ten ways to prevent problems

Allow teenagers to have some (0)....*freedom*.... . It's the hardest lesson for a caring parent to learn.	FREE
Trust them. If you tell teenagers you think they are not (1).......................... , they won't try to be.	TRUST
If you disapprove, be (2)...................... . You might not approve, but your comments can hurt. They'll trust you more if you (3).......................... criticize.	TACT / RARE
If they're having a party, disappear for a while. Their social success is (4)......................... on not having over-anxious parents around.	DEPEND
Discuss rules together.	
Agree to make their bedroom their (5)......................... This helps to ensure their (6)......................... . In return, they should agree to keep the rest of the house tidy.	RESPONSIBLE / PRIVATE
Don't impose your opinions on them.	
Don't dictate. It is far more important to encourage your child to learn how to put forward an (7)..................... and be able to take part in a reasoned (8)..................... .	ARGUE / DISCUSS
Make them feel that you understand. What's unimportant to you may seem (9)......................... important to them.	DESPERATE
Above all, you must never show their baby photos to their friends. This can only cause them real (10)........................ .	EMBARRASS

B **Read the text again and use the words at the end of each line to form a word that fits in the space in the same line.**

Example: (0) freedom

WP 2

2 Error correction

A **Read the advice about how teenagers should treat their parents. Take no notice of the numbers at the beginning of the lines or any mistakes you come across. Which piece of advice do you think is the most useful?**

ten *ways to avoid* UPSETTING *your* parents

0	**Arrive** home when you've agreed to get at home.
00 ✓	They'll be happier to let you stay out late if you
1	stick to agreed times.
2	**Introduce** them to your friends. They'll be less likely
3	to be worry if they know them. If they feel involved
4	with, your life will be easier.
5	**Tell** to them where you're going. They'll be more
6	tolerant about your social life even if you can reassure
7	them you're not with total strangers.
8	**Be** a model student. If you will work hard at school
9	or college, your parents won't have to nag you about
10	poor exam grades, will they?
11	**Help** around the house. Do your bit, and because
12	of they feel you are supporting them, you'll find your
13	life is suddenly much easier.
14	**Don't** overuse the telephone. How would you feel
15	as if you had to pay for a huge bill and you never got
16	the chance to use the phone?
17	**Don't** go behind their backs. If they forbid you to do
18	something and you defy them, you can say goodbye
19	to your freedom!
20	**Don't** make them feel as if they are out of a touch
21	with your emotions.
22	**Shouting** won't get you anywhere. You'll earn the their
23	respect if you express yourself after a deep breath and
24	with a too calm voice.
25	**Sulking** won't help. This will simply confirm you are
26	still a child.

B **Now read the text again. Some of the lines are correct, and some have a word which should not be there. Tick (✓) the lines which are correct and underline the unnecessary words. There are two examples at the beginning (0 and 00).**

WP 3

GRAMMAR ZOOM

Modals

1 Modals and meaning

Match sentences 1–10 with their meanings a–g. More than one answer may be possible.

1 You should always try to do the homework the teacher sets.

2 I'm amazed that you can speak six languages fluently.

3 I could meet you tomorrow afternoon if you're free.

4 You must be at the airport two hours before take-off.

5 You may leave the room if you want to.

6 You must not stay out after 10.30 pm.

7 If you hurry, you might just catch the train.

8 You needn't come to the party if you don't want to.

9 I really think you ought to ring Oliver up and apologize.

10 It may rain this afternoon.

a *you know how to do it*

b *it is possible*

c *this is probably the right thing to do*

d *it is not allowed/important not to do it*

e *you have my permission to do it*

f *you have got to/are obliged to do it*

g *it is not necessary for you to do it*

2 *Must, have (got) to, should/ought to*

A Read these sentences carefully.

1 I *must* buy a new diary.

2 I really *should* phone my sister.

3 I *have to* be at a meeting at 6.30.

4 I suppose I *ought to* do my homework.

5 I*'ve got to* write a composition by tomorrow.

Which of the words in *italic* suggests that:

a you have no choice?

b you may or may not do this?

B In small groups, tell your partners:

three things you must/have (got) to do.

three things that you ought to do/should do.

3 *Mustn't, don't have to, needn't*

A Match the words in *italic* with meanings a–b.

1 You *mustn't* eat or drink in the school library.

2 You *don't have to* do your homework tonight.

3 You *needn't* wait for me – I'm going to be a long time.

a It's not necessary for you to do this.

b You're not allowed to do this.

B Complete these sentences with a suitable comment using *mustn't, don't have to* or *needn't*.

1 .... without locking the front door.

2 .... come to school tomorrow as it's a study day for the exam.

3 .... because I've already phoned them.

4 .... if you don't want to.

5 .... because we're going out for a meal.

4 *Should(n't), needn't, could*

TASK 1	TASK 2
How to be a good friend	**How to be a good student**
In small groups, use the modals *should(n't), needn't, could*, to explain how to be a good friend to others. Here are some ideas to help you:	**In small groups, use the modals *should(n't), needn't, could*, to explain how to be a good student. Here are some ideas to help you:**
be trustworthy	hand your work in on time
lend them money	get top marks
phone them every day	be a genius
understand their problems	write in your textbooks
help when necessary	be late for lessons
tell them your secrets	try to get on well
tell others their secrets	play about in class
borrow things from them	be enthusiastic

1 Talking about yourself

How independent are you? Do you live your life according to your own rules, or do you let yourself get talked into things that you later regret? In pairs, take it in turns to read the statements to each other, then tick the five statements that apply most to you.

- ☐ **a** When you've made up your mind, you rarely change it.
- ☐ **b** People think you're really confident, but you aren't.
- ☐ **c** You hate to let people down.
- ☐ **d** Your friends are better at getting their own way than you.
- ☐ **e** You're an individual – no one makes decisions for you.
- ☐ **f** You prefer being with people to being on your own.
- ☐ **g** You believe in fate.
- ☐ **h** You often say you agree with people, when deep down you don't.
- ☐ **i** You'd say almost anything to avoid a row.
- ☐ **j** It's important to keep an open mind.
- ☐ **k** Some friends have a bad influence on you.
- ☐ **l** You hate being rushed.
- ☐ **m** You really depend on your friends.
- ☐ **n** You don't stand up for yourself, which annoys you.
- ☐ **o** You do what you think is right, even if friends don't agree.
- ☐ **p** Sometimes you get confused.
- ☐ **q** If you don't agree with friends, you keep quiet.
- ☐ **r** It's easier to give in than stand up for yourself.
- ☐ **s** You often lack confidence.
- ☐ **t** You've got strong views.

Now look on page 171 and add up the points for your statements. Read the descriptions and find out how independent you are.

Do you agree with the description?

2 Talking together

In small groups, talk about the people in the pictures below. What do you think they depend on each other for? In which picture do they look as if they need each other most? Try to persuade others in your group to agree with you. Use the words in the Phrase Box to help you.

Although it is not always necessary to agree with your partner(s) in the exam, it is a good idea to encourage your partner(s) to take part in the discussion by inviting comments on your opinions.

Persuading and convincing

I'm sure you'd agree that the (people) in picture ... couldn't manage without each other.

Surely the (people) in picture ... don't really need each other?

Don't you think the (people) in picture ... need each other the most?

The (person) in picture ... really needs (help), doesn't he/she? But the (people) in picture ... don't, do they?

WP 4&5

In small groups, discuss these questions.

1 How many really good friends is it possible to have?

2 At what age do you think people should start going out with each other?

3 Why do some relationships between girlfriends and boyfriends break up?

Do you remember what kinds of questions you may be asked in Part 1? Some examples were given in Unit 8 on page 81. Some other possibilities are:

- say what the speaker's opinion is.
- identify the main point of the conversation.
- work out the purpose of the conversation.

---

1 Multiple choice

You will hear people talking in eight different situations. For questions 1–8, choose the best answer A, B or C.

1 You hear someone talking about her boyfriend. What is the problem?

  A He has found another girlfriend.
  B He has no time for her.
  C He wants her to go to football matches.

  [ ] 1

2 You hear a woman giving a girl advice. What does she say about boys?

  A They don't tell their parents about their girlfriends.
  B They sometimes go out with two girls at the same time.
  C They don't like friends finding out that they have a girlfriend.

  [ ] 2

3 You hear someone talking about his parents. What are they trying to do?

  A prevent him going out
  B make him work much harder
  C break up his relationship

  [ ] 3

4 You hear someone talking about a problem. What is it?

  A He misses his bus in the morning.
  B He is not doing well at school.
  C He can't remember things.

  [ ] 4

5 You hear a girl talking about a boy she's just met. What has he done?

  A fallen in love with someone else
  B changed his appearance
  C made the wrong decision

  [ ] 5

6 You hear someone talking about her younger brother. What is he always doing?

  A having accidents
  B getting into trouble at school
  C shouting at his parents

  [ ] 6

7 You hear someone talking about his friends. What does he say about them?

  A They are always short of money.
  B They have designer clothes and shoes.
  C They argue with their parents about money.

  [ ] 7

8 You hear someone talking about a difficult situation. How does she feel about it?

  A indifferent
  B annoyed
  C depressed

  [ ] 8

Listen again and check your answers.

2 Multiple matching

You will hear five different people talking about their neighbours. For questions 1–5, choose from the list A–F how the speakers now feel about their relationships with their neighbours. Use the letters only once. There is one extra letter which you do not need to use.

A feels grateful to them   Speaker 1 [ ] 1

B gets on quite well with them   Speaker 2 [ ] 2

C is going to report them to the police   Speaker 3 [ ] 3

D has accepted the situation for the time being   Speaker 4 [ ] 4

E is moving home to get away from them   Speaker 5 [ ] 5

F is angry about what's happened

Listen again and check your answers.

3 The same or different?

At least one of the words in each pair below appeared in the listenings. Write S beside the words which are pronounced the same, and D beside those which are different.

1 caught / court   5 stare / stair
2 copying / coping   6 wear / where
3 prices / prizes   7 wondering / wandering
4 threw / through   8 whether / weather

Writing an informal letter

In Part 2 of the writing paper, you may be asked to write an informal letter to a friend.

1 Sample task

Read the sample task and make brief notes on what you would include in your answer. When you have finished, compare your notes in pairs.

You have been doing an English course in London for two months. Write a letter to an English-speaking friend who has asked you to tell him or her how the course is going and to describe some of the things you have been doing in your free time.

Write your **letter** (120–180 words).

2 Sample answer

Read the letter and answer the questions.

Analysis

Discuss these questions. Support your decisions with examples from the text.

1 How good is the content of the letter? How well does it answer the question?

2 Can you see any words and phrases that you could use again in an informal letter? Underline them – they would be useful to learn.

3 The letter contains various mistakes in word order. Find them and correct them.

Dear Christina,

Many thanks for your letter. I'm sorry I haven't written for so long, but I've been very busy, and we have at the end of the month exams.

Anyway, you'll be pleased to hear the course has been going really well. I like very much the teachers, and we have also classes about British culture – they're really interesting. I've been practising pronunciation in the language lab and watching videos too a lot.

As for my social life, it couldn't be better. I've met on the course lots of really nice people, and we all get on well together. We go out to films and restaurants together, and we organize now and again trips to the country. Last weekend we went to Wales for the weekend, which was great. We may go next month to Cornwall.

Anyway I'd better go now as I want to catch the post. Do write again soon.

Lots of love

Andrea

P.S. By the way, give my best wishes to Ben if you see him.

(172 words)

3 Language study

Word order

A One of the problems with the letter is that the word order is wrong in several places. Do you know any rules for word order? Look at the following pairs of sentences and put the words in order. Check your answers and then complete the rule.

1 a Jackie He yesterday saw

....

b dog bone eating The is a

....

The object goes .... the verb.

2 a concerts interesting are The always

....

b usually have at home lunch I

....

Single-word adverbs of frequency go .... the verb and .... the verb *to be*.

3 a went Danny cinema yesterday to the

....

b on Last week holiday were we

....

Expressions of time can be placed .... or .... of the sentence.

4 a dancing we go Every two weeks out

....

b meet each other once a month They

....

Longer phrases of frequency go .... or .... of the sentence.

5 a played The beautifully orchestra

....

b knew him well very She

....

Adverbs of manner go .... the verb (and object).

B Correct each of these sentences.

1 I met the other day Peter.
2 I am tomorrow meeting some friends for lunch.
3 I have just read about Russia a very interesting book.
4 Here is terrible the weather.
5 I don't go out in usually the evenings.
6 If you don't reply I will write never to you again.
7 We go now and then to the country.
8 I like from time to time to visit museums.
9 Last weekend I had with Mary a long talk.
10 Never I watch TV.

4 Writing task

Writing an informal letter
You have been working as an au pair girl/boy with a family abroad. Write a letter to an English-speaking friend telling them about the family you are staying with and what work you are doing.
Write your **letter** (120–180 words).

Notes...

Work through the notes and prepare your letter.

- Remember that the letter has two main parts, but you should also have suitable opening and closing lines.

- Keep the style suitably informal so avoid words like *firstly, on the other hand, what is more,* etc.

- You may find some of the following phrases and sentences useful:

  I'm so sorry I haven't written ...

  Thanks for your letter. It was great to hear that ...

  Well, that's all my news for now – I'll write again soon.

  Give my love to ...

  I'd better finish now.

When you have finished, check your writing for spelling, punctuation and grammar mistakes.

WORD POWER

1 Vocabulary

Choose the best word to complete the sentences below.

1 All the students *passed/succeeded* the English exam.
2 Mary is going to *take/have* the FCE next July.
3 The students are all *going/attending* to university.
4 My son *goes/is* at university in Bristol.
5 After three years' hard work, Brian *managed/got* a degree.
6 Sue *graduated/left* from university last year.

2 *Make, let* and *allow*

A Two of the sentences below contain a mistake. Can you find them?

1 My mother made me tidy up my room.
2 You have made me very happy.
3 My parents let me to go on holiday alone.
4 Let me go – I'm ticklish.
5 The staff allowed the students use the tennis courts at the back of the school.

B Which of the verbs in 1–5 means:

a did not stop sb from doing sth?
b gave official permission for sb to do sth?
c forced sb to do sth?
d caused sb to do/be sth?
e stop holding/restraining sb?

C Use *make, let* or *allow* in its correct form to complete the sentences below.

1 My brother won't .... me borrow his CDs for the party.
2 Students are not .... to take dictionaries into the exam.
3 I am not going to go to bed early and you can't .... me!
4 The police can't prove Jim stole the money so they'll have to .... him go.
5 What you said .... me very angry.

3 Words easily confused

Look at these two sentences.

1 If couples talk about their problems, they can often *prevent* their relationship *from* breaking up.
2 The best way to get on well with people is to *avoid* having arguments.

Which of the words in *italic* above means:

a to keep away from or to try not to do sth?
b to stop sth happening or to stop sb doing sth?

Use one of the words to complete the sentences below.

1 I'm sure Tim is .... Susie. He crosses over to the other side of the road every time he sees her.
2 I think John's father is trying to .... him from marrying Sally.
3 My parents never tried to .... me from enjoying myself.
4 It is usually better to try to .... discussions with people who have very strong opinions about everything.

4 Phrasal verbs/expressions with *up* and *down*

Complete these sentences with either *up* or *down* and then match the phrasal verbs and expressions with the meanings below.

1 My babysitter really *let me* .... the other evening so we couldn't go out.
2 When I was a child I always *looked* .... to my grandparents, who were wonderful people.
3 You have to try to *stand* .... for yourself at school, otherwise you'll be bullied.
4 Carol couldn't *make* .... her mind about what she wanted to do when she left school.
5 Bad weather really *gets me* ....
6 Simon asked Lucy to marry him but she *turned him* ....
7 After seven years at secondary school I was *fed* .... with being a student.
8 When Sally's boyfriend told her he didn't love her any more, she *broke* ....

a respect	d disappoint sb/not to do sth you promised	
b decide	e refuse or reject	g burst into tears
c depress	f be tired of sth	h defend yourself

5 Question tags

Question tags are often used when you expect people to agree with you, or to check that what you think is correct. Complete these sentences with a suitable word or phrase and add an appropriate question tag.

1 We should try to make our own .... , ... ?
2 You must always keep an open .... , ... ?
3 Sometimes it isn't easy to stand up for .... , ... ?
4 Some people hate being .... , ... ?
5 You have to be tactful when .... , ... ?
6 Mike and Rosie have had a terrible .... , ... ?
7 Sue and Pete split up because .... , ... ?
8 I'm always late for .... , ... ?

UNIT 10 ➤ LET'S REFLECT!

1 Error correction

Read the text and look carefully at each line. Tick (✓) the lines which are correct and underline the unnecessary words. There are two examples at the beginning (0 and 00).

thoughts for teenagers

0   Here are some issues a school asked <u>of</u> pupils about

00 ✓ themselves to find out why teenagers feel happy or sad.

1   Think of something that can make you to happy or content.

2   Think of one thing that might cause you to be worry.

3   Name two things you do with which give you confidence.

4   Write down an occasion when you did not feel confident.

5   Who can you go to in order to discuss about your feelings?

6   Who would you go to if you felt you needed the advice?

7   If you would feel low, what do you do to cheer yourself up?

8   Have you ever felt out of a touch with what is going on?

9   What would you like to be able to do in the future?

10   Which people do you consider to be some your best friends?

(10 marks)

2 Vocabulary

A Form adjectives from the following words by writing the appropriate ending.

1 trust ...   3 depend ...   5 care ...

2 tact ...   4 remark ...   6 tolerate ...

B Write another word which sounds the same as those below but has a different spelling and meaning.

1 caught   2 stair   3 wear   4 whether

(10 marks)

3 Question tags

Complete the following sentences with an appropriate question tag.

1 Some people make friends easily, ... ?

2 You should always try to tell the truth, ... ?

3 It didn't rain yesterday after all, ... ?

4 Students have to be in class by 9 o'clock, ... ?

5 I'm here to help, ... ?

(10 marks)

4 Modals

Use *mustn't, needn't, shouldn't, don't have to* or *can't* to complete these sentences.

1 I .... meet you tomorrow because we're going away for the weekend.

2 You .... really hand in homework which looks a mess.

3 We .... hand in that homework until next week, do we?

4 You .... park there. It's illegal.

5 You .... bother turning up for the meeting if you don't feel like it.

(10 marks)

5 Key word transformations

Use the word in **bold** to complete the second sentence so that it has a similar meaning to the first. Write between two and five words.

1 The children were so noisy that they were asked to leave the party.

   such

   The children .... that they were asked to leave the party.

2 Patrick wasn't allowed to go out with Sarah.

   prevented

   Patrick's parents .... out with Sarah.

3 Maria can't decide whether to come to the party or not.

   mind

   Maria still hasn't .... whether to come to the party or not.

4 In my day, parents were always respected by their children.

   looked

   In my day, children .... their parents.

5 Chewing gum is not allowed in lessons.

   must

   Students .... in lessons.

(10 marks)

Total: 50 marks

LEAD-IN ▶

A magazine asked its readers a simple question: 'What is your main ambition?' Look through some of the answers they received and answer the questions below.

to climb Mount Everest

to get married and have a family

to become famous

to learn to fly

to get rich

to run my own company

to travel round the world

to go to the best university in the country

1 Some people's ambitions can provide information about a person's character, age, interests, personality, etc. Choose one of the ambitions above. What can you guess about the sort of person who hopes to achieve this?

2 Do you share any of the ambitions in the list above? Why? Why not?

3 Write down three of your main ambitions. In pairs, discuss:

   a whether you think you will ever achieve them.

   b how you will achieve them.

1 Multiple matching

A **This is a true story, even though you may find it hard to believe. Read the article quickly and answer these questions. Take no notice of gaps 0–7.**

1 How did Larry Walters manage to achieve his ambition?

2 What went wrong?

3 How was he saved?

UP UP AND AWAY

| 0 | *I* |

Larry Walters was a lorry driver, but he had always wanted to fly. After leaving school, he wanted to become an Air Force pilot, but unfortunately, he was turned down because of his poor eyesight. So he had to make do with watching others fly the fighter jets that
05 criss-crossed the skies over his backyard. As he sat there in his garden chair, he dreamed about the magic of flying.

| 1 | |

Then one day, Larry came across an advertisement in the local paper and realized there was a way of making his dreams come true. He went to a specialist store and bought forty-five weather balloons and
10 several tanks of helium. These were not brightly-coloured party balloons, but large spheres measuring more than one metre when fully inflated. His plan was to float lazily into the sky, and spend the afternoon sunning himself 10 m above his girlfriend's garden before eventually coming back down to earth.

| 2 | |

15 When he returned home, he attached the balloons to his garden chair, tied the chair to his car, and filled the balloons with helium. Then he packed a few sandwiches and drinks and took his air gun so that he could burst a few balloons when it was time to return to earth.

| 3 | |

When his preparations were complete, Larry sat in his chair and cut
20 the cord. But he made a mistake in his calculations and things did not turn out quite as he had planned. He did not float up as gently as he had expected: within seconds, he passed the 10 m altitude that he had hoped to reach, rising quickly to 30 m and then 300 m. He climbed and went on climbing until he finally levelled off at 3,000 m.

4 [   ]

25 At that height, he did not want to risk shooting any of the balloons because he was afraid it might unbalance his aircraft and send him crashing to the ground. So he stayed up there among the clouds, sailing around for fourteen hours, desperately trying to come up with a solution to the problem
30 of how to get back to earth.

5 [   ]

Eventually, many hours later, he drifted into the main approach corridor for Los Angeles International Airport. Fortunately, a Pan Am flight passed him and air traffic control was alerted. The pilot explained that he had just seen
35 an armed man floating in a garden chair at 3,000 m just outside the plane. Understandably, the air traffic controller found this difficult to believe, but a few minutes later a Delta Airlines pilot called with the same message. Radar confirmed the existence of an unidentified flying object above the
40 airport and the authorities sent for a Navy helicopter to investigate.

6 [   ]

As night began to fall, offshore breezes began to blow Larry out to sea, and when the helicopter arrived, the wind from the propeller kept pushing his home-made aircraft further
45 and further away. Eventually, they hovered several hundred metres above him and managed to drop down a line, with which they were able to pull him gradually back to safety.

7 [   ]

As soon as Larry hit the ground, he was taken away by the police and charged with invading Los Angeles' International
50 Airport airspace. But as he was being led away in handcuffs, a television reporter called out, 'Why did you do it?' Larry stopped, looked at the man and explained. 'I've been dreaming of flying for years. I just got tired of waiting.'

B Choose the most suitable heading from the list A–I for each part (1–7) of the article. There is one extra heading that you do not need. There is an example at the beginning (0).

A **No way down**

B **An incredible report**

C **A difficult rescue**

D **Free as a bird**

E **Under arrest**

F **A bright idea**

G **Heading for the clouds**

H **Getting ready for take-off**

I **A lifelong ambition**

2 Phrasal verbs

A The phrasal verbs a–e were used in the text. Match them with their meanings.

a *turn out* (line 21)   1 to ask to come and help

b *go on* (line 24)   2 to think of (an idea)

c *come up with* (line 29)   3 to shout

d *send for* (line 40)   4 to continue

e *call out* (line 51)   5 to be the result

B Complete the following sentences using the correct form of the phrasal verbs above.

1 I saw her on the other side of the street and .... her name.

2 She was worried about the exams, but everything .... all right in the end.

3 If you .... wasting time like this, you'll never get your work done.

4 We discussed the problem, and my sister .... some very good suggestions.

5 I'm sure my leg isn't broken – there's no need to .... an ambulance.

WP-1

3 Activity

With your partner, write a short dialogue based on the information below and act it out in pairs.

Student A   You are the pilot of a jumbo jet and have just seen Larry in his garden chair outside your cockpit. Your co-pilot has confirmed that he really is there and that you are not imagining things. Radio air traffic control with your message. Begin with these words:

This is the pilot of flight PA326. You're not going to believe what I've just seen, but …

Student B   You are one of the air traffic controllers at Los Angeles International Airport. You are thinking about a newspaper report you read recently which said that a lot of pilots suffer from stress. A pilot from a jumbo jet is on the radio to you.

LEAD-IN

**Which comedians are famous in your country?
Why are they funny?**

1 Open cloze

Read the following text about the comic actor Rowan Atkinson
and think of one word which best fits each space.

Example: (0) one

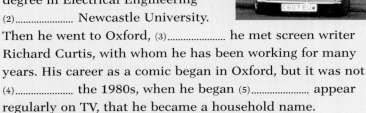

ROWAN ATKINSON

Rowan Atkinson has been (0)......*one*......
of Britain's most popular comedians
for many years. He was born in the
North of England, and (1).................... a
degree in Electrical Engineering
(2).................... Newcastle University.
Then he went to Oxford, (3).................... he met screen writer
Richard Curtis, with whom he has been working for many
years. His career as a comic began in Oxford, but it was not
(4).................... the 1980s, when he began (5).................... appear
regularly on TV, that he became a household name.

One of the things that makes Atkinson such (6)....................
exceptional actor is that he is always trying new ideas, and
each of his new comic characters (7).................... completely
different to anything that he has done before. He (8)....................
has a wonderful range of facial expressions, and he can
(9).................... people laugh simply by raising an eyebrow.
(10).................... one of his TV programmes, *Mr Bean*, he makes

(11).................... most of these skills. It is
mostly a silent comedy
(12).................... is similar in many
ways to the old Charlie Chaplin
films. The show is based
(13).................... a series of
disasters that happen to the
unfortunate Mr Bean, and it has
(14).................... very popular not
only in England (15).................... also
outside the UK. Recently
Atkinson has made a feature film
in the USA, and he is also
planning a new situation
comedy for TV.

WP 2

GRAMMAR ZOOM

Periods of time up to the present

1 Uses

A Read these sentences and answer the questions that follow.

Atkinson has been a professional comedian for many years.

Atkinson has been making TV programmes for many years.

1 What period of time are we talking about in these sentences – is it finished or did it start in the past and continue up to the present?

2 Which sentence refers to an activity of some kind? What tense is used?

3 Which sentence refers to a state? What tense is used?

B Rephrase the following sentences using the verb in brackets in the present perfect continuous or, in the case of stative verbs, the present perfect simple.

1 I started playing the guitar three years ago. I still play it. (play)

2 I met Anna ages ago. I know her now. (know)

3 Peter and Jane started going out six months ago. They are still going out. (go out)

4 He bought that car when he was a student. He has still got it. (have)

5 They got married 20 years ago. They are still married. (be)

6 I started waiting for the taxi 40 minutes ago. I am still waiting for it. (wait)

C In pairs, use your own ideas to make short dialogues using *How long* and either the present perfect simple or present perfect continuous.

How long have you been smoking?

Example:

A: I still don't understand the present perfect continuous.

B: Really? How long have you been learning English?

A: Six years.

1 It's my parents' wedding anniversary next month.
2 I don't think the bus is ever going to arrive.
3 I think I might move house soon.
4 I'm giving a piano recital next month.
5 My grandmother thinks my brother and his girlfriend should get married.
6 I think I should leave the bank and start looking for another job.

2 Completed or uncompleted actions?

A Read these sentences and answer the questions.

He has been making a film in Kenya.

He has made a film in Kenya.

1 Which sentence could mean that he is still making the film?
2 Which one tells us that the film is finished?

B Fill in the spaces with the verbs in brackets. Use the present perfect simple or the present perfect continuous.

1 This traffic is terrible. We .... (drive) nearly all day and we .... (only/do) about 20 miles.
2 Do you think Danny is all right? He .... (only/answer) six questions and he (do) .... the test for over an hour now.
3 I .... (try) to find a job for three months now, and I .... (have) about 12 interviews.
4 I .... (ring) my friends all morning to tell them that the party is off. I .... (manage) to get through to most of them.
5 I .... (meet) some really interesting people since I started the course and we .... (study) together in the evenings.

3 Recently completed activities

We sometimes also use the present perfect continuous to ask or talk about an activity that has just finished, especially when there is some evidence of it.

Example:

A You're covered in mud! What on earth have you been doing?

B I've been playing football in the rain.

A Match the halves of the sentences in 1–6 with those in a–f to make six sentences.

Example: 1c

1 I'm terribly tired because
2 My coat's soaking wet because
3 The office is in a terrible mess because
4 The room smells awful because
5 I've lost a lot of weight because
6 Your shoulders are burned because

a you've been smoking again.
b you've been sitting in the sun too long.
c *I've been working very hard.*
d you haven't been doing the filing.
e it's been raining.
f I haven't been eating much.

B Using the present perfect continuous, write four short paragraphs by finishing the sentences below and writing some more of your own.

Example:
You can see that the tourist season is nearly over …
the crowds have been getting smaller and the restaurants have been closing early. The airport has been getting quieter, and the weather has been getting colder.

1 I look much fitter and healthier than I have for ages and that's because …

....

....

....

2 You can tell that the students have got exams coming up soon as …

....

....

....

3 My sister looks exhausted, but it's not surprising as …

....

....

....

4 My English is a lot better now, and that's because …

....

....

....

1 Talking about yourself

Name the cartoon characters and say which you find funny and what you think makes them so popular.

WP 3

2 Taking a long turn

These pictures show entertainers who make people laugh.

Work with a partner. Take it in turns to talk about the pictures for one minute, and then answer the question about your partner's pictures. You have about 20 seconds to do this.

> Remember to listen carefully when your partner has their long turn. In the exam you will be asked a question about their pictures after they have finished.

HELP LINE

Student A   Compare and contrast pictures 1 and 2, and say if you find people or events like these funny.

Student B   In which of the pictures do you think the audience is enjoying the entertainment more?

Student B   Compare and contrast pictures 3 and 4, and say how you think the audiences are feeling.

Student A   Do you enjoy watching events like these?

3 Talking together

Look at some entries in a funny photograph competition. In pairs, talk about why you think the pictures are funny or not and decide which you think is the funniest. Use the expressions in the Phrase Box.

Comparing and contrasting
PHRASE BOX

This photograph seems ... whereas this one ...
One or two of the photographs are ... but the others ...
Although all the photographs are ... , only one or two ...

1   What kind of jokes do you enjoy the most?

2   Can you think of any jokes you know in your own language that would be funny when translated into English?

1 Multiple matching

Listen to the following news reports giving details of true but unusual stories. Match the statements from the list A–F with the speakers 1–5. Use the letters only once. There is one extra letter which you do not need to use.

Which speaker mentions ...

A   a medical condition that cannot be explained?   Speaker 1 [1]

B   an apparent miracle that can be explained?   Speaker 2 [2]

C   something that looks human but is not alive?   Speaker 3 [3]

D   a human that looks like an animal?   Speaker 4 [4]

E   someone whose real identity is unclear?   Speaker 5 [5]

F   a case of animals wearing clothes?

Listen again and check your answers.

2 Who said what?

You will hear an interview with a comedian who is about to star in a new TV show. For questions 1–7, write either I (for interviewer), C (for comedian) or N (for neither) in the boxes provided.

1   Who says that not many new TV comedians are successful?   [1]

2   Who says that it is important to learn from experience?   [2]

3   Who mentions finding the money for the show?   [3]

4   Who mentions the difficulties of raising children?   [4]

5   Who talks about the disadvantages of working late?   [5]

6   Who mentions the name of a recent festival?   [6]

7   Who complains about local audiences?   [7]

Listen again and check your answers.

3 The same or different?

At least one of the words in each pair below appeared in the listenings. Write S beside the words which are pronounced the same, and D beside those which are different.

1   angry / hungry

2   seat / sit

3   possible / passable

4   sight / site

5   thirty / thirteen

4 Speaking

In pairs or small groups, answer these questions.

1   What is your favourite comedy programme on TV at the moment?

2   Are there any comedy programmes that are no longer on that you used to like?

3   Give a brief description of a funny moment in a TV comedy that you remember well.

Writing a report (2)

If you choose to write a report, remember that the use of headings or numbering can help to make your answer more organized.

1 Sample task

Read the sample task.

You are in charge of the video evenings at your language school and have been asked to find out about video clubs in the area from which you will be able to hire videos. Write your **report** (120–180 words).

2 Sample answers

Read both reports and answer the questions.

Analysis

1 What do you notice about the way the ideas are organized in the two answers? Which one is better?

2 In sample answer A, each of the three main paragraphs follows a similar pattern, and provides at least five main pieces of information. Make a list of five things that each paragraph deals with.

3 What do you notice about the use of informal and formal language? Can you give examples of language in sample answer B that are not really suitable for a report?

Sample answer A

TO: Helen James
FROM: Jean Parillaud

Local video clubs
I was asked to visit a number of video clubs to select one for the video evenings. My recommendations are as follows:

Cinema International
This is about ten minutes' walk from the school. It has a wide selection of popular films. It specializes in comedy, and has both new releases and classic comedies. Annual membership is £10 and films are £3.00 per day.

Magic Eye Videos
This is also fairly near the school, and its selection of videos is quite impressive. These are mostly old black and white films, but there seem to be few new releases. Membership is £10 per year, and films cost £2.50 per day.

Silver Screen Videos
Although this is the closest club to the school, the range of films is relatively poor. It specializes in kung-fu and war films. Films cost £2.00 per day. Membership is free.

I therefore suggest that we join Cinema International, which will meet our needs because it is fairly convenient and offers the best selection.

(174 words)

Sample answer B

I have been to three video clubs and Cinema International was quite good. Basically, the problem with Silver Screen was that the man in charge there seems to like kung-fu films and hasn't got much else. This is a pity, you know, because it's much closer than Cinema International, and would really be quite convenient, but he isn't really very keen on English or American films. Magic Eye is quite cheap, about £10 a year, and it has quite a lot of black and white films. They cost the same as other films, about £2.50, and membership of the Silver Screen is free. Anyway, I think it would be a good idea to choose Cinema International, although it is quite a long way from school.

(126 words)

Focus on tenses

As you have seen, in reports we usually use the simple present tense. Likewise, when we relate the story of a film, we normally use one of the present tenses, such as the simple present, the present continuous, the present perfect simple or the present perfect continuous.

A Read the film review.

Mrs Doubtfire

FILM REVIEW

…is a comedy that is suitable for all the family and is great fun. The basic story involves an actor who has lost his job. Then his marriage comes to an end and his children stay with their mother. He decides to dress up as an elderly British nanny and manages to get a job looking after the children. There are a lot of funny scenes, and one of the most memorable comes when the family eventually find out who he really is.

B Read another film review and put the verbs in brackets into the correct tense. Use the simple present or present perfect simple or continuous.

Honey, I Shrunk the Kids

…is a fun-filled science fiction comedy. The story is about a scientist, Rick Moranis, who .... (be) married to Marcia Strassman. He .... (work) for some time on a special kind of ray that .... (make) people smaller. One day, the ray accidentally .... (hit) his children and some of their friends, who immediately .... (shrink). They .... (end) up in the garden, which .... (look) like a jungle to them because they .... (become) so small. The rest of the film .... (deal) with the children's adventures and Moranis' attempts to find them.

FILM REVIEW

Set texts

If you answer a question about a set text, you will need to use the present tenses to describe what happens or to talk about a character.

You will mainly use the simple present, but you may also need the present continuous, present perfect simple and present perfect continuous to relate the different events.

HELPLINE

4 Writing task

Writing a report

You are in charge of your language school's English Club and, for the end of term, you have been asked to find out about two videos (in English) that you could show to the whole school (11–18 year-olds). You need to write a report for the head of the English Department giving details of the films and recommending one of them.

Write your **report** (120–180 words).

Notes...

Work through the notes and prepare your report.

- In pairs, decide what information should be in each paragraph.
- Next, write a plan individually.
- Check you have included everything in your plan and then write your report.

When you have finished, check your writing for spelling, punctuation and grammar mistakes.

WORD POWER

1 Phrasal verbs with *come* and *go*

A Read the following pairs of sentences. In which sentences do the verbs *come* and *go* have their usual meanings, and in which sentences does the meaning change?

1 a You'd better make sure you know these verbs because they always come up in the exam.

b When you come up to bed, could you bring the paper that's on the kitchen table?

2 a Have you come across any good stories in the paper?

b If you come across the fields, be careful of the bull.

3 a If you wait a minute, the Princess will come round the corner in her coach.

b The Princess fainted when she kissed the frog and it took her several minutes to come round.

4 a Put your gun on the floor and come out with your hands above your head.

b The garden always looks lovely when the roses come out.

5 a Philip went off on holiday without saying goodbye.

b This meat smells absolutely revolting. It must have gone off.

6 a Go through the main door, down the corridor and the library's on the left.

b I'm going through a difficult time with my girlfriend – we seem to do nothing but argue.

7 a At the end of the lesson, the teacher went over the main points again.

b He hit the ball so hard that it went over the roof of the stadium into the road.

8 a It's the school dance on Saturday – who are you going to go with?

b Don't get me wrong – the polka dot skirt is nice, but it doesn't really go with your striped blouse.

B Match the phrasal verbs in the sentences above with their meanings.

1 *suffer or endure*

2 *occur or arise*

3 *match*

4 *explain again*

5 *become conscious again*

6 *come into flower*

7 *find by chance*

8 *go bad (referring to food)*

C Complete these sentences with your own ideas, using some of the phrasal verbs in A.

1 It's lovely when spring arrives, because …

2 If you don't keep the milk in the fridge, …

3 It's a good idea to look through old exam papers, because …

4 It's a lovely hat, but …

5 I didn't quite understand that exercise. Could you …

2 Word grades

Arrange the following words in the table below. Put all the verbs in the left-hand column and all the adjectives in the right-hand column.

cry   delighted   dissatisfied   ecstatic   giggle
frown   laugh   miserable   pleased   satisfied
smile   sob   unhappy

		Verbs of laughing and crying	Adjectives of happiness and sadness
Happiest	1	....	1 ....
	2	....	2 *delighted*
	3	....	3 ....
	4	*frown*	4 ....
	5	....	5 ....
	6	....	6 ....
Saddest			7 ....

3 *Fun* and *funny*

Look up the words *fun* and *funny* in a dictionary. Complete these sentences using the correct words or phrases.

1 I play the piano but I've never wanted to take any exams or anything. I just do it ....

2 A: Do you think anything has happened to Mrs Smith? I haven't seen her for ages.

B: Well, ..., I'd been thinking just the same thing and then I bumped into her yesterday.

3 Jenny is very sensitive about her glasses. It was very unkind of you to .... her like that.

4 I shouldn't have eaten those oysters. I'm feeling a bit ....

5 The film was so .... that I laughed from beginning to end.

6 I'm not surprised that they've split up. I had a .... feeling that she was seeing someone else.

7 It was a brilliant holiday and the children .... lots of ....

8 I think it would be .... to go camping for the weekend.

UNIT 11 ► LET'S REFLECT!

1 Open cloze

Read the text and think of one word which best fits each space.

Example: (0) has

• GOLDEN SUMMER

Golden Summer is a light–hearted romantic comedy that
(0)........*has*........ been available in video shops (1)...................... the
beginning of the year. The central character, Danny, is a banker who has
(2)...................... working and living alone in New York (3)......................
several years, and is beginning to get tired (4)...................... his lifestyle.
(5)...................... day at a party, he meets Rosita, a girl he used to know
many years (6)...................... when he was a child. Rosita is the daughter
of one of the (7)...................... important underworld bosses in the city,
but she dreams (8)...................... getting away from the world of crime
and meeting someone (9)...................... can make her dreams
(10)...................... true. The two fall (11)...................... love and plan to
run away together, much to the annoyance of Rosita's father. He
disapproves of Danny, and although he is (12)...................... arrest, he
manages (13)...................... send orders that they should be prevented
from seeing each other. The rest of the film is about the funny things that
happen to (14)...................... while they're on the run, but in the end,
things turn (15)...................... well for everyone.

(15 marks)

2 Key word transformations

Use the word in bold to complete the second sentence so that it has a similar meaning to the first. Write between two and five words.

1 I started to learn Spanish a couple of years ago.
   for
   I have .... a couple of years.

2 Jo and I are old friends – we met years ago.
   known
   Jo and I are old friends – we .... years.

3 Mark thought of a way of solving the problem.
   came
   Mark .... to the problem.

4 Do you realize that's your third coffee in an hour?
   three
   Do you realize that .... in an hour?

5 The roads are bad because of the recent heavy snow.
   it
   The roads are bad because ....
   heavily.

6 I rather suspected that he had another girlfriend.
   funny
   I .... that he might have another girlfriend.

7 When did you last see your cousin?
   since
   How .... you last saw your cousin?

8 She sings so well that she has been asked to make a record.
   such
   She .... that she has been asked to make a record.

9 When did your sister get married?
   has
   How .... married?

10 What TV programme do you like best?
   favourite
   What .... TV programme?

(20 marks)

3 Spot the mistake

Correct each of these sentences.

1 I don't know the town very well because I am only here since last week.

2 I couldn't stop laughing because his jokes were so fun.

3 I've only learned the piano for a year, so I'm not very good yet.

4 We've been taking 20 photos, so there are only four left on the film.

5 Jack's been in Adelaide since nearly a year now.

(5 marks)

4 Phrasal verbs

Complete each sentence with a word from row A and a word from row B. Put the verbs in their appropriate form.

A go   come   go   go   turn
B over   off   out   up with   with

1 Could you .... my homework with me? I don't really understand it.

2 We should buy the red curtains, because they would .... the carpet really well.

3 I'm throwing that chicken out because it's ....

4 The story has a surprising end – it doesn't .... as you would expect.

5 You would make a lot of money if you could .... a new and useful invention.

(10 marks)

Total: 50 marks

LEAD-IN

In pairs, discuss these questions.

1 What kind of music do you like (classical, pop, country and western, rock, heavy metal, reggae, soul, blues, jazz, traditional music from your country, etc.)?

2 What kind of music don't you like?

3 Have you ever been a fan of a particular singer or group? Who? Which?

1 Gapped text

A You are going to read an article about a rock fan. Look through the main text quickly and answer these questions.

1 What does Claire do?

2 Who else in the article is a fan of The Wildhearts?

DEVOTION

Shut your mouth and use your brains is the title of one of The Wildhearts' most popular songs. I would be tempted to describe The Wildhearts as a heavy metal band, but they don't like to use the term.

0	*H*

05 That was three years ago, and since then she has devoted her life to following the group. Now 20, she still buys all their albums in every format (even though she doesn't have a CD player), collects every magazine that mentions them, and writes frequently to the band members.

1	

10 Claire is unemployed but spends what little money she has on her Wildhearts obsession. She doesn't see it as a problem – it's what she wants to do. She's the sort of person for whom the word fanatic was invented, although she still leads a normal family life.

2	

15 Still, it was by doing this that she converted her next door neighbour, James, who became a Wildhearts fan after listening to the records through the wall. He is the only other fan she knows, as The Wildhearts have not yet achieved the massive following of bands like Aerosmith.

3	

20 Claire, however, does not see it that way. 'I don't think they realize the effect they have on people like me, although they should know by now – I tell them all the time in my letters … It's almost a spiritual thing.'

4	

'One reader wrote in and said he thought I wasn't
25 particularly attractive and he was surprised that some of the band have had their photo taken with me. But it was only his opinion. The band aren't worried about fame or women and they're not interested in money.'

5	

Although it's hard, she insists that it's worth it, and she
30 makes the most of the concerts she goes to. She usually travels with her next-door neighbour James. She insists on getting there early in order to see the band arrive at 4 pm. Her next priority is to get a place at the front of the queue so that she can get a spot at the foot of the stage. Then,
35 for the next few hours she is in heaven.

6	

These thoughts usually go on for a week or so. She only begins to get better when she thinks about the next concert and starts counting the days until she will see the band again.

B Now read the missing paragraphs A–H and choose the one which best fits each gap (1–6). There is one extra paragraph which you do not need. There is an example at the beginning (0).

A She once actually received a letter from the band's bass player, Danny, in reply to a card she sent him when he was ill. This treasured possession is pinned up in her bedroom, where the walls are covered in Wildhearts posters and magazine cuttings.

B They may not be, but for Claire, who likes to go and see them whenever they are on tour, money is a big issue. It can take her six months, trying to save about £10 a week, to pay for the tickets, transport and somewhere to stay.

C The feeling does not last long. 'When a concert finishes, I still feel great for an hour or so afterwards, but when I get home it's a real anti-climax. I keep thinking – this time yesterday I was with them, this time yesterday I was seeing them. I just want to go off with them in their tour bus and never come back again.'

D It doesn't bother her that they have not gained this sort of popularity. The Wildhearts make her happy. Their philosophy 'Just do what you want and it doesn't matter what anyone says' is now her philosophy, but their lead singer, Ginger, says 'We are not gods, we are just ordinary blokes.'

E The tour was meant to start a few months back, but was postponed when Ginger broke his arm hitting a kitchen cupboard. As soon as she found out the new dates, she phoned the Bristol box office every day until the tickets finally came on sale.

F In fact she still lives at home in Yeovil with her parents and younger brother. They do not seem to share her enthusiasm, which is probably more of a problem as they have to put up with Claire endlessly playing songs like Caffeine Bomb at full volume.

G She has met all The Wildhearts in person and has all their autographs. She even had her picture taken with Ginger and Rich, the drummer, and had it published in a magazine.

H This, according to Claire Templeman, is because they don't like people putting labels on their work. And she should know, because she has been The Wildhearts' number one fan ever since she heard their first song.

2 Vocabulary

A Work in pairs.

Student A   Look through the main text and find the words defined in the first list.

Student B   Look through the missing paragraphs and find the words or phrases defined in the second list.

LIST 1

1 a group of musicians
2 a word or expression
3 dedicated
4 inability to think of anything else / over enthusiasm
5 made someone change their opinion about something

LIST 2

1 articles taken from a newspaper, etc.
2 an important matter
3 to trouble, worry or upset
4 men (informal)
5 signatures of famous people

B Read the definitions to your partner. Can they guess the words?

WP 1

Read through this list of noises and answer the questions in pairs or small groups.

neighbours playing music late at night

low-flying aeroplanes

traffic on a busy road/motorway

ambulance or police sirens

loud music being played at a disco

birds singing early in the morning

children playing in a school playground

1   Which of these noises do you regularly hear where you live? How do you feel about them?

2   Are there any noises that get on your nerves? Can you do anything about them?

3   Have you ever complained to anyone about the noise they were making? Has anyone complained about you?

1   Multiple-choice cloze

Read the newspaper article about someone who was disturbed by noise and decided to solve the problem herself. For questions 1–15, decide which answer A, B, C or D best fits each space.

Example: (0) A

0	A	practising	B	revising	C	repeating	D	acting
1	A	loud	B	strong	C	big	D	large
2	A	red	B	green	C	yellow	D	white
3	A	doing	B	making	C	having	D	playing
4	A	denied	B	refused	C	ignored	D	rejected
5	A	lowered	B	dropped	C	fell	D	felt
6	A	collected	B	found	C	raised	D	brought
7	A	on	B	to	C	with	D	from
8	A	spread	B	developed	C	came	D	increased
9	A	total	B	all	C	part	D	full
10	A	wonder	B	surprise	C	astonishment	D	fright
11	A	action	B	effect	C	fight	D	battle
12	A	harm	B	injury	C	damage	D	wound
13	A	hate	B	object	C	dislike	D	detest
14	A	come on	B	go on	C	take on	D	let on
15	A	pleased	B	satisfied	C	delighted	D	proud

WB 2

THE LAST
straw

One peaceful afternoon in the Cotswold village of Ebrington, as some Morris dancers were (0)......*A*...... in the garden of the village hall, they were interrupted by a terrifyingly (1)...................... shout from behind the garden wall. When they went to see who it was, they found an old lady who was (2)...................... with rage. Gracie Mitchell, 64, complained that they were (3)...................... so much noise that it was driving her mad. She asked them to stop, but as their practice session had only just begun, the dancers (4)...................... .

Gracie Mitchell returned home to plan her revenge. When darkness (5)...................... , she returned to the village hall, armed with a hammer. After breaking into the store room, she (6)...................... up all the Morris dancers' costumes, sticks and the accordion; she then put everything into a big pile in the garden and set it (7)...................... fire.

When news of the blaze at the village hall (8)...................... , reporters were soon on the scene, eager to hear the (9)...................... story of the elderly vandal. It soon became clear that the attack had not been a complete (10)...................... . One of the Morris dancers explained that there had been a long-running battle between Mrs Mitchell and the dancers and she had often threatened to take (11)...................... .

Mrs Mitchell admitted at once that she had caused the (12)...................... . 'I am fond of music and don't mind Morris dancing,' she said, 'but I do (13)...................... to these practice sessions. They (14)...................... for so long that you can't hear yourself think.' She said she was not (15)...................... of what she had done, but that in the end, she had had no choice.

GRAMMAR ZOOM

Reported speech

1 Tense changes

A When we report what someone has said and use a verb in the past tense, (e.g. *she said, he told me*) we need to make certain changes to the tenses. Look at these sentences. What do you think the speaker's actual words were?

Reported speech	Actual words
1 She said the Morris dancers were driving her mad.	*'The Morris dancers are driving me mad.'*
2 She said she couldn't think.	....
3 She told reporters she had caused the damage.	....
4 She said she was not proud of what she had done.	....
5 She said she had had no choice.	....

B Look at the sentences and answer the questions.

John told me he was going to a concert in Sheffield *tomorrow*.

John told me he was going to a concert in Sheffield *the following day*.

1 What is the difference between these sentences? In which has the concert already taken place?

2 What changes might you need to make to these words when you use reported speech?

a today	....	e next month	....
b tomorrow	....	f here	....
c yesterday	....	g this	....
d last week	....		

C Fill in the spaces to report these statements.

1 'I don't like pop music very much,' he said.

He said that he .... pop music very much.

2 'I'm feeling too tired to go out to the concert,' she said.

She said she .... too tired to go out to the concert.

3 'I gave Claire a CD for her birthday,' Amanda said.

Amanda said that she .... Claire a CD for her birthday.

4 'I have never been to a pop festival before,' Paul said.

Paul said that he .... to a pop festival before.

5 'I was feeling sad until I heard the record on the radio,' said Shima.

Shima said that she .... sad until she heard the record on the radio.

6 'I'll buy the tickets tomorrow,' James said last week, but he never did.

Last week James said he .... the tickets .... , but he never did.

D In pairs, think of a time when you have had an argument with a friend or member of your family. Explain what the problem was and then, using reported speech, report:

• what the other person said about the problem.

• what you said to the other person about the problem.

2 Reported questions

A When we report questions, we either use a question word such as *who, what, where, when, how, why,* or *if/whether*. Read these examples and match the direct questions in 1–6 with the reported questions in a–f.

1 Where did you learn to play the piano?

2 Where have you been learning to play the piano?

3 Do you study at music school?

4 Did you study at music school?

5 Who teaches you?

6 Who do you teach?

a I asked her if she studied at music school.

b I asked her who she taught.

c I asked her where she had learned the piano.

d I asked her who taught her.

e I asked her where she had been learning the piano.

f I asked her if she had studied at music school.

B What do you notice about the word order in reported questions after question words and *if/whether*?

C Imagine that one of the reporters who interviewed Mrs Mitchell wrote these short notes about the answers she gave. In pairs or groups, say what you think the reporter asked her.

Example:

0 64 He asked her how old she was.

1 *Honeysuckle Cottage, Ebrington*

2 *in the afternoon*

3 *a hammer*

4 *because the noise was driving me mad*

5 *yes, many times – but they just ignored me*

1 ....

2 ....

3 ....

4 ....

5 ....

WP 3

1 Talking together

Work in pairs and complete Tasks 1 and 2. One of you is Student A the other is Student B.

TASK 1	TASK 2
Student A: Look at the advert below and ask Student B for information about: a the instrument b the fees c the days and times of the lessons.	Student B: Look at the advert below and ask Student A for information about: a dates available b the prices of the tickets c the times of the performances.

Student B   Look at page 172 and answer Student A's questions.

Student A   Look at page 171 and answer Student B's questions.

FANCY PLAYING AN UNUSUAL INSTRUMENT?

Expert tuition by professional musician

Reasonable fees

Some hours still available

TEL: 889 3524

HAMMER HEAD TOUR

TICKETS STILL AVAILABLE FOR SOME CONCERTS

various prices
evening performances
Tel: 01189 567046

2 Taking a long turn

The pictures in the next column show people practising and performing different things.

Work with a different partner. Take it in turns to talk about the pictures for about one minute. When your partner has finished talking, answer the question about their pictures. Remember you have about 20 seconds to do this.

> Remember to organize what you are going to say. Think about the points you want to make and the order in which you will make them.

Student A   Compare and contrast the different things the children are learning to do in pictures 1 and 2, and say whether you think it is more difficult to learn to play a musical instrument or to sing.

Student B   Do you think young children should be encouraged to learn to play a musical instrument?

Student B   Compare and contrast the different kinds of entertainment in pictures 3 and 4, and say which one is more popular in your country.

Student A   Which of these performances would you prefer to go to?

3 Discussion

In small groups, discuss these questions.

1 Which do you think would be more interesting for a musical entertainer: recording an album in a studio or giving a live concert?

2 What would be some of the advantages of being a famous entertainer?

3 What would the disadvantages be?

4 What would you like to be famous for?

LEAD-IN ►

Work in pairs. Write down the titles of your three favourite songs of all time. Take it in turns to ask and answer questions about one of the songs. Find out:

who it is by.

what language it is in.

what appeals to them most – the music or the words.

how long ago they first heard it.

how the song makes them feel.

1 Note taking

You will hear an extract from a talk about the music of the Caribbean. For questions 1–10, complete the notes.

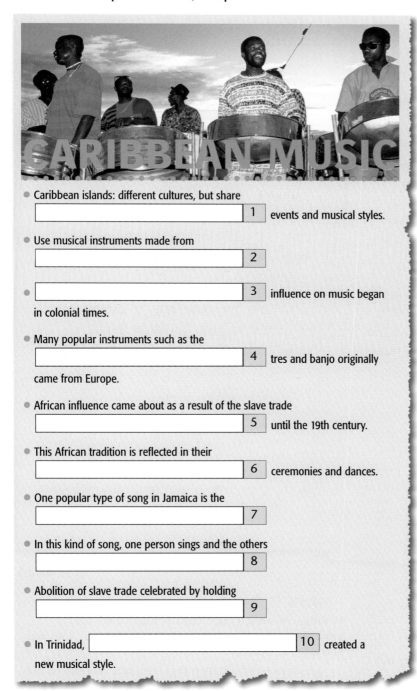

CARIBBEAN MUSIC

- Caribbean islands: different cultures, but share [1] events and musical styles.

- Use musical instruments made from [2]

- [3] influence on music began in colonial times.

- Many popular instruments such as the [4] tres and banjo originally came from Europe.

- African influence came about as a result of the slave trade [5] until the 19th century.

- This African tradition is reflected in their [6] ceremonies and dances.

- One popular type of song in Jamaica is the [7]

- In this kind of song, one person sings and the others [8]

- Abolition of slave trade celebrated by holding [9]

- In Trinidad, [10] created a new musical style.

Listen again and check your answers.

2 Multiple choice

You will hear an interview with Hans Zimmer, who writes soundtracks (that is the music) for films. For questions 1–7, choose the best answer A, B or C.

1 The film directors he deals with appear to be mainly
   A confident.
   B nervous.
   C aggressive.   [1]

2 He was chosen to write the music for *The Lion King* because
   A he was recommended by a famous composer.
   B he had experience of working with animation.
   C he had written some music which the directors liked.   [2]

3 When Zimmer writes music for films, he tries to
   A make the story easier to follow.
   B express things the director hasn't shown.
   C forget about parts of the story.   [3]

4 Zimmer says the best tunes come to him
   A when he is relaxed.
   B when he is in the bath.
   C when he gets up early.   [4]

5 He says that he produces most of his work
   A when he is under pressure.
   B by working regularly.
   C when he has plenty of time to think.   [5]

6 How long does it take Zimmer to write the soundtrack for a film?
   A several years
   B three to four weeks
   C it varies   [6]

7 What does Zimmer say he is going to do?
   A take a two-month holiday
   B refuse most new projects
   C work for a further five years   [7]

Listen again and check your answers.

WP 4

Writing a transactional letter (3)

In the transactional letter in Part 1, you may be required to give or ask for information.

Read the sample task.

You have received a letter from an English speaking friend who is coming to your country to attend a music festival. Read the extract from the letter and the notes. Write a suitable **letter** in reply, answering all your friend's questions (120–180 words).

Anyway, the reason I'm writing is to say that I'll be in your area for a music festival next April. It goes on for three days, and I've got an extra ticket that you could have if you want. Let me know quickly if you want to come. If not, I'll give it to someone else.

Free most of the month

hope so – exact dates?

Who's playing? Price of ticket?

Also, I was wondering if I could stay with you for a few days after the festival. I've got a week off and I thought it'd be nice to spend some time with you.

Yes, no problem – I'd love to have you stay.

By the way, what's the weather like in April? As I've only ever been to see you in the summer, I'm not sure what clothes to bring.

Do you remember ...

Read the letter and answer the questions.

With reference to your letter of 18 November, it was great to hear that you are coming over again.

I think the festival sounds like a great idea, and I anticipate that I shall be able to attend. I'm free for most of the month, and could you let me know how much the tickets are? I would also be grateful if you could inform me who is playing.

It gave me great pleasure to hear that you would like to stay with me for a few days after the concert. I can't see any problem, we can talk about it nearer the time. I will try to organize some free time, so that we can be together.

In April the weather is warm, but it tends to rain quite a lot. I would suggest light clothes and either a raincoat or an umbrella to keep you dry.

Hope to hear from you soon.

Yours

Jo

(156 words)

Task interpretation

1   What questions will you need to answer?
2   What questions will you need to ask?
3   What else will you need to include at the beginning and at the end?
4   What sort of language would be appropriate for this letter – formal or informal? Why?

Analysis

In some ways it is a good reply because there are no grammatical mistakes, but in other ways it is not. Can you find any examples of:

1   questions or information that the writer has missed out and should have included?
2   words or expressions that are not really appropriate?

3 Language study

Asking for information

When we write a letter asking for information, we often begin a question with an expression like *Do you know…?* or *Could you tell me…?*

These are called *indirect questions*.

A Look at these examples and answer the questions below.

1 a 'When does the festival begin?'

   b 'Could you tell me when the festival begins?'

2 a 'Will Jane be free?'

   b 'Do you know if Jane will be free?'

What do you notice about the word order in 1b and 2b?

Which extra word has been included in 2b?

B Rewrite these questions beginning with the given words.

1 What time are you arriving?

   Could you let me know ....

   ....

2 How long are you planning to stay?

   Could you also tell me ....

   ....

3 Do you want to go out on Saturday?

   Could you tell me ....

   ....

4 Do you need a lift from the airport?

   Could you let me know ....

   ....

5 How much will it all cost?

   Do you know ....

   ....

6 Could you give me a ring tomorrow?

   Do you think ....

   ....

4 Writing task

Writing a formal letter

You and your class are planning to give a surprise party for your English teacher, Chris Wilson, who is leaving at the end of term. Read the last part of a letter from Mrs Wilson, your teacher's wife, and the notes written on it. Write a letter to Mrs Wilson giving her details of what you have arranged and asking for any information you need.

Write your **letter** (120–180 words).

Thanks for agreeing not to say anything.

As I said on the phone, Chris will be really delighted by this surprise party you are planning, and I promise not to mention it. A little nearer the time, could you let me know when and where it will be? I know our last week will be very busy with all the packing, but I'll make sure we get there.

School, Friday 25 March at 6.30 pm

Is Friday OK? If not, we can change the day.

I look forward to seeing you all again.

Yours,

Janet Wilson

Suggestions for a leaving present:

Notes…

Work through the notes and prepare your letter.

In pairs discuss what you think you should include in paragraphs 2 and 3.

Paragraph 1

Begin your letter by thanking Mrs Wilson for her letter and for promising not to mention the surprise party. It would be appropriate to address her as *Mrs Wilson*, although you can refer to your teacher as *Chris* or *Mr Wilson*.

Paragraph 2

....

....

....

Paragraph 3

....

....

....

Paragraph 4

Finish the letter in a suitable way.

Now write your letter, making sure you include all the relevant information.

When you have finished, check your writing carefully for spelling, punctuation and grammar mistakes.

WORD POWER

1 Phrasal verbs with *put*

A Read these sentences. Underline the phrasal verbs and match them with the meanings (a–g).

1 I didn't want her to come to the concert so I put her off by saying she wouldn't enjoy it.

2 I hate our new teacher. She's always putting me down in front of the other students.

3 His children play their music so loud – I don't know how he puts up with it.

4 The band had to put the tour off until May because the drummer broke his arm.

5 Are you sure I can stay? I don't want to put you out.

6 Sorry, I wanted the Sales Department. I must've been put through to the wrong extension.

7 Don't stay in a hotel – we can put you up for a few days.

a	tolerate	e	connect to someone on the phone
b	postpone	f	have someone to stay
c	discourage	g	say bad things about someone
d	inconvenience		

B Read these sentences. Correct the ones which are incorrect.

1 Do you think your brother would mind putting me out for a couple of nights?

2 You want extension 2317? I'll put you off now, sir.

3 I don't want to put you through, but there will be quite a lot of people you won't like at the party.

4 She never says anything nice about her friends – she's always putting people down.

5 If Fatima doesn't get back in time, we'll have to put the meeting up until next week.

6 She's so rude to her parents – I don't know how they put up with her.

2 *Say, talk, speak, tell*

Complete the sentences with the correct form of *say, talk, speak* or *tell*.

1 I'm very good at French, but I don't .... German very well.

2 Even the twins' mother finds it hard to .... the difference between them sometimes.

3 I'm sorry I left without .... goodbye.

4 It's your own fault. I .... you that you would miss the train if you didn't hurry.

5 Jane is upset. What did you .... to her?

6 Did he .... you what he was doing today?

3 Reporting verbs

When we report speech, we often use other reporting verbs apart from *say* or *tell*. Match the speech bubbles with the list of verbs below.

1 If I were you, I'd have a holiday.

2 Don't go into the garden – I've just seen a snake.

3 All right, we will have a meeting if you really want.

4 Don't forget to lock the door.

5 If you don't stop annoying me, I'll scream.

6 It wasn't me who broke the window.

7 No, I won't do any more homework. I'm sick to death of it.

8 It was me who took the money.

9 Go on, let's see how fast this car can really go.

10 I assure you I will give you the money back next week.

a	advising sb to do sth	....
b	warning sb not to do sth	....
c	encouraging sb to do sth	....
d	reminding sb to do sth	....
e	threatening to do sth	....
f	promising to do sth	....
g	agreeing to do sth	....
h	refusing to do sth	....
i	admitting doing sth	....
j	denying doing sth	....

4 Verbs and prepositions

Complete the spaces using an appropriate verb and preposition.

1 You don't really .... ghosts, do you?

2 The new group .... a lead singer, two guitarists, and a drummer.

3 Can I see you later? There's something I'd like to .... with you.

4 Rob's new CD player is great, but he .... a lot of money .... it.

5 This is a great song – why don't we .... the lyrics and try to learn them.

6 Last night I .... flying a plane.

7 I'm not sure if I'll be able to come to the concert – it .... my work.

8 I must .... my mother, because I haven't written for ages.

UNIT 12 ► LET'S REFLECT!

1 Word formation

Use the word given in capitals at the end of each line to form a word that fits in the space in the same line.
Example: (0) inventors

One of the best-known (0)...*inventors*... **INVENT**
of the last century was Thomas Edison.
He (1)............................ came up with new **REGULAR**
inventions in his life – 1,093 in all – but his
(2)............................ remained the phonograph, **FAVOUR**
a machine for recording sound. He was very
(3)............................ about the possibilities for **ENTHUSE**
his machine, which could be used for recording
(4)............................ of music, dictating letters, **PERFORM**
making toys – the possibilities seemed
(5)............................ . Although the machine was **END**
quite (6)............................ and the sound quality **EXPENSE**
was not particularly good, the phonograph
quickly gained great (7)............................ . The **POPULAR**
(8)............................ success of the phonograph **MASS**
encouraged others, and in 1887 the gramophone
was invented. This used a (9)............................ **DIFFER**
system, a flat disk instead of a cylinder. Other
improvements (10)............................ led to a **FINAL**
machine that could reproduce high quality sound.

(10 marks)

2 Key word transformations

Use the word in **bold** to complete the second sentence so that it has a similar meaning to the first. Write between two and five words.

1 It's your own fault – I told you it was dangerous to go near the dog.

   not

   It's your own fault – I warned .... near the dog.

2 The twins look exactly the same to me.

   tell

   I can't .... the twins.

3 My father said: 'Did you enjoy the party?'

   enjoyed

   My father asked me .... the party.

4 Of course we'd be happy to have you to stay for a few days.

   up

   Of course we wouldn't mind .... for a few days.

5 The electrician said, 'I'll come tomorrow and fix the lights.'

   following

   The electrician told me he .... and fix the lights.

6 When does this train get to Blackpool? Do you know?

   gets

   Do you know .... to Blackpool?

7 How much did your computer cost?

   pay

   What .... your computer?

8 'Who were you talking to?' I asked Jane.

   been

   I asked Jane .... to.

9 The man admitted stealing the money.

   said

   The man .... the money.

10 The teacher asked Peter, 'Who is picking you up from school?'

   was

   The teacher asked Peter .... up from school.

(20 marks)

3 Spot the mistake

Correct each of these sentences.

1 I asked him to help me but he simply rejected.
2 I was surprised to see Ken – I thought he is on holiday.
3 Excuse me, could you tell me what is the time?
4 He said he would ring tomorrow, but he never did.
5 Did Jenny say you where she was going?
6 They've warned motorists to don't drive too fast this morning.
7 Could you put me down for a few days until I find a flat?
8 Aunt Mary's on the phone – do you want to tell hello?
9 We may be able to go – but it depends from the weather.
10 How many different languages can you talk?

(10 marks)

4 Vocabulary

Find a word or phrase from this unit that means:

1 to rearrange for a later date (phrasal verb)
2 a street party regularly held in Trinidad
3 to tolerate (phrasal verb)
4 to say that you have not done something
5 to say you will not do something

(10 marks)

Total: 50 marks

13 Good luck, bad luck

FRAME 1 ▶ READING

LEAD-IN ▶

Discuss these questions in pairs.

1   In your country, what is supposed to bring good or bad luck?

2   Do you have anything or do anything to bring you good luck?

3   Do you think of any numbers as lucky or unlucky?

4   Do you know what your star sign is? Do you take any notice of your horoscope?

1   Multiple choice

A   Read this article about a person who seems to have had a lot of bad luck. For questions 1–7, choose the correct answer A, B, C or D.

THE UNLUCKIEST WOMAN IN THE COUNTRY

Marie Rawsthorne may be the unluckiest woman in the country. In an 18-month period her house caught fire twice and, just before she got
05 married, the church burned down. She has had so many car accidents – including eight crashes and near-misses in one 50-mile journey – that she has lost count. A few years ago,
10 she fell and broke her arm, so it was strapped up. Almost immediately, she broke her leg. At the same time, she was made homeless.

Her daily life is like a long list of
15 annoying incidents: the car won't start, she loses her keys, she gets stuck in traffic jams. When she visits friends she breaks mirrors or knocks pictures off the walls. Electrical equipment
20 fails for no reason when she tries to operate it, and everything she buys goes wrong. 'These things don't seem so extraordinary to me any more. They're just part of everyday
25 life.'

Marie, who is 29, is one of the subjects taking part in a two-year study of the psychology of luck. Richard Wiseman, who is directing the research, is trying
30 to find out whether some people do have better luck than others or whether 'lucky' people are simply those who only remember the good things that happen to them.

35 Many people believe that luck or chance is a strong force that can give people things or take them away as it likes. Lucky people are given good fortune at birth; unlucky people are
40 marked by the hand of fate, and we avoid them in case some of their bad luck rubs off on us. This, of course, is illogical, but it does seem strange that there are people as unlucky as Marie
45 whereas others are at the other end of the scale. There are some people, for example, who have to give up buying tickets in local raffles because they win so often that it becomes
50 embarrassing.

Successful people often say that 'you make your own luck', and the first results from Wiseman's study suggest that this is true. If people believe that
55 they are lucky, then they are more likely to continue trying until they succeed at something. Those who think they are unlucky, on the other hand, do the opposite. They don't buy
60 lottery tickets because they 'know' they will not win, and therefore they can never succeed. Luck is also a matter of interpretation. When one of Wiseman's other subjects fell down
65 the stairs and broke his arm, he did not think that this was unlucky. On the contrary, he was actually extremely fortunate – if he had fallen differently, he might have broken his
70 neck.

Wiseman is carrying out a number of different tests on his subjects. He starts with a questionnaire which helps to show whether or not people
75 think they are lucky. He then tests this against random events: for instance, how often they can predict the result of tossing a coin. In another test, his subjects have to guess the shape of a
80 drawing hidden in an envelope, and the earliest results seem to show that lucky people do better at this.

In the end, Wiseman is hoping to work out why some people think of
85 themselves as lucky, and to find ways in which unlucky people can improve their lives. He believes that certain childhood events could hold the answer, and that there may be certain
90 ways of bringing up children that can affect the rest of their lives.

Marie thinks she was definitely affected by her childhood, which was difficult. Although she did well at
95 school, she recently found out that she was dyslexic. Sometimes this condition can upset your balance, and this side-effect might explain why she is so accident-prone. She says that
100 taking part in the project has helped her because she can now explain some of her bad luck.

1 The writer suggests that Marie is particularly unlucky because

   A she has nowhere to live.
   B she has had eight car accidents.
   C a lot went wrong in a fairly short space of time.
   D her house burned down after her wedding.

2 It appears that Marie

   A has got used to her minor misfortunes.
   B does not know how to drive.
   C is rarely invited to her friends' houses.
   D tends to break most of the things she buys.

3 What does the writer find surprising?

   A People's luck can change so rapidly from good to bad.
   B There are such great differences between how much luck people have.
   C We prefer to avoid being in close contact with unlucky people.
   D We are born either lucky or unlucky and are unable to change this.

4 The first results from the study seem to show that 'lucky' people

   A are always successful.
   B are usually optimistic.
   C rarely buy lottery tickets.
   D rarely have serious accidents.

5 What does Wiseman ask his subjects to do?

   A fill in several questionnaires
   B draw various objects
   C complete several tests
   D predict their test results

6 The main aim of Wiseman's research is to find out

   A which childhood events are important.
   B the best way of bringing up children.
   C why some people have more luck than others.
   D how to help 'unlucky' people.

7 Marie now believes that

   A her failure at school was not her fault.
   B her luck is unlikely to improve in the immediate future.
   C she will now become a lucky person.
   D some of her bad luck may be due to a medical problem.

B Look at the text again and discuss which of the things that happen or have happened to Marie might be connected with her problem of balance. Which of them are just bad luck?

2 Vocabulary

A Match these words and phrases from the text with their meanings.

1 *near-misses*   a unable to remember how often something has happened

2 *accident-prone*   b stops working properly

3 *goes wrong*   c situations in which an accident is only just avoided

4 *lost count*   d more likely to have accidents than other people

5 *side-effect*   e a lot of vehicles moving very slowly or not at all

6 *traffic jam*   f secondary, usually unpleasant effect of something

B Using the words and phrases above, answer these questions.

Example: *Why do you say he's a dangerous driver? He brought you to school safely, didn't he?*

              'Yes, but he had five near-misses!'

1 How many compositions do you think you have written in your life?

2 Why do you think your mother needs a new car?

3 Why on earth did it take you two hours to get here?

4 Why has the doctor changed the pills she was giving you?

5 Why do you put all the glasses away when Marie comes to visit?

3 Language study

Regrets about the present and the past

A When we express regrets about the present or the past, we can use the expressions *I wish* and *If only*. Look at the examples of some of the things Marie might say.

I wish these things didn't keep happening to me.
If only I wasn't so unlucky.
I wish I had stayed at home today.
If only I had been more careful.

1 Which sentences refer to the present? What tense is used?

2 Which sentences refer to something that happened in the past? What tense is used?

B Using *I wish* and *If only*, tell your partner about something …

                          Examples:

1 you would like to be/not to be.   *I wish I was/were better at maths.*

2 you would like to have/not to have.   *If only I didn't have so much homework to do.*

3 you would like to be able to do.   *I wish I could speak Chinese.*

4 you regret doing in the past.   *If only I hadn't stayed up so late last night.*

5 you regret not doing in the past.   *I wish I had studied harder for my exams.*

WP 1

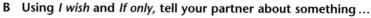

1 Error correction

Read the following text about a famous diamond. Some of the lines are correct, and some have a word which should not be there. Tick (✔) the lines which are correct and underline the unnecessary words. There are two examples at the beginning (0 and 00).

THE CURSE OF THE HOPE DIAMOND

0	✓	The Hope Diamond is one of the most notorious gems in history. It
00		was mined in India, and was said to be cursed because <u>of</u> it had
1		been stolen from a statue of the Hindu goddess Sita. In 1668,
2		the diamond was brought to France by a man he called Tavernier
3		who has sold it to King Louis XIV. Tavernier might have lived longer
4		if he had listened up to the warnings about the curse, but he
5		ignored about them. On his next trip to India, he was killed by wild
6		dogs. The diamond was inherited by King Louis XVI and Marie Antoinette.
7		They were executed during the French Revolution and the diamond it was
8		stolen, together with all the other French crown jewels. In 1830,
9		the diamond reappeared in to London. Henry Hope bought it, and since
10		then it has been called as the Hope Diamond. It was sold to an Eastern
11		European prince; he gave it to an actress whom he later shot her. The
12		next owner, was a Greek millionaire, plunged to his death over a cliff.
13		Harry Winston bought the diamond in the 1947. He was fully aware
14		of the diamond's terrible history and eventually donated it to the
15		Smithsonian Institution – no doubt with a great sense of the relief.

WP 2

GRAMMAR ZOOM

Third conditional

1 Uses

We use the third conditional to talk about events in the past that did not happen, and to talk about how the results would have been different.

A Look at the example sentences and answer the questions.

Past event	*Harry Winston gave the diamond away.*
Past result	*He did not have a nasty accident.*

We can join these two sentences as follows:

Different past event	*If Harry Winston had not given the diamond away,*
Different past result	*he would have had a nasty accident.*

1   What tense do we use to talk about different events in the *if* clause?

2   What tense do we use to talk about the different results in the other clause?

3   What other verbs can we use instead of *would have*?

B Read through these sentences. Some of them contain a mistake. Tick the ones that are right, and correct the ones that are wrong.

1   If I hadn't got up so late, I wouldn't have missed the first lesson.

2   If she wasn't wearing a seat belt, she might have been killed.

3   I couldn't have succeeded if you wouldn't have helped me.

4   If I had seen her, I would have told you.

5   I'm sure I would have passed if I hadn't have been so nervous.

6   If you would have followed my advice, you wouldn't have got into trouble.

7   I might have got the job if I'd applied for it.

8   I would have enjoyed the party more if you had been there.

C In pairs, write a short paragraph about:

1 a time when you had some good luck

or

2 a time when you had some bad luck.

Use one third conditional sentence in your paragraph.

Example:

I first met my girlfriend quite by chance. I was supposed to go to a party one evening, and as the car had broken down, I decided to take the bus. I was just standing there in the queue when she came up and stood behind me. Somehow we got chatting, and we got on really well. So we arranged to meet again and that's how it all started. But it's strange to think that if the car hadn't broken down, I might never have met her.

2   Word formation

HELPLINE

Usually you only need to make one change to the word in capitals. For example, you may need to change a noun into an adjective, FAME – *famous*.

However, you may need to make two changes to the word in capitals. For example, you may need to change EVENT into an adjective *and* use the negative form – *uneventful*.

A Complete the table below, filling in the positive and negative adjectives from the base words. Sometimes more than one answer may be possible.

base	positive	negative
luck	*lucky*	*unlucky*
fashion	....	....
logic	....	....
sympathy	....	....
reason	....	....
responsibility	....	....
success	....	....
fortune	....	....

B Read the text and use the words at the end of each line to form a word that fits in the space in the same line.

Example: (0) believers

FENG SHUI

According to (0).....*believers*..... in the Chinese science   BELIEF
of *feng shui*, houses and other (1)..........................   BUILD
should be arranged in a certain way. Some of the basic
(2)........................... of *feng shui* experts are as follows: RECOMMEND
it is considered (3)........................... if a stove can be   LUCK
seen from the front door as stoves are (4)........................   CLOSE
associated with death; similarly, a staircase pointing
towards the front door can bring (5)...........................   FORTUNE
because it means money will (6)........................... flow   CONSTANT
out through the door. Until (7)..........................., people   RECENT
might have dismissed the idea of *feng shui* as
(8)..........................., but builders and estate agents in   LOGIC
the USA are taking *feng shui* masters (9)...........................   SERIOUS
as the number of buyers from the East is rising and they
are (10)........................ becoming more influential.   RAPID

1 Talking about yourself

In pairs, discuss these questions.

1 Have you ever had a lucky escape?

2 What happened?

3 Whose fault do you think it was?

2 Taking a long turn

The pictures below show situations in which people have had a lucky escape. Working with the same partner, take it in turns to talk about your pictures and answer the question about your partner's pictures.

Student A Compare and contrast pictures 1 and 2, and say what you think might have happened. (You have about one minute.)

Student B In which situation do you think the people have had the luckiest escape? (You have about 20 seconds.)

Student B Compare and contrast pictures 3 and 4, and say what you think might have happened. (You have about one minute.)

Student A In which situation do you think the people have had the luckiest escape? (You have about 20 seconds.)

3 Talking together

Talk together in groups of three about the pictures in 2. Decide who or what you think was to blame for what happened, and which of the four pictures you think shows the luckiest escape. Before you begin the task, check that you've understood what you have to do. Use the ideas in the Phrase Box below.

> **HELPLINE**
>
> In the exam, you can check with the examiner that you have understood the task.

> **PHRASE BOX**
>
> **Checking that you've understood**
> *So, I / We have to …*
> *Do you want me / us to …?*
> *Am I / Are we supposed to …?*
> *Should I …?*

4 Discussion

In small groups, discuss these questions.

1 If you could have changed one thing about your life so far, what would it have been?

2 What do you think would (not) have happened as a result?

> **HELPLINE**
>
> If you do not hear exactly what the examiner asks you and you want to hear the question again, ask her or him to repeat it. See the Phrase Box below for expressions you can use.

> **PHRASE BOX**
>
> **Asking someone to repeat**
> *I'm sorry. I didn't quite catch that.*
> *Would you mind repeating that, please?*
> *Could you say that again, please?*

FRAME 4 ►LISTENING

1 Multiple choice

You will hear people talking in eight different situations. For questions 1–8, choose the best answer A, B or C.

1 You hear part of a radio programme. Who is the speaker?

   A   a fireman
   B   a policeman
   C   an ambulance man | 1 |

2 You overhear a woman talking on the phone. The person she is talking to

   A   dislikes holidays in the sun.
   B   is at the hotel.
   C   originally planned to be there with her. | 2 |

3 You hear two people talking at the airport. What have they left behind?

   A   their luggage
   B   their tickets
   C   their money | 3 |

4 You hear an advertisement on a radio. What is being advertised?

   A   a book
   B   a course
   C   a programme | 4 |

5 You hear someone talking about a time when she went to stay with a family abroad. What does she regret most?

   A   that the family were not friendly
   B   that she did not get the chance to speak French | 5 |
   C   that it took so long to meet people she liked

6 You hear part of a local radio interview. Who is being interviewed?

   A   a journalist
   B   an actor | 6 |
   C   a film director

7 You hear a critic talking about a new film. What is her overall opinion of it?

   A   It was badly produced.
   B   It was a bit disappointing. | 7 |
   C   It was amusing.

8 You hear two people talking at the entrance of a restaurant. The man who wants a table

   A   has not made a reservation.
   B   will not get a table tonight. | 8 |
   C   must wait before getting a table.

Listen again and check your answers.

2 Multiple matching

You will hear five people talking about events that made them choose a particular career. For questions 1–5, choose from the list A–F the profession of each speaker. Use the letters only once. There is one extra letter which you do not need to use.

A   a doctor   Speaker 1 | 1 |
B   a teacher   Speaker 2 | 2 |
C   a TV reporter   Speaker 3 | 3 |
D   a banker   Speaker 4 | 4 |
E   a lawyer   Speaker 5 | 5 |
F   an architect

Listen again and check your answers.

3 The same or different?

A   At least one of the words in each pair below appeared in the listenings. Write S beside the words which are pronounced the same, and D beside those which are different.

1 some / sum   5 heat / hit
2 fair / fare   6 steal / still
3 wrote / rode   7 reel / real
4 scene / seen   8 career / carer

B   Read the following sentences which appear in the second listening and fill the spaces with an appropriate word from the list above.

1 *He never used to .... them, but he was very cruel.*

2 *I .... an article in the school magazine about it.*

3 *But I had a .... battle – my teachers suggested I could become a police officer, but I was more ambitious than that.*

4 *I studied law, although I never intended to pursue it as a ....*

WP 3

Writing a story (3)

If you choose to write a story in Part 2, it is important to try to make it as interesting as possible.

1 Sample task

Read the sample task.

You have decided to enter a short story competition. The rules state that the story must end with the following words:

'I can't believe my luck,' she said. 'I don't know what I would have done without you.'

Write your **story** (120–180 words).

2 Sample answers

Read both stories and answer the questions.

Analysis

Which one is better, A or B? Say why.

Compare the two stories from the point of view of detail. Discuss these questions.

1 What time markers and expressions are used in each text to make the sequence of the story clear? Underline them.

2 Underline examples of adjectives and adverbs used in both stories. How do the two versions differ in the use of these?

3 In what other ways is the first version more detailed than the second? Underline the extra details.

Sample answer A

When the supermarket closed and all the staff had left, the security guard went on his rounds. As he was walking slowly down one of the long dark corridors at the back of the store, he noticed that the door to one of the large walk-in fridges had been left slightly open.

'Some people are so careless,' he muttered, slamming the heavy metal door shut.

It was several hours later, just before dawn, that he heard a noise. As he walked down the corridor, the sharp metallic noise grew louder. Suddenly he realized what was wrong.

He ran to the door of the walk-in fridge and opened it hurriedly. There, blue with cold, but still alive, was one of the shop assistants.

'Oh, thank you,' she cried. 'I thought I was going to die. I was getting some lamb out, but the door slammed shut. It was the wind, I suppose.'

The guard did not reply. The girl smiled.

'I can't believe my luck,' she said. 'I don't know what I would have done without you.'

(175 words)

Sample answer B

The guard went on his rounds. As he was walking around the back of the store, he noticed that one of the walk-in fridges had been left open.

'Some people are so careless,' he said, shutting the door.

Later he heard something. As he walked down the corridor, the noise grew louder. He realized something was wrong and went towards the fridges. He opened one of the fridge doors. There was a shop assistant. She was still alive.

'Oh, thank you,' she cried. 'I thought I was going to die. I was getting something when the door shut.' The guard did not reply. The girl smiled.

'I can't believe my luck,' she said. 'I don't know what I would have done without you.'

(122 words)

Adding details

Rewrite each of the following sentences, adding a few more details to make them more interesting. Be careful not to add too many because it will sound unnatural.

Example:

He went to his car and drove away.

He walked slowly towards his red Mercedes sports car, got in and drove off towards the motorway.

1   He got up, went downstairs, and saw the letter on the table.

....
....
....
....
....
....
....
....

2   She opened the door and saw the man.

....
....
....
....
....
....
....
....

3   I saw the animal and ran away.

....
....
....
....
....
....
....
....

Answer the following question.

Writing a story

You have decided to enter a short story writing competition. The rules state that the story must end with the following words.

If you had listened to my advice, none of this would have happened.

Write your **story** (120–180 words).

Notes...

Work through the notes and prepare your story.

* Plan the outline of the story, and make a few notes about the most important things that happen.

* You will need to consider the following:

  1   What has happened? It does not have to be something bad like an accident – it could be something wonderful.

  2   Who is in the story and who is speaking? The sentence given allows you to choose the speaker. You could be the one saying this, or someone could be saying it to you. Remember also that the story does not have to be written in the first person.

  3   You need to try to think of a story that will allow you to mention the 'advice' (whatever that may be) at an early stage.

  The main part of the story will be about what happened when the character in the story did not listen to the advice.

  4   What is the setting of the story, and how soon after the events in the story did the speaker say these words?

* Think of some of the points that you will describe in more detail, and write more notes about each of these.

* Start writing your story, adding the detail as you write. Take care with paragraphs and punctuation.

When you have finished, check your story carefully for any mistakes.

WORDPOWER

1 Words easily confused

A Match the words *chance, opportunity, possibility* and *occasion* with the sets of sentences. The word must fit all three sentences in the set.

Set A

There's a good .... that you will do well in the exam.

The other day I ran into Emma quite by ....

We don't stand a .... of winning.

Set B

There is a distinct .... that I will fail.

It is now a very real .... that we will have to cancel our holiday.

There is now no .... of finding any more survivors.

Set C

I had the .... to go to England, but I decided not to.

This job offer is a wonderful .... , so make the most of it.

I will tell him how you feel at the earliest ....

Set D

I last saw her in July and on that .... she seemed very happy.

The wedding was an .... I didn't want to miss.

My parents' anniversary was a memorable ....

B Complete these sentences with one of the four words from A.

1 My mother and father met by ....

2 You can easily win a few pounds on the lottery, but you only have a small .... of winning the big prize.

3 We have to face the .... that we might not make it to the top.

4 The New Year celebrations were a memorable ....

5 I never drink champagne except on special .... such as weddings or at Christmas.

6 You should accept their offer – it's a great ....

C In pairs, answer these questions.

1 On what occasions do you have to wear special or formal clothes?

2 Tell your partner about two things that have happened to you by chance.

3 When do you have the opportunity to speak to native English speakers?

4 What is the possibility of it raining over the next few days?

2 Neutral and negative adjectives

A In Frame 2, the Hope Diamond was described as being *notorious*. This is similar in meaning to *famous*, except that it suggests that it is famous for bad rather than good reasons. Divide the following adjectives into two groups. Put the adjectives which have a negative meaning on the right.

famous	slim	timid
arrogant	shocked	skinny
notorious	pleased	obsessed
surprised	shy	smug
interested	confident	

neutral		negative	
famous	....	*notorious*	....
....	....	....	....
....	....	....	....
....		....	

B Read the following sentences. Choose the option that fits in best with the rest of the sentence.

1 The *famous / notorious* murderer was sentenced to life for his terrible crimes.

2 Claudia is tall, *slim / skinny* and elegant, and has beautiful long hair.

3 I was terribly *surprised / shocked* by the news of her tragic death.

4 He has made excellent progress and is a very *confident / arrogant* speaker.

5 You passed the test but there's no reason to be so *pleased / smug* about it.

C Using some of the adjectives above and others of your choice, describe someone you know whom you like or dislike a great deal.

3 *Have* or *take*

A Look at the list of words and phrases below. Do we use these with *have* or with *take*?

fun	part in
sth for lunch	a good time
a good idea	sth in common with sb
a photo	place
action	care of sb

B Write five sentences using some of the phrases above.

1 Multiple-choice cloze

For questions 1–15, read the text and decide which answer A, B, C or D best fits each space. *Example: (0) C*

TWINS

Science magazine (0)..........C.......... published a report by researchers at Minnesota University. The researchers studied identical twins who had been separated at (1)..................... and had been taken (2)..................... of by different families. The results showed that the twins were often very similar, not only in (3)..................... but also in intelligence and personality.

More (4)..................... , however, were the other coincidences which were almost (5)..................... to explain. For example, one set of female twins met again for the first time when they were 39. They both (6)..................... the same dress, had seven rings on their fingers, and the same bracelets. There were also some male twins who (7)..................... part in the study. They too (8)..................... a great deal in common. Both of them worked in the police force, and (9)..................... their holidays in Florida. They drove the same kind of car and had a dog called Toy. (10)..................... of them had married and divorced women called Linda, and their second wives were called Betty.

The researchers intend to (11)..................... out more studies in the future. This is because these coincidences are so remarkable and have occurred so often with twins that they have almost (12)..................... count. The coincidences are so extraordinary that it is (13)..................... to simply say that they happen because of (14)..................... . It seems that there must be a more (15)..................... explanation, but so far nobody has found out what it is.

	A		B		C		D
0	newly		lately		recently		freshly
1	first		beginning		start		birth
2	care		responsibility		concern		worry
3	look		sight		appearance		form
4	disgraceful		shocking		insulting		surprising
5	impossible		incredible		unlikely		dissimilar
6	carried		wore		put		dressed
7	held		came		took		played
8	did		were		had		made
9	passed		spent		stayed		went
10	All		Each		Two		Every
11	bring		follow		do		carry
12	dropped		fallen		missed		lost
13	illiterate		illegal		illegible		illogical
14	opportunity		chance		possibility		occasion
15	correct		logical		intelligent		proper

(15 marks)

2 Key word transformations

Use the word in bold to complete the second sentence so that it has a similar meaning to the first. Write between two and five words.

1 I really regret being so unkind to her.
been
I .... so unkind to her.

2 They seem to have enjoyed their holiday.
time
They seem to have .... on holiday.

3 It's such a pity I can't have a few weeks off.
only
If .... a few weeks off.

4 It's such a pity there isn't anything I can do.
there
I wish .... do.

5 It's a pity I don't know when they are going to arrive.
were
I wish I .... to arrive.

(10 marks)

3 Spot the mistake

Correct each of these sentences.

1 We would have enjoyed our last holiday more if the weather was better.

2 I would have called you if I would have had your number.

3 Would you have been angry if I have took a photo of you?

4 My husband had been very annoyed if I had forgotten our anniversary.

5 Oh dear, if only you would have come to see me when this problem started.

(10 marks)

4 Sentence completion

Finish these sentences in a suitable way.

1 She would have passed the exam if …

2 My mother is being unreasonable. I wish …

3 It's OK being at school, but sometimes I wish …

4 It's just as well you reminded me about the party. If you hadn't …

5 I don't often get the opportunity …

(15 marks)

Total: 50 marks

In pairs, take it in turns to describe the pictures in the article.

1 Multiple matching

A Read the article about King Tutankhamun, taking no notice of gaps 0–6. Find out:

1 how old he was when he came to the throne.

2 when his tomb was discovered.

3 how he might have died.

4 what happened to some of the people who discovered his tomb.

B Choose from the list A–H the sentence which best summarizes each part (1–6) of the article. There is one extra sentence which you do not need to use. There is an example at the beginning (0).

> **HELPLINE**
> Matching summary sentences to parts of a text is similar to the matching headings task. Both have the same aim, which is to get you to find the main points of a paragraph. Read the whole paragraph for clues before making your decision.

A Was it dangerous to break into a Pharaoh's tomb?

B It is difficult to decide what caused the King's death.

C Could robbers have entered the tomb?

D Who could have committed the crime?

E Why might the young King have been murdered?

F A new and astonishing fact is revealed.

G Let us examine the case more closely.

H An exciting find results in a strange and disturbing theory.

WHO KILLED TUTANKHAMUN?

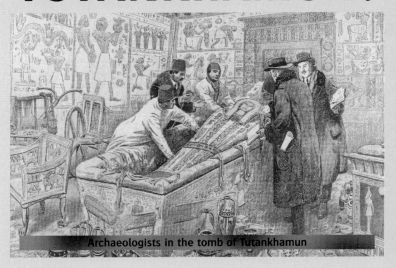

Archaeologists in the tomb of Tutankhamun

0	*H*

Scotland Yard is investigating startling new medical evidence which reveals that the boy Pharaoh, Tutankhamun, who came to the throne aged nine and reigned for only ten years, could have been murdered. His body was discovered by British archaeologists Howard Carter
05 and the Earl of Carnarvon in 1922. While digging in the Valley of the Kings in Egypt, they came across 'the greatest treasure ever found'. Peering into a tomb, they saw 'strange animals, statues and gold', but the most important discovery was the magnificent gold mask of the King. The tomb, however, hadn't given up all its secrets. Nearly
10 half a century later, X-rays showed possible evidence of damage to the brain.

1	

Reopening the case after 3,000 years, Scotland Yard is examining the evidence and trying to identify the killer. Several people might have wanted to get rid of the young King. Ay, his chief adviser, who
15 may have been related to him, took over the throne after his death and married his widow. There was also General Horemheb, the most likely person to succeed the childless Tutankhamun. Horemheb later became Pharaoh after Ay. He destroyed the monuments of Tutankhamun and the young King's father-in-law, and added the
20 years of their reigns to his own.

2	

The man leading the investigation is a former Detective Inspector on the murder squad. So, what facts are there for him to look at? A mummified corpse with a head injury and no mention of the King in official records suggest a possible cover-up. Someone must have
25 wanted Tutankhamun and his father-in-law written out of the

records. Did it require a conspiracy or could one person do it alone? In order to kill a king, you must be able to get past the guards. This type of murder, a blow to the head, could be hidden and not easily seen. But whoever did it would need help. Perhaps from the army?

3 [ ]

30 What is needed is a pathologist's report. A 3,000 year-old 'whodunnit' is not an easy case. There is no scene of the crime to dust, little scope for forensics, and no witnesses to interview. All the evidence is circumstantial.

4 [ ]

Several weeks after the start of the investigation, the pathologist is
35 able to confirm that a close examination of the X-ray of the head shows that the fracture to the skull was there before the King died. He agrees that this could have been the cause of death. It doesn't prove absolutely that the King was murdered but it's as near as we are going to get!

5 [ ]

40 What brought all this about is unclear. Tutankhamun was the ruler of one of the greatest nations in the ancient world. But his father-in-law was a dictator who had rejected the old religion and tried to force a new one on the people. Once Tutankhamun was on the throne, the old priests regained their power and life returned to
45 normal. Were people worried that Tutankhamun might start to re-introduce his father-in-law's ideas? The priests could have worked together with Ay and Horemheb to commit this crime. The reason for the murder can't have been power because Ay was old. It must have been for what they thought was the good of the country.

6 [ ]

50 It is perhaps significant that many people who were involved in the discovery of the tomb of the young King met with an untimely death themselves. This may simply be coincidence or superstition, or it may have something to do with the fact that the tomb, once opened, gave off harmful gases which had been buried for thousands of years.
55 There was even a suggestion that those who opened the tomb were cursed. This, however, is something that could never be proved!

Removal of treasures from the tomb.

2 Vocabulary

A These words from the text are all connected with committing and solving crimes. Can you explain what they mean? Use a dictionary if necessary.

a *an investigation* (line 21)

b *a corpse* (line 23)

c *a cover-up* (line 24)

d *a pathologist's report* (line 30)

e *a case* (line 31)

f *forensics* (line 32)

g *witnesses* (line 32)

h *evidence* (line 33)

B Which verbs below can be used with the words above?

1 interview	3 lead	5 examine
2 carry out	4 identify	

WP 1

C Which of these adjectives from the text and sentences, might you use with the nouns below?

a *startling*	d *dangerous*	
b *magnificent*	e *astonishing*	
c *ancient*	f *disturbing*	

1 building   *magnificent, ancient, dangerous*

2 monument ....
....

3 activity ....
....

4 piece of news ....
....

5 invention ....
....

LEAD-IN ➤

In small groups, discuss which of the following you would do if you saw someone shoplifting.

- call the police
- try to stop the thief
- tell the person not to steal
- look the other way

1 Open cloze

A Read the article about two women who saw someone stealing some money and think of **one** word which best fits each space.

Example: (0) were

STOP THAT THIEF!

Two netball coaches, Denise Ellis and Ruth Mogford, (0)......*were*...... supervising their team of teenagers at a tournament, when they saw a man steal the cash box (1)..................... a stall selling netball gear. 'I noticed him as I walked into the tent (2)..................... the stall had been set up,' said Denise. 'I don't know (3)..................... he stood out so much, but he must have looked suspicious (4)..................... some reason. Somehow I just knew he couldn't have been (5)..................... of the parents. I thought he might have been a helper but he looked as (6)..................... he was up to no good.' Suddenly he ran off (7)..................... the cash box. Denise and Ruth ran after him, tackled him and brought him to the ground. 'We shouldn't have done it. We could have been seriously injured (8)..................... we just didn't stop to think,' said Denise. 'He was not as tall (9)..................... us but he put up a good fight until the police arrived.' The two netball coaches were commended (10)..................... the police for their bravery and prompt action. And they must have inspired their team, who went on to take third place (11)..................... the tournament. Unfortunately, the thief can't (12)..................... sentenced as he's disappeared. (13)..................... he was later charged with theft and was due to appear in court, he failed (14)..................... attend, and a warrant has now been issued for (15)..................... arrest. Denise said afterwards, 'We needn't have gone to all that trouble, but I'm glad we did!'

B How many questions can you answer without looking at the article again?

1 What were the two women doing when the theft happened?
2 What did the thief steal?
3 What did Denise and Ruth do?
4 How did the man react?
5 What were the two women commended for?
6 What has happened to the thief?

WB 2

GRAMMAR ZOOM

Past modals

1 Must have (done), can't/couldn't have (done)

A Look at these sentences from the article *Stop that thief!*

1 ... he <u>must have looked</u> suspicious ...
2 ... he <u>couldn't have been</u> one of the parents.

Which of the underlined verbs means:

it is impossible that this was the case?
this is a logical explanation for what happened?

B Look at the drawings below. Make sentences about them using either *must have (done)* or *can't/couldn't have (done)*.

Example:
Picture 1: They must have had an argument.

2 Might have (been), could have (been), may have (been)

Read the explanation and suggest what *might*, *could* or *may have* happened in the sentences below.

In *Stop that thief!*, Denise says, *... he might have been a helper ...* and *... we could have been seriously injured. Might have, could have* and *may have (done/been)* suggest a possible but not certain explanation for what happened.

1 Maisie opened her purse and found that there was no money in it.

2 As Samara was getting into bed, she heard a loud bang and a sound of breaking glass.

3 The phone rang twice, then suddenly stopped.

4 Jim looked through the post but there was no letter from Frances.

5 The man the police wanted to arrest disappeared.

6 There was a horrible smell coming from the kitchen.

3 Should(n't) have (done), needn't have (done), didn't need to (do)

A Look at these sentences from the article *Stop that thief!*

1 *We shouldn't have done it.*

2 *We needn't have gone to all that trouble.*

Which underlined verb suggests that:

it was an unnecessary thing to do but we did it?

it was the wrong thing to do but we did it?

B Complete these sentences using one of the structures above.

1 You .... Nobody else has arrived yet.

2 Kim .... buy a new dress for the wedding as she'd just bought one the week before.

3 Russell .... We actually had plenty of food in the house.

4 You were way ahead of everybody in that race. You ....

5 The boys .... their homework as the maths teacher wasn't in school this morning.

6 You .... checked the flight times because I'd already done it.

7 We .... leave home early because we were catching a midday flight.

8 We forgot to lock the front door. We .... before we left.

4 Speaking

In small groups, tell your partners about something you:

1 think you must have done last weekend because you always do this.

2 know you can't/couldn't have done yesterday morning because you never do this.

3 think you might have done when you were younger but you can't remember.

4 know you could have done in the past but didn't want to.

5 admit you should have done recently but didn't have time to.

6 realize you needn't have done over the last month but did anyway.

5 Police investigation

Imagine that on Saturday night there was a burglary in the street where you live and the police are questioning some of the people who live in the area. Divide into groups of four. Students A and B are police officers, Students C and D are residents.

Students A and B
You are going to ask questions to find out:

1 what people were doing on Saturday night.

2 if anyone heard anything suspicious before the burglary.

3 if anyone noticed anything suspicious.

4 if anyone saw any strangers in the area on the day of the burglary.

Student C   Look at page 171.

Student D   Look at page 172.

Use the information you find to answer the questions.

When you have finished, decide who might have committed the crime and what preparations they might have made beforehand.

1 Talking together

A In pairs, look at the pictures below and decide whether the people are doing the right or the wrong thing. If appropriate, say what they should or should not have done instead.

Example:
These people are doing the wrong thing. They shouldn't have lit a cigarette. They should have gone outside to smoke.

B In small groups, decide who the people in the pictures below are, whether they are breaking the law and if so, how.

Example:
This person is a pickpocket and he is breaking the law because he is stealing something from a woman's coat.

C Now decide which of the crimes you identified is the most serious and which the least.

D In the same groups, decide what might be a suitable punishment for the crimes you identified in B. Use the ideas below and the expressions in the Phrase Box to help you.

> In the exam, you may be asked to express your opinion about something that you know very little about. Don't panic! Admit that you don't know much about it, but try to say something which will express what you think.
>
> HELPLINE

imprisonment (how long?)

a fine (how much?)

probation (how long?)

working in the community (what kind of work?)

electronic tagging (does it work?)

anything else? (a warning?)

> **Saying you don't know**
> *I have to say I know very little about ... , but ...*
> *I don't actually know a great deal about ... , but ...*
> *... is something I don't know very much about, but ...*
>
> PHRASE BOX

LEAD-IN ▶

How good an eyewitness would you be? Imagine you witness the scene in the picture on page 173. Look at it for about one minute then close your books and see if you can answer the questions the teacher asks you.

1 Note taking

You will hear an eye-witness describing what happened on a busy motorway one morning. For questions 1–10, fill in the missing information on the incident sheet.

TRAFFIC POLICE INCIDENT SHEET

Name of witness: *Charles Goodman*

Date of incident: [ ] **1**

Weather conditions: [ ] **2**

Place of incident: *about* [ ] **3**

from Newbridge.

Car registration: [ ] **4**

REPORT OF INCIDENT

Car was moving quickly from

[ ] **5**

Passenger: a [ ] **6**

Woman driver was chasing

[ ] **7** *in outside lane.*

Woman eventually stopped other vehicle against the

[ ] **8**

Passenger was lifted into vehicle through the

[ ] **9**

Afterwards the witness rang

[ ] **10**

Listen again and check your answers.

WP 3

2 True or false?

Now listen to a news report of the incident on the motorway. For questions 1–7, say whether the statements are true or false.

1 Trina was too worried to pay any attention to other drivers on the road. [ ] **1**

2 The toddler had been well when Trina left home. [ ] **2**

3 Trina stopped the ambulance by braking hard in front of it. [ ] **3**

4 The ambulance driver was slightly injured. [ ] **4**

5 The ambulance door couldn't be opened. [ ] **5**

6 The ambulance was not properly equipped to help the toddler. [ ] **6**

7 Trina watched her son's life being saved. [ ] **7**

Listen again and check your answers.

3 The same or different?

At least one of the words in each pair below appeared in the listenings. Write S beside the words which are pronounced the same, and D beside those which are different.

1 place / plays
2 raising / racing
3 warn / worn
4 sick / six
5 breathe / breath
6 brakes / breaks
7 past / passed
8 week / weak

4 Everyday expressions

The underlined expressions appeared in the listening. They are used when we want to change or correct something we have said.

1 *It must have been about 8, <u>no, sorry</u>, 8.30.*

2 *... it was about half-way between Junctions 3 and 4, <u>or was it</u> 4 and 5?*

3 *No, <u>on second thoughts</u>, it was definitely ...*

4 *... it could only have been about two, <u>well</u>, <u>maybe</u> three ...*

Imagine you have witnessed an incident on a busy road or motorway. Make sentences using the expressions above and the ideas below.

a the colour of a vehicle
b the time the incident happened
c where it happened
d the driver of the car
e what the driver did
f what happened next

Writing a composition (2)

In Part 2 of the writing paper, you may be asked to write a composition discussing a given topic, but not in the form of for and against, advantages and disadvantages, etc.

1 Sample task

Read the sample task and answer the questions.

Your teacher has asked you to write a composition on the following subject:
What is the purpose of prison?
Write your **composition** (120–180 words).

Task interpretation

1 What sort of language do you think would be suitable for this composition – formal or informal?

2 Does the question ask you to give a balanced argument (advantages and disadvantages)?

3 What does it ask you to do?

4 In pairs, plan your answer to this question. Think of the following:

   points to include

   organization of these points – write brief notes for each paragraph.

2 Sample answer

Read the composition and answer the questions.

Prison has been an important feature in almost every society, and in this composition I will look at some of the main purposes it is meant to serve.

Firstly, many people believe that the threat of prison helps to reduce crime. In my opinion, it does and there would probably be many more crimes committed if people were not afraid of being punished. Prison also helps to reduce crime by keeping the most dangerous criminals away from society.

The second purpose of prison is to punish people who have done something wrong. This type of punishment should only be used for people who have committed very serious crimes. Other punishments should be used for less serious offences.

The final aim of prison is help criminals become responsible citizens. Many prisons now have educational programmes, and prisoners can learn new skills to prepare them for life when they leave prison.

In conclusion, it can be seen that prison has a number of different purposes, and it will certainly continue to play an important role in society for years to come.

(179 words)

Analysis

1 Is it similar to how you planned your answer?

2 Underline the three most important sentences of this composition.

3 What pattern do the three main paragraphs follow?

4 What is the writer doing in the second sentences of paragraphs 2 and 3?

Lead sentences

Look at the following sentences. They are taken from a composition entitled:

Should there be stricter punishment for students who behave badly in class?

Work out which three sentences should open the three paragraphs and which give more information about each of the lead sentences. Then complete the table below.

A Under these circumstances, it is better for the teacher to encourage the student to talk about the problem rather than to simply punish them.

B First of all, students sometimes behave badly because they find the lessons too difficult.

C Finally, students are not always to blame for discipline problems in a class.

D There are also times when a student behaves badly because he or she is having personal problems such as arguments with parents.

E In cases like this, stricter punishments are not likely to solve the problem; what the students need is extra help so that they can understand the lessons more.

F Sometimes it is the teacher who is at fault and it is the teacher who needs to make the lessons more interesting and easier to understand.

The correct order is as follows:

Paragraph 1: ....

Paragraph 2: ....

Paragraph 3: ....

Read the following question.

Writing a composition

Your teacher has asked you to write a composition on the following subject:

What can be done to reduce the amount of crime committed by young people?

Write your **composition** (120–180 words).

Before you read through the notes, write down your ideas for the three main points to include in your composition. Compare your answers in pairs. There is no correct answer, but some points may be more relevant than others. These notes will help you plan your essay.

Notes...

Work through the notes and prepare your composition.

The best way to answer this type of composition is to base it around three main points.

Paragraph 1

Introduction. Make a general statement about the topic of juvenile crime and say what you are going to look at in your composition.

As a general rule, you can often start a composition by making a general statement about the subject.

Examples:

Nowadays many people are worried about juvenile crime…

Over the centuries, many people have tried to solve the problem of juvenile crime…

Juvenile crime has been a problem in almost every society…

Paragraphs 2–4

Introduce each one with one of your *lead* sentences. These should summarize the main points that you have to make. Introduce the most important one first. Remember to add any relevant opinions or details after each of the lead sentences. Remember to use suitable link words at the beginning of each paragraph to make your composition clearer.

In pairs, think of suitable link words to use.

Examples: Firstly … To sum up …

You may also find the following phrases useful when presenting your argument:

It's generally accepted that…

It's safe to say that…

Most people would agree that…

Paragraph 5

Write a short sentence to conclude the composition.

Check your writing carefully for spelling, punctuation and grammar mistakes.

WORD POWER

adjectives expressions
phrasal verbs nouns

1 Words connected with crime and punishment

What's the difference in meaning between the pairs of words below? Choose the best word in its correct form to fill in the spaces in these sentences.

1 **judge**   **jury**

The .... decided that the accused had committed the crime and the .... sentenced him to five years in prison.

2 **defence**   **prosecution**

The .... lawyer argued that the accused was an honest and trustworthy person but the .... lawyer had a different story to tell.

3 **murder**   **manslaughter**

If it can be proved that the accused planned the crime, then she will be charged with .... If it was accidental, then the charge will be ....

4 **in jail/prison**   **under arrest**

Although the thief is .... , it is unlikely that he will spend much time ....

5 **criminal**   **petty thief**

This kind of minor crime is usually committed by a .... and not a dangerous ....

6 **guilty**   **innocent**

After the trial, Mrs Black was found .... of trying to obtain money that did not belong to her, but her husband had not been involved in the crime and he was found ....

7 **rob**   **steal**

I've been .... ! That woman's .... my handbag!

8 **robbery**   **burglary**

There were a lot of .... in this area the week before the local bank ....

2 Expressions with *good* and *bad*

A Complete the sentences below using either *good* or *bad*. Then match the expressions with meanings a–h.

1 Although they seem like the perfect couple, Sue and John are going through a .... patch at the moment.

2 It's no .... trying to phone Peter now. He's gone out.

3 The children were no trouble when I baby-sat last time. They were as .... as gold.

4 That super holiday in Spain really did me ....

5 We've missed the plane, so we'll just have to make the best of a .... job and go by train instead.

6 It's too .... that you weren't able to come to the party at the weekend. We had a great time.

7 William's a very kind person. He'll do anybody a .... turn.

8 I just couldn't believe it when I heard that I'd got a place at university. It seemed too .... to be true.

a *experiencing a time of problems or unhappiness*

b *do what we can in difficult circumstances*

c *do sb a favour*

d *there is no point in doing this*

e *so fantastic that it is beyond belief*

f *very well-behaved*

g *it's a pity/a shame*

h *help sb relax/recover*

B Choose four of the expressions, two with *good* and two with *bad*, and write sentences of your own.

3 Phrasal verbs with *on*

A In the examples below, choose the verb which means the same as the explanation at the end of the sentence.

1 Geoffrey decided to *keep/carry/call on* his old friend to see if he was at home. (visit)

2 Please *hang/carry/count on* with your story. We're all dying to hear what happened next! (continue)

3 You can always *look/hang/count on* me if you need any help. (rely)

4 Can you remember what the suspect *tried/had/took on* when he ran out of the bank? (be wearing)

5 I'm afraid we have *put/taken/tried on* too much and we're not managing things very well. (agree to do)

6 If you would like to *take/try/carry on* the dress, we have some changing rooms over there. (put on and see if it fits)

B Put a suitable verb with *on* in its correct form in the spaces below. The first letter is given.

1 Why do people t...................... clothes on?

2 Who can you c...................... on in times of trouble?

3 She always c...................... on me, when she's in the area.

4 Please c...................... on with your work while I go and fetch a dictionary from the library.

5 Have you ever t...................... on too much responsibility?

6 Do you usually remember what people h...................... on at parties?

UNIT 14 ▶ LET'S REFLECT!

1 Open cloze

Read the text and think of **one** word which best fits each space. *Example: (0) who*

THE FORGOTTEN PHAROAH 👁 👁

No one knows (0)......*who*...... originally found Tutankhamun's body or even the place in (1)...................... it was found. The reason it might have (2)...................... buried in haste, in the grave of someone (3)...................... , is unclear. The coffin was made (4)...................... badly that the lid cracked as it was lowered into place; it wasn't one of (5)...................... most magnificent royal funerals. The dead King's enemies wanted (6).................. forget he ever existed, so they wrote (7).................. name out of the records. It was January 1,323 BC (8)...................... Tutankhamun died. His young wife survived him, but he left (9)...................... living child to tell his story, and no-one was ever arrested for the crime (10)...................... charged with his murder. The sands of Egypt blew over his tomb in the Valley of the Kings (11)...................... 3,000 years. Tutankhamun might (12)...................... simply disappeared for ever but the Pharaoh's enemies (13)...................... not take into account one thing: human greed. You can't bury huge quantities (14)...................... treasure, even in a tomb, and not expect visitors. Over the centuries, grave robbers crept into the tomb in the Valley of the Kings and ran off (15)...................... whatever they managed to find. 👁 👁

(15 marks)

2 Words which go together

A Complete the following expressions. They are all connected with crime and punishment.

1 appear in c...............   4 be given a prison s...............

2 carry out an i...............   5 arrest a s...............

3 interview a w...............   6 examine the e...............

(6 marks)

B Use each of the expressions in a sentence of your own.

(6 marks)

3 Everyday expressions

Write three everyday expressions you can use to change your mind when you are speaking.

1 ....

2 ....

3 ....

(3 marks)

4 Key word transformations

Use the word in **bold** to complete the second sentence so that it has a similar meaning to the first. Write between two and five words.

1 The evidence shows that the robbers did not enter the bank until after midnight.

   entered

   The robbers .... the bank until after midnight.

2 The children behaved very well last night.

   gold

   The children .... last night.

3 Don't try to phone the station – the line's engaged.

   good

   It's .... phone the station – the line's engaged.

4 I feel better after that holiday, you know.

   did

   That holiday really .... , you know.

5 It was illegal to park on double yellow lines.

   should

   The car .... on double yellow lines.

6 We're looking forward to seeing Tom and Janet when we visit Glasgow.

   call

   We can't wait ....Tom and Janet when we visit Glasgow.

7 What a shame you couldn't come – it was a great party.

   bad

   What a great party – it's .... come.

8 I'm always here if you need help.

   count

   You .... if you need help.

9 I think Tutankhamun was possibly murdered by a member of his own family.

   may

   Tutankhamun's murderer .... a member of his own family.

10 It wasn't necessary to bring the book back.

   brought

   You .... the book back.

(20 marks)

Total: 50 marks

LEAD-IN ▶

A In small groups, discuss these questions.

1   Have you ever seen a magician perform? Did you enjoy it? Why? Why not?

2   What kind of things do magicians do?

B   Look at this picture and say what is unusual about it.

1 Multiple matching

A   You are going to read an article about tricks and illusions. Read the text quickly and find out what the optical illusion is in each trick.

Example:
In A, the optical illusion is that a girl appears to be sawed in half.

PROMISE you won't tell how it's done

There are a few great tricks which go back centuries – and a lot of modern variations. If you want to know how they're done, read on!

A SAWING A WOMAN IN HALF

👁 THE ILLUSION This is probably the most famous of illusions, but it is in fact quite a modern one, first performed in London in 1921 by the great P. T. Selbit. In his original version, the woman was tied by ropes, which the audience held so they could feel her wriggling. She was
05 then locked in a long box and 'sliced up' with a huge, two-handled saw. One famous magician arranged for ambulances and stretchers to be close by when he did the act.

☆ THE TRICK There are two classic versions. In the first, the victim goes into quite a deep box, sticks her head out from one end and
10 draws her legs up to her chin. The feet at the far end of the box belong to a second woman, wearing identical clothes, in a secret compartment beneath her. The second version uses a wider but flatter box – made to look even thinner by clever optical illusions – in which the victim is curled up on her side at the one end, while the feet and
15 legs are, in fact, remote-controlled mechanical models.

B THE CHINESE LINKING RINGS

👁 THE ILLUSION To the audience, this one looks really impossible. This is the trick with eight solid-steel rings, which the magician links and unlinks before our very eyes. It's amazed audiences since ancient times.

☆ THE TRICK Only two of the eight rings are actually solid, and these are the ones the audience is invited to examine closely. The next two rings are already linked to each other, and so are the next three. The eighth is the 'key' ring and it has a small opening to allow it to attach to or separate from the others. By distracting the audience at the right
25 moment, a skilled magician can seemingly produce chains of two, three, four, five or six linked rings.

C THE ZIG ZAG LADY

👁 THE ILLUSION Another fairly recent illusion, first performed by Robert Harbin in 1965, is where the lady goes into a three-part cabinet, her head visible in the top section, her waist in the middle,
30 and her foot waggling out of a hole in the bottom section. Then the middle is slid away to one side ... taking her waist with it.

☆ **THE TRICK** Because we've watched the girl step into the box and face us, we assume she's stayed in that position. In fact, when the middle section slides over, it
35 only moves a very short way – the edges of the box are usually painted black to confuse us and make us think that it has moved further – and the girl turns to one side and bends with it, fitting into another small part of the box.

D LEVITATION

👁 THE ILLUSION This is what it says, lifting someone in mid-air without any visible means of support.

☆ THE TRICK This usually relies on 'invisible' wires to hold the subject, so stage lighting has to be carefully controlled. In the classic 'floating lady' levitation, the
45 assistant lies on a couch and the magician distracts the audience by waving a cloth, while a thin, clear, body-shaped cover is lowered on wires over her. While the magician covers her with the cloth, the assistant actually slips into a compartment in the couch, leaving
50 the body-shaped cover in her place. As the shape 'levitates', the couch is wheeled off stage. Finally, with a flash of light, the magician quickly lifts the cloth away to reveal that the lady has 'vanished' in mid-air.

E WALKING THROUGH A WALL

👁 THE ILLUSION This illusion was originally performed
55 on stage, but more recently David Copperfield walked through the Great Wall of China.

☆ THE TRICK Most magicians perform this by having a screen put up against one side of the wall. The magician goes behind the screen, changes his clothes so as to look
60 like one of the assistants, slips out and joins them as they take the screen to the other side of the wall to re-build it. He then miraculously emerges from behind the screen. It's a simple trick but needs clever movements and organization.

B Read the text again. For questions 1–14, choose from the illusions and tricks A–E. Where more than one answer is required, these may be given in any order. There is an example at the beginning (0).

Which statement refers to which illusion or trick?

The amount of light is important.	**0**	D
It was performed at a famous landmark.	**1**	
A piece of material is needed to do this.	**2**	
Colour plays an important part in the deception.	**3**	
It is not actually a very old trick.	**4**	**5**
It is a very old trick.	**6**	
It was performed with the emergency services nearby.	**7**	
The helpers are dressed in the same way as another person.	**8**	**9**
The audience participated.	**10**	**11**
In this trick the assistant vanishes.	**12**	
The identical objects are not what they seem.	**13**	
It has puzzled people since it was first performed.	**14**	

C Which of these tricks and illusions do you find the most impressive?

2 Vocabulary

These words are used in the article to describe people's movements:

wriggle	(line 4)	*bend*	(line 38)
stick out	(line 9)	*lower*	(line 47)
curl up	(line 14)	*lift*	(line 52)
waggle	(line 30)	*emerge*	(line 62)

Use one of the verbs in its correct form to complete the sentences below.

1 In some countries, it's considered very rude to .... your tongue ....

2 The cat .... on the sofa and went to sleep.

3 Be careful when you're .... anything heavy because you might hurt your back.

4 Stop .... ! The injection isn't going to hurt you.

5 Now, ... over and see if you can touch your toes.

6 The injured man was .... carefully from the helicopter to a waiting ambulance below.

7 The actress .... from her room in the afternoon.

8 My friend Marcus can .... his ears.

WP 1

LEAD-IN

Look at these pictures of lasers being used at work. Take it in turns to match their uses with the descriptions below.

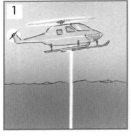
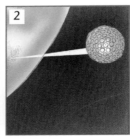

The lasers are being used to:

a   find out about road conditions.

b   pay for making phone calls.

c   record movements of the earth's surface.

d   record fingerprints.

e   measure sea depth.

1 Error correction

Read the text about lasers and CDs. Some of the lines are correct, and some have a word which should not be there. Tick (✓) the lines which are correct and underline the unnecessary words. There are two examples at the beginning (0 and 00).

• Lasers and CDs

0	The word LASER stands ~~up~~ for Light Amplification by the Simulated
00 ✓	Emission of Radiation. Lasers produce narrow beams of either intense
1	light or infra-red rays. When the laser was invented in 1960, it was a little
2	more than a useless scientific curiosity. Now they are the common. Every
3	home with a compact disc (CD) player has a laser, and at every
4	supermarket checkout with bar-code readers has them, together with
5	computer data and phone lines. The compact disc, was introduced in 1980,
6	gradually replaced the vinyl records which used in home stereo systems.
7	But, instead of a sharp stylus moving along a record groove, CDs are 'read'
8	by a beam of laser light. Nothing touches the disc, so if it cannot wear out.
9	(Video discs, working on a similar principle, they are used instead of
10	video tape to store films.) Although CDs have only one recording side,
11	they are capable of holding more over an hour of music. In addition,
12	because they can store large amounts of information, CDs are also used
13	up in personal computers, storing, for example, the text and pictures from an
14	encyclopaedia. There are but also multi-media CDs containing text, still
15	pictures, sound and video. There is certainly in no doubt that the laser is here to stay!

The passive and the causative *have*

1 Meaning

Match the sentences with the explanations.

1   I repaired the video yesterday.

2   The video was repaired yesterday.

3   I had the video repaired yesterday.

4   I had already repaired the video yesterday.

a   *We are interested in the action – not who did it.*

b   *This action happened before another in the past.*

c   *I actually did it myself.*

d   *I paid or told someone to do this.*

2 The passive: form

A   Which of these sentences is passive and which active?

1   A Dutch scientist built the first pendulum clocks in 1656.

2   The first pendulum clocks were built by a Dutch scientist in 1656.

When the sentence changes from active to passive:

a   what happens to the verb?

b   what extra word is needed?

c   how does the word order change?

d   how does the meaning of the sentence change?

B   Change the sentences below into the passive.

1   Swiss craftsmen make these watches.

2   They will produce the new car in Japan.

3   Computers are going to drive cars in the future.

4   They first made marmalade in Portugal.

5 Someone has broken into our house.

6 The Olympic runner broke the world record.

7 More and more young people are buying mobile phones.

8 People were using computer technology years ago.

In which four sentences do you not need to refer to the agent? Why not?

3 The passive: use

Why is the passive used in these sentences? Match sentences 1–5 with explanations a–e.

1 All the equipment is checked regularly by maintenance engineers.

2 Our products are sold all over the world.

3 Several computers were stolen from one of our offices last week.

4 It is thought that working at a computer for long periods of time can be dangerous.

5 The paper is placed into the feeder tray of the facsimile machine.

a *Nobody knows who did this.*

b *Both the action and the special people who do it are important.*

c *It is obvious or unimportant who does the action, so the writer or speaker does not need to mention them.*

d *This is what people think generally.*

e *The writer or speaker is describing how to do something.*

4 Practice

A Put the verbs in the passage into the active or the passive.

In 1970 a different way of reading information about goods (1)............................ (introduce): the bar code. This is a label which (2)............................ (print) with a series of black or coloured stripes and white spaces. There (3)............................ (be) one on the cover of this book! The thickness of the stripes and spaces (4)............................ (correspond) to a code which can (5)............................ (understand) by a computer. For example, many libraries now (6)............................ (use) bar codes. When you (7)............................ (borrow) a book, the bar codes on your library ticket and book (8)............................ (scan) with a light pen, which (9)............................ (shine) an infra-red laser beam onto the bar code. Only the white spaces (10)............................ (reflect) the light. When the light pen (11)............................ (move) over the bar code by the librarian, the reflected rays (12)............................ (pick) up by a sensor, which (13)............................ (send) a series of messages to the scanner. The information (14)............................ (go) to a central computer which (15)............................ (record) when the book (16)............................ (borrow) and the date it (17)............................ (be) due back. If the book (18)............................ (become) overdue, you (19)............................ (receive) a card, which (20)............................ (print) by the computer, requesting you to return the book.

B A newspaper reporter has made the following notes for a news story about a new anti-pollution scarf. Rewrite the notes in the passive for an article to be included in tomorrow's edition of the newspaper.

Anti-Pollution Scarf
- everyone will admire you
- nobody will recognize you
- Harry Cole / inventor
- will increase your chances of breathing fresh air
- you can wear it every day
- you can wash it
- original purpose of invention: for motorcyclists
- you wear it with a nose clip
- you can bend the nose clip for a good fit
- Cole based idea on a device to protect against chemical warfare

WP 2

5 The causative *have*: form

Instead of saying *I paid someone to repair the video for me*, you can say *I had the video repaired* (*have* + the object + the past participle).

What other word can you use instead of *have* or *had* in these sentences?

1 I had my hair dyed green last week.

2 I'm going to have my ears pierced.

3 I think we'll have a swimming pool built in the back garden.

6 The causative *have*: use

In small groups, take it in turns to decide where to go and what to have/get done in the following situations.

Example: The car hasn't been running well lately. I'll go to the garage and have/get it serviced.

1 Your jumper has got a stain on it.

2 The heel's come off your shoe.

3 You have toothache.

4 You need a passport-size photograph for your student card.

5 You can't see as well as you used to.

6 You have finished the film in your camera.

7 Your watch strap has broken.

8 Your passport has run out.

9 Your hair looks a mess.

10 The ring you're wearing is too loose.

1 Talking about yourself

A In pairs, name the objects in the pictures below.

If you can't remember a word, try to paraphrase it.

B With the same partner, take it in turns to ask and answer the following questions.

1 Have you ever used any of the things, or done any of the activities shown in the pictures?

2 Would you like to use or do any? Why? Why not?

2 Talking together

Work in groups of three. Each choose one of these objects: a mobile phone, a surfboard or a camera. Explain to the rest of the group in a simple way how the object works and/or how to use it.

Describing how something works/how to use something

First, you …

Then you …

Next, the … can/should be …

Finally, you …

3 Discussion

In the same groups, discuss these questions.

1 Where would it be best to advertise objects like those above?

• in newspapers and magazines

• on radio or TV

• in public places, e.g. trains, buses

2 What kind of advertisements attract your attention?

3 Why is it necessary to advertise?

4 Do you think advertising should be allowed to interrupt TV or radio programmes? What are the alternatives?

LEAD-IN

Look at the picture below and, in groups of three, decide where the people are, what they are doing and why the activity might be dangerous.

1 Note taking

You will hear part of a radio programme about someone called Andrew Sneath and his new invention. For questions 1–10, complete the missing information.

Listen again and check your answers.

2 Multiple matching

You will hear five different people talking about learning how to handle different types of transport. Choose from the list A–F what each speaker says about their first attempt. Use the letters only once. There is one extra letter which you do not need to use.

A I broke my leg.	Speaker 1	1
B I forgot what to do.	Speaker 2	2
C I had a terrifying experience.	Speaker 3	3
D I wanted to have another try.	Speaker 4	4
E I decided I didn't like the instructor.	Speaker 5	5
F I wore the wrong clothing.		

Listen again and check your answers.

Which of these types of transport would you like to try out?

3 The same or different?

At least one of the words in each pair below appeared in the listenings. Write S beside the words which are pronounced the same, and D beside those which are different.

1 damp / dump   5 sell / cell
2 our / hour   6 hit / heat
3 wear / where   7 right / write
4 slip / sleep   8 bored / board

WP 3

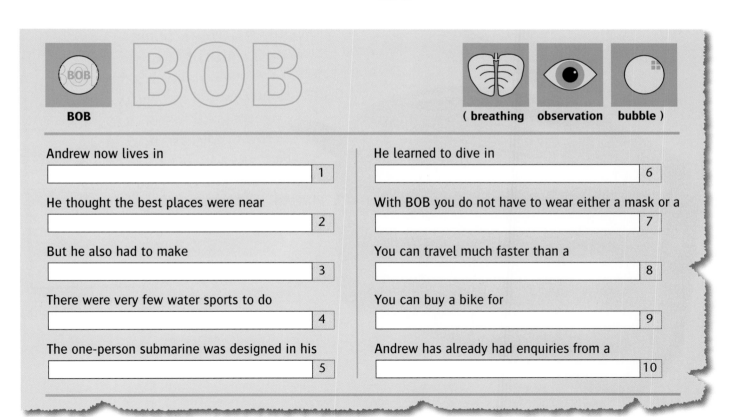

BOB

(breathing   observation   bubble)

Andrew now lives in [1]	He learned to dive in [6]
He thought the best places were near [2]	With BOB you do not have to wear either a mask or a [7]
But he also had to make [3]	You can travel much faster than a [8]
There were very few water sports to do [4]	You can buy a bike for [9]
The one-person submarine was designed in his [5]	Andrew has already had enquiries from a [10]

Writing an article (3)

If you choose to write an article, think carefully about:

- the target audience – title, level of formality
- organization – paragraphing, logical order of information, introduction and conclusion.

1 Sample task

Read the sample task.

A magazine for young people is planning to publish a series of articles about technology. Write an article about an example of technology that you think is particularly important. You should include information about how it works, what it is used for, why you think it's important and any other facts you know about it.

Write your **article** (120–180 words).

2 Sample answer

The paragraphs in this article are in the wrong order. Read them, put them in the correct order and answer the questions.

Analysis

1 Can you think of a title for the article?
2 What information is included in each paragraph?
3 Three of these paragraphs are suitable for the target audience. Which is not? Why?

That's certainly the case with inventor Trevor Bayliss' new idea. He was developing a radio for remote parts of Africa, where it's sometimes very hard to get hold of batteries, when he suddenly came up with the idea of using clockwork.

The result is a radio that can be used in any location. It is inexpensive, and in addition, the sound reproduction is of high quality. A key is turned, and sufficient electricity is produced to power the radio. The product is simple to operate and it can always be re-charged.

When you think about inventions, you probably think about things like new computer-controlled gadgets or space-age machines and so on. But things needn't always be so complicated – some of the best ideas use old technology rather than anything modern.

That's one of the great things about clockwork, and of course it's completely environmentally-friendly too. In the future, we'll probably see all sorts of other uses for Trevor Bayliss' new idea, but we can be sure of one thing – we haven't heard the last of clockwork yet.

(180 words)

3 Language Study

A In certain articles, depending on your target audience, you may need to use informal language. Read these guidelines.

1 Use contractions, e.g. say *won't* as opposed to *will not*.

2 Use intensifiers like *very*, *really* or *absolutely* rather than *most*, *extremely*, *highly*, etc.

3 Use phrasal verbs instead of more complicated formal verbs, e.g. use *put up with* rather than *tolerate*.

4 Only use the passive when it is necessary. It can often be avoided by saying *you do this, you do that*, etc.

5 Avoid the more formal link words such as *moreover*, *in addition*, etc. Instead, use words and phrases like *what's more* or *too*.

6 Use short, simple words rather than more complicated vocabulary, e.g. use *plane* rather than *aeroplane* or *fridge* rather than *refrigerator*.

B Look back at the article. Can you find examples of the six points mentioned above?

C Now read the following sentences. They are mainly informal, but each one sounds slightly wrong because a part of it is too formal. Rewrite each one so that it sounds less formal.

1 Jack's new car looks very nice. Moreover, it goes really fast.

2 I think we had better leave now, do you not?

3 I'll investigate what's happened and get back to you as soon as I can.

4 The examination was quite hard, but I think I'll pass.

5 I was most surprised to see Jenny at the party.

6 I'll show you how it works – a coin is put into the slot, then the lever is pulled.

4 Writing skills

Timing your writing

In the exam, you have 45 minutes to answer each question. In pairs, discuss how long you think you should spend on each of these activities:

- reading the question
- writing
- planning
- checking your writing

Checking your writing

Here are a few points to remember when checking your writing.

Spelling and punctuation

- common mistakes (*there / their, it's / its, sincerely, faithfully*)

Vocabulary

- the right words (try not to translate from your own language as you could choose the wrong words)

Grammar

- verb forms and tenses
- word order, especially the position of adjectives and adverbs
- articles *a*, *an* and *the* (there are probably several differences with the use of articles in your own language)

Many mistakes are made because you translate from your own language. Try to think in English and keep it relatively simple.

5 Writing task

You have **45 minutes** to answer the following question.

Writing an article

An international magazine for young people is holding a competition for writers. The rules say that you must write an article about a useful gadget that you use a lot. You should include information about how it works, what it is used for, why you think it's important and any other facts you know about it.

Write your **article** (120–180 words).

Notes...

Plan and write your article.

Remember to give your article a heading and underline it.

Paragraph 1

This needs to catch the reader's attention. As this is about a product that is useful in your daily life, you could talk about what it is and how often you use it. Since this is an article for a magazine for young people, the language and style need to be fairly informal, and you may address the reader directly if you like.

Paragraph 2

Talk about what the product does and how it works. If possible, give some of the history of the product or talk about how long you have had it.

Paragraph 3

Say a little about some of the other advantages of the product, and explain how it has changed your life.

Paragraph 4

You could finish by addressing the reader – say how much the reader would probably like it, give details about where it can be bought, etc.

Check your writing for spelling, punctuation and grammar mistakes.

WORD**POWER**

1 Phrasal verbs with *into*

A Here are some sentences which contain verbs with *into*. Match the phrasal verbs with the meanings below.

1 Thieves broke into the house about midnight last night.
2 Peter came into a lot of money when his uncle died.
3 You'll never guess who I ran into the other day!
4 Imagine what we could do if we could turn a piece of stone into a bar of gold!
5 The car went out of control and ran into a lamp-post.
6 William is really into modern jazz music.
7 The police are looking into the case of the forged banknotes.

a *crash into*
b *meet by chance*
c *transform/change ... into*
d *investigate*
e *enter by force*
f *be interested in/keen on*
g *inherit*

B Now use one of the phrasal verbs in A to complete the sentences below.

1 I was coming out of the post office when I .... an old school friend.
2 There was a flash and the magician's balloon .... a white dove.
3 The bus swerved quickly and .... a stationary car.
4 Most of my friends seem to .... 'clubbing'.
5 Sally has recently .... a lot of money.
6 Someone .... our garage and stole my bicycle.
7 We have no idea what has happened to your missing cheque but we will .... the matter.

2 Forming words

Make nouns from the verbs below using these suffixes:

| -ing | -tion | -ion | -ment | -y | -er | -or | -r |

More than one answer may be possible. You might need to change the spelling.

VERB	NOUN	VERB	NOUN
1 invent	....	5 discover	....
2 introduce	....	6 decorate	....
3 develop	....	7 move	....
4 produce	....	8 build	....

When you have finished, make up a sentence for each noun you have made.

Example: The wheel was an important invention.

3 Which way?

Match the expressions with the drawings below, then write a sentence to describe what is happening in each picture.

upside down	back to front
inside out	bumper to bumper
side by side	round and round in circles

UNIT 15 ▸ LET'S REFLECT!

1 Word formation

Use the word given in capitals at the end of each line to form a word that fits in the space in the same line.

Example: (0) deception

MAGICAL ILLUSIONS

Magicians enjoy using their own skills to
create a (0)..... *deception* ..... . That's why   DECEIVE
modern technology is not (1)............................. REAL
vital for their magic. (2)............................   ILLUSION
Wayne Dobson remembers seeing two
magicians on TV doing a (3)...........................   FAME
Victorian trick called the Blue Room, in
which ghosts (4)............................ appear and   MIRACULOUS
float around. 'I can imagine it being
(5)............................ in a live theatre,' he says. AMAZE
'But on TV it was just too (6)............................ . PROBABLE
It looked like a camera trick.' Like most
magicians, Dobson tends to feel that the old
tricks are the (7)............................ of all. It's GOOD
not that technology doesn't put in an
(8)............................ in modern magic, but   APPEAR
most illusions are performed with the help
of (9)............................ . The truth is you can't ASSIST
really make people (10)............................ or   VISIBLE
change their bodies. So you have to cheat!

(10 marks)

2 Vocabulary

A Write another word which sounds the same as those below but has a different spelling and meaning.

1 our   3 right   5 sell
2 wear   4 bored

(5 marks)

B Use one of these verbs in its correct form to complete the sentences below.

| bend | curl up | lift | wriggle | stick out |

1 Stop .... while I try to fasten your tie for you.

2 I was trying to .... a heavy suitcase when I injured my back.

3 Susan .... over her son's bed to give him a goodnight kiss.

4 In the winter I like to .... on the sofa with a good book.

5 You shouldn't .... your head .... of the window in a moving vehicle.

(5 marks)

3 Word stress

A Mark the main stressed syllable on the pairs of words below.

verb	noun
1 advertise	advertisement
2 discuss	discussion
3 desert	desert
4 decorate	decoration
5 invent	invention

(10 marks)

B Now use one of the words in each pair in a sentence of your own.

(10 marks)

4 Key word transformations

Use the word in **bold** to complete the second sentence so that it has a similar meaning to the first. Write between two and five words.

1 Who did your hair at the weekend?
   have
   Where did .... at the weekend?

2 Electric power will drive cars in the future.
   be
   Cars .... electric power in the future.

3 People think that someone checks the electrical equipment regularly.
   is
   The electrical equipment .... regularly.

4 This trick made its first stage appearance in the 1920s.
   seen
   This trick .... stage in the 1920s.

5 To open the box, insert the key in this opening.
   should
   To open the box, ... in this opening.

(10 marks)

Total: 50 marks

Practice test

PAPER 1 ► READING

Part 1

You are going to read a newspaper article about a computer hacker (someone who uses a computer illegally to find out information stored on another computer). Choose from the list **A–H** the sentence which best summarizes each part of the article (**1–6**). There is one extra sentence which you do not need to use. There is an example at the beginning (**0**).

Mark your answers **on the separate answer sheet**.

A A lawyer explained how an investigation led to the discovery of the hacker.

B The teenage hacker was considered too young to be sentenced.

C He started hacking when he was certain he would have nothing to pay.

D The bright teenager was able to read top-security papers.

E The hacker refused the offers of fame and fortune he received.

F Pryce had not intended to cause any trouble.

G The hacker did not make things difficult for those who came to pick him up.

H There was a world-wide search for the teenage computer hacker.

FOUND: SPY WHO HACKED INTO PENTAGON

| 0 | *H* |

A sixteen year-old schoolboy using a cheap computer sparked an international hunt for a spy ring, said prosecution lawyer Simon Dawson in court yesterday. Richard Pryce, a music student, known to his fellow hackers as 'Datastream Kid', had
05 hacked into military computers in the USA from his north London bedroom on at least 200 occasions before he was arrested.

| 1 | |

'He was a very able hacker and he had a fascination for military sites. It caused enormous worries for the American
10 authorities,' Mr Dawson said. There was no suggestion that Pryce – who pleaded guilty to 12 charges of gaining illegal access to computers and was fined £1,200 – had destroyed the files. 'A substantial number of military files that Pryce had transferred from the US military would have covered 2,000 to
15 3,000 A4 pages, and some of these files he looked at would have contained state secrets,' he said.

| 2 | |

Mr Dawson told the court that several years ago the US Office of Special Investigation had discovered a large number of illegal entries, particularly in air force computers. This had
20 been very worrying. They had identified several individuals by the names they used to make these entries on their computers and were now looking for the Datastream Kid – whose real identity was, of course, Pryce.

| 3 | |

So how did he manage it? Pryce, who was taking exams in
25 computer studies and music, had been given a £750 computer to help him. Although he had a particular talent for playing the double bass, and spent most of his free time playing the instrument, he had become interested in hacking and spent more and more time on his computer using the Internet. To
30 help him do this without being detected, he had a piece of equipment which fools the telephone exchange into giving a freephone number. The free use of the telephone
35 left Pryce secure in the knowledge that his parents would never receive the bill for all the telephone calls he made.

| 4 | |

40 After weeks of investigations, Pryce was eventually arrested by Scotland Yard officers at his home following a tip-off from officials in the United States. Mr Dawson said he was co-operative when he was arrested and he admitted everything that he had done. In order to repair their security systems,
45 the US Air Force would have to spend at least £200,000.

| 5 | |

Police were convinced they had found a master spy who might have been passing official secrets to an international spy ring. However, they needn't have worried. After pouring out from more than half a dozen cars and racing up the stairs
50 to the attic room, they were astonished to find a sixteen year-old schoolboy sitting in front of his computer screen. Geoffrey Robertson, defence lawyer, said that Pryce was a sheltered boy who spent a lot of time on his own. 'He meant no harm, made no money out of his hobby, and the last thing he was
55 thinking about was trying to become a spy,' said Robertson.

| 6 | |

Robertson went on to say that Pryce could have accepted offers amounting to £30,000 from a tabloid newspaper for his story, film and book rights but he had turned them all down because he wanted to pursue his career as a musician.
60 Robertson argued that this was a quite extraordinary case which could only happen against a background of advancing technology and it should be a warning to others.

Part 2

You are going to read a magazine article about wildlife in Africa. For questions **7–14**, choose the correct answer **A**, **B**, **C** or **D**.

Mark your answers **on the separate answer sheet.**

7 What were the lions doing when the writer first became aware of them?

  A walking in single file
  B following the visitors
  C running quickly
  D going round in circles

8 When the stork first appeared, the writer and his friends

  A had no idea what it was.
  B were absolutely terrified.
  C dropped onto their knees.
  D decided to follow it.

9 What does *them* in line 25 refer to?

  A herds
  B elephants
  C thickets
  D tracks

10 When the writer first saw the elephants, what were they doing?

  A tramping through the thicket
  B protecting their young
  C feeding in a clearing
  D circling round the party

11 What did the lions do at first?

  A They watched the people suspiciously.
  B They continued feeding.
  C They walked right up to the party.
  D They took no notice of the party.

12 The writer and his friends were surprised that

  A Gavin could imitate every animal and bird call.
  B the lions had walked away so soon.
  C Gavin could communicate with the lions.
  D one of the lions seemed to be lost.

13 What did one young male lion do?

  A He called for his lost companion.
  B He walked round in circles.
  C He came and stared at the party.
  D He ran away from the pride.

14 How did the party feel about their encounter with the lions?

  A horrified
  B worried
  C excited
  D puzzled

THE MAN WHO TALKS TO LIONS

We were a party of six, on the trail of a pride of 16 lions in the heart of Hwange National Park. Walking in single file, we
05 followed our leader, Gavin Ford, one of Zimbabwe's famous trackers. We first heard them as they were moving like lightning through the bush. They knew we
10 were behind them. If they became annoyed, they might circle back and give us a little reminder of who was king of the jungle.

15 Suddenly Gavin dropped to one knee to examine the ground. A large maribou stork crashed through the vegetation. Before we had even recognized what it was, Gavin was back on his feet. If you are going to track lions, you have to have reactions as fast as a lion, and Gavin had
20 been tracking lions – and elephants, rhinos and Cape buffaloes – for most of his life. Thanks to Gavin, we became more skilled at walking through the bush and our chances of close encounters with wild animals increased with our skill.

One morning Gavin came across tracks of a herd of elephants. He studied
25 them carefully and inspected the surrounding thickets and, within minutes, he announced that we were on the trail of a maternal herd travelling with several babies. Gavin knew precisely when they had moved on. We followed him in silence. After about ten minutes, we came into a clearing where, directly in front of us, were several sets of huge feet
30 sheltering the baby elephants in a circle. We crept within metres of the herd and soon they began feeding.

After several days on the trail, however, we still hadn't got close to any of the lions. Then, suddenly, on our final day, a pride of nine strolled out in front of us. They didn't even bother to look at us but merely carried on
35 with their morning walk. As we frantically scrambled for our cameras, Gavin turned to us with a smile and asked, 'Would you like me to call the lions back?'

We had heard him imitate every animal and bird call perfectly, but didn't realize he could talk to lions as well. A soft, low, throaty noise came from
40 Gavin and the lions stopped dead. 'This is the call of the lost lion,' Gavin whispered to us. He continued to call and the lions crept towards us. They were looking around for a missing companion and seemed puzzled that none was in sight. The older, cautious lions hung back, but one young, bold male approached closer and closer until he was just a metre or so
45 away. He examined us steadily and then looked away across the landscape before he returned his gaze to us. He couldn't work things out.

The rest of the pride was uneasy and still hung back but, for what seemed like ages, the young male continued to gaze at us. We tried to appear relaxed but were inwardly alarmed. We stood there hardly daring to
50 breathe. Eventually, the mystery was too much and, much to our relief, the lion strolled away with an occasional backward glance. We couldn't explain to him that he had simply encountered Gavin Ford.

You are going to read a newspaper article about an unusual woman. Eight sentences have been removed from the article. Choose from the sentences **A–I** the one which fits each gap (**15–21**). There is one extra sentence which you do not need to use. There is an example at the beginning (**0**).

Mark your answers **on the separate answer sheet.**

A gift of giving

She is a silver-haired washerwoman who has spent most of her unremarkable life in poverty, in a run-down terraced house in Mississippi. **0** **I**

05 After a lifetime of being very careful with money, Oseola had somehow saved more than £100,000, and in one humble gesture, gave it all away to a local university. **15**

This generous act has captured the heart of a nation where most people think that greed is
10 good and kindness like this is very rare, and she has become one of the most famous figures in the country. **16**

She has also been all over the country accepting awards and honorary degrees from universities.
15 Despite her new-found fame, she remains very modest. 'I am surprised at being treated like a celebrity. I gave what I had, but I don't think there's any reason to be too proud,' she said.
17

20 If it is astonishing how a single act of charity can repay Oseola a thousand times, it is even more astonishing that she saved such a fortune in the first place. She had known nothing but hard times. Her family was poor and she was one of eight
25 children. **18**

She still lives in the same house her uncle left her in 1947, and since her aunt's death 30 years ago, she has lived there alone. She worked hard and saved whatever she could, always putting away a
30 few dollars a day. **19** She didn't go out on dates, and she never married or had children.

She had originally intended to use the money to look after her grandmother. **20** She never thought of going on a cruise or buying a new car,
35 and eventually decided to give it away to help under-privileged children get the education she was denied.

The act has transformed her life, but Oseola is still the same. She only turns on the air conditioning
40 when visitors call. **21** She doesn't need much to live on and seems happy with the little that she has. 'I am at peace with my life and my work,' she says. 'I don't think I have any enemies.'

A 'It was simply the right thing to do. What did I need all that money for?'

B However, when she died, and Oseola was left alone, she carried on saving anyway.

C She asked for nothing in return, except that the money should be used to give poor children a better education.

D The only apparent change is a small colour television instead of the old black-and-white one.

E 'It's not the big earners like that who make fortunes,' she says, 'it's the people who know how to save.'

F She had to leave school when she was eight to work and help support them.

G She has been to the White House to meet the President, and has carried the Olympic torch.

H She never spent money on herself, and would always walk the five miles to the nearest store.

I But one extraordinary act of kindness a year ago turned 87 year-old Oseola McCarty into a national hero.

Part 4

You are going to read a magazine article about bargain holidays in different countries. For questions **22–35**, choose from the holiday destinations **A–E**. There is an example at the beginning (**0**).

Mark your answers **on the separate answer sheet**.

DIFFERENT DESTINATIONS

So you want to get away for a while. We've combed the brochures for glamorous getaways at reasonable prices ... and not a theme park in sight!

A FRANCE

You'll feel like royalty in one of these marvellous
05 apartments in the Château de Grezan, in the south of France. Surrounded by vineyards, with the beach only a short trip away, this is just the place if you're desperate to escape from city life. The Château consists of only four luxury apartments (so hurry before they're all
10 snapped up!), an excellent restaurant and a swimming pool. If you can't resist the urge to go and mix with the extremely rich, St Tropez is just a few hours' drive away. Prices are based on seven nights self-catering with five people sharing an apartment and include return
15 scheduled flights and car hire for the week. Cost is £325 per person departing mid-June with Crystal Holidays.

B EGYPT

If you're the type of tourist who enjoys a bit of sightseeing, Egypt is fascinating with its vast cultural attractions and the legendary River Nile. Luxor, the
20 ancient city of Thebes, and the centre of Egyptian power for over 1,400 years, is not as busy as the more popular resorts. Luxor itself is extremely relaxing and, from there, you can take some fascinating excursions, which even include a Sound and Light Show. Seven nights at
25 the New Emilio in Luxor cost £279 per person, departing in May and June, including return flights, airport transfers and bed and breakfast (B&B).

C KENYA

The magnificent wildlife of Mombasa's famous game reserves undoubtedly attracts most tourists to this more
30 exotic area, but the beaches and coconut trees swaying in the wind are also a welcome addition. With busy street markets, historic monuments and over 20 miles of white sand, Mombasa is a paradise. However, if you're after an alternative to sunbathing and swimming in the
35 clear blue sea, there's lots to do – including a tour of Mombasa or a safari in Tsavo National Park. Seven nights at Mombasa's Jadini Beach Hotel cost from £399 per person. Departures in April. Price includes return flights, airport transfers and B&B.

D MEXICO

40 With its tropical scenery, Spanish churches and markets full of Indian delights, Mexico is becoming an increasingly popular place to visit. The West Coast is a diver's paradise, but even if you aren't into water sports, the beaches around Cancun offer silver sands with a
45 taste of the Caribbean. If you're up to it, the nightlife is pretty wild, too. A 14-night stay with half board at the Sona Hotel in Cacun, in early May, costs from £449. Flights are also available on request.

E ITALY

For real peace and tranquillity, whisk yourself away
50 to Selva in the Italian Gardena Valley, amidst the breathtaking Dolomites and just a short trip away from the pine National Forest. Take a chair-lift up above the tree tops and enjoy the beautiful scenery – pure escapism and the ideal location if you're the type who
55 is keen on keeping fit and into walking. Selva is also the perfect base for excursions to Venice and border-hopping trips to Austria and Switzerland. Go for 10 nights B&B in June, including flights, from £408 per person.

Which statement refers to which holiday?

The price includes the rental of your own transport.	0 A
You can have an exciting time in the evenings.	22
There are fewer tourists here than in other parts of the country.	23
Here you can explore the underwater world.	24
No meals are included in this holiday price.	25
This is a very quiet place.	26
You can eat really well here.	27
If you are interested in animals, this is the place for you.	28
Accommodation here is limited.	29
Flights are not included in the price.	30
Take a trip to get a good view of the countryside.	31
Here you can live like a king or queen.	32
Here you can shop out of doors.	33
More and more people are visiting this place.	34
This is convenient for travelling to other countries, too.	35

Part 1

You **must** answer this question.

1 You are planning to travel around Britain with an English-speaking friend next year. You have seen the advertisement below and phoned for more information (see notes).

Read the advertisement and the notes and write a letter to your friend suggesting that you spend some time working there. Say why you think this would be a good idea and give full details of the work.

BERRY FARM

If you need some extra money,
why not get a job picking strawberries?
Based in the south of England, we offer:

- good rates of pay
- free accommodation

Pickers needed in May and June –
no experience needed.
Write soon if you
are interested.

Notes:

no interview

must be reasonably fit

length of stay optional

check if visa is required

accommodation and cooking facilities provided

Write a **letter** of between **120 and 180** words in an appropriate style. Do not write any addresses.

Part 2

Write an answer to **one** of the questions **2–5** in this part. Write your answer in **120–180** words in an appropriate style.

2 A tourist magazine for young people has asked you to write an article about the best way for a visitor (aged 15–20) to spend a day in the place where you live. Take into consideration that many people of this age are students, so include ideas which do not involve a lot of expense.

Write your **article** for the magazine.

3 You have decided to enter a short story competition in a newspaper. The competition rules say that the story must end with these words:

Although it happened a long time ago, I will always remember it as one of the happiest days of my life.

Write your **story** for the competition.

4 Your English teacher has asked you to write a report making suggestions about how to improve the facilities and equipment at your language school. A substantial amount of money has been allocated and all students have the opportunity to express their opinion.

Write your **report**.

5 **Background reading texts**

Answer **one** of the following two questions based on your reading of **one** of the set books.

Either (a) Who is your favourite character in the book? Write a **composition**, describing what the character is like and giving examples of some of the things that the character does.

Or (b) What is the most memorable scene in the book? Write a **composition**, saying what happens in the scene and explaining why it is so important to the book as a whole.

Part 1

For questions **1–15**, read the text and decide which answer **A**, **B**, **C** or **D** best fits each space. There is an example at the beginning (**0**).

Write your answers **on the separate answer sheet**.

THE FIRST TRAVEL AGENT

The **(0)** ...... *A* ...... of modern tourism began on July 5, 1841, when a train carrying 500 factory workers **(1)** .... off from Leicester towards Loughborough, 12 miles away. This modest excursion had been **(2)** .... by a young man called Thomas Cook, who had neither money **(3)** .... formal education. He had **(4)** .... to persuade the Midland Railway Company to **(5)** .... him charter a train on the condition that he would pay them back once he had sold all the tickets. His motive was not to **(6)** .... a profit, but to try and improve society. **(7)** .... , he argued, would broaden the mind and **(8)** .... people from getting into trouble with the police or causing other social problems.

The success of Cook's first excursion led to other trips to neighbouring towns and the **(9)** .... As these were so popular, he took the **(10)** .... to charge his customers a small fee for the **(11)** .... that he had done. Cook soon realized that the middle classes, who could **(12)** .... to travel, might be **(13)** .... in travelling further, so he began to organize tours to Switzerland and Italy, and so the first travel agency was born.

The business **(14)** .... off rapidly and Cook launched his own travel magazine. By 1872, he was selling 100,000 copies a year, and Cook was regarded as a hero of the modern industrial **(15)** ....

0	A history	B	tale	C	past	D	record
1	A got	B	set	C	put	D	came
2	A decided	B	agreed	C	developed	D	arranged
3	A none	B	no one	C	neither	D	nor
4	A succeeded	B	could	C	managed	D	achieved
5	A leave	B	let	C	allow	D	permit
6	A make	B	do	C	have	D	take
7	A Transport	B	Travel	C	Journey	D	Voyage
8	A avoid	B	escape	C	defeat	D	prevent
9	A wildlife	B	environment	C	countryside	D	nature
10	A occasion	B	possibility	C	opportunity	D	probability
11	A work	B	job	C	post	D	position
12	A earn	B	cost	C	gain	D	afford
13	A interested	B	dedicated	C	enthusiastic	D	keen
14	A went	B	took	C	came	D	stood
15	A time	B	age	C	term	D	season

Part 2

For questions **16–30**, read the text below and think of a word which best fits each space. Use only **one** word in each space. There is an example at the beginning **(0)**.

Write your answers **on the separate answer sheet**.

SENSITIVE TO SPIRITS

When Betty Puttick was three years **(0)**.........*old*........., she woke one night to see a man sitting on the bed. 'I thought it was my father,' recalls Betty. 'I held out my hands to him, but **(16)**......................... I did, he smiled, got up and just faded away. At the time, I thought it must **(17)**......................... been a dream. Then, **(18)**......................... day, a long time afterwards, I saw an oil painting of my grandfather **(19)**......................... had died young, long **(20)**......................... I was born. He looked exactly **(21)**......................... the man I had seen in my bedroom.' Only recently, just a few months **(22)**........................., in fact, Betty was taking her dog for a walk in the countryside near her home. Everything was strangely quiet. 'Suddenly, I heard the sound of horses and shouting. But **(23)**......................... was nothing to see.' Turning round, she saw a man leaning against a tree. He was wearing leather clothes and in **(24)**......................... hands were a bow and arrow. 'He was very quiet and seemed to be **(25)**......................... pain. Then he began to fade away and he vanished **(26)**......................... few seconds later,' said Betty. The place had been the scene of a terrible battle in the 15th century, and Betty is in **(27)**......................... doubt that she somehow became part of it. 'It's amazing **(28)**......................... many people tell you that they have actually either seen, felt **(29)**......................... heard ghosts. Luckily for me, **(30)**......................... are often happy to talk about their experiences,' says Betty, who publishes her third book about ghosts tomorrow.

Part 3

For questions **31–40**, complete the second sentence so that it has a similar meaning to the first sentence, using the word given. **Do not change the word given**. You must use between two and five words, including the word given. There is an example at the beginning **(0)**.

Write **only the missing words on the separate answer sheet**.

0 Peter was too nervous to say anything.

that

Peter was *so nervous that he could* not say anything.

31 I'm sure that somebody saw what happened.

must

Somebody .... what happened.

32 The painter you recommended is redecorating the house.

having

We .... by that painter you recommended.

33 'Do you know where Tom is staying?' she asked.

where

She asked me if .... staying.

34 I'm really looking forward to leaving school.

wait

I .... school.

35 My sister can't vote because she's too young.

enough

My sister .... vote.

36 George's composition was inaccurate.

some

George .... his composition.

37 Football doesn't interest me very much.

interested

I .... football.

38 I've had enough of listening to all your complaints.

fed

I'm .... to all your complaints.

39 When did you start playing the piano?

been

How .... the piano?

40 Travelling first class is too expensive for me.

afford

I .... first class.

Part 4

For questions **41–55**, read the text below and look carefully at each line. Some of the lines are correct, and some have a word which should not be there. If a line is correct, put a tick (✓) by the number **on the separate answer sheet**. If a line has a word which should **not** be there, write the word **on the separate answer sheet**. There are two examples at the beginnning (**0** and **00**).

Examples:

0	*had*
00	✓

ONE OF MY FAVOURITE STUDENTS

0	I was only 22 when I had started teaching and I was very nervous
00	at first but the teachers and pupils were warm and welcoming.
41	This may be why I remember Siobhan well, as she was one of the
42	first pupils I ever taught. She had a mind of the her own, even
43	then. She was a natural performer and always played at the piano
44	enthusiastically, despite of a few wrong notes. I remember one
45	concert when some boys outside the hall started to tapping on the
46	window. Siobhan saved the day. She turned round and started
47	singing for them. They decided to come in and listen her instead.
48	She always said she was nervous of playing or singing in the
49	front of people, but all she needed was a little encouragement. She did
50	never let me down. She had long hair, which it was right down her back.
51	When playing piano duets, she was used to fling her hair back and it
52	would wrap itself around the other girl's neck, almost strangling her.
53	She would often come up to the music room to discuss about her
54	problems. I have always had a several pupils who like to sit and talk
55	to me. That's one of the things I like best about to teaching. I love it
	when some pupils feel comfortable enough to come and talk to me.

Part 5

For questions **56–65**, read the text below. Use the word given in capitals at the end of each line to form a word that fits in the space in the same line. There is an example at the beginning **(0)**.

Write your answers **on the separate answer sheet**.

Example: | 0 | *difficulties* |

THE CHIEF CONSTABLE

Selecting the right kind of job can cause **(0)** *difficulties* for young people.   DIFFICULT

But, for Susan Thomas, the second woman to rise **(56)**............................   SUCCESS

through the ranks to become a Chief Constable, it was **(57)**............................   POSSIBLE

to consider doing anything else. Her **(58)**............................ had been different.   EDUCATE

She changed schools 11 times! But it taught her to be **(59)**............................ .   ADAPT

After university, she joined an accelerated police **(60)**............................ scheme.   PROMOTE

She only realized later what an **(61)**............................ it was to pass the exam.   ACHIEVE

If you answered a question **(62)**............................ you had to do another one!   CORRECT

The training was exhausting. The job itself is **(63)**............................ than most   TOUGH

people imagine. **(64)**............................, Susan works a 10-hour day. But she is   TYPICAL

convinced that her **(65)**............................ of career was the right one.   CHOOSE

PAPER 4 ► LISTENING

First Certificate Listening Test

Hello. I'm going to give you the instructions for this test.

I'll introduce each part of the text and give you time to look at the questions. At the start of each piece you'll hear this sound:

[tone]

You'll hear each piece twice.

Remember, while you're listening, write your answers on the question paper. You'll have time at the end to copy your answers onto the separate answer sheet.

The tape will now be stopped. Please ask any questions now, because you must not speak during the test.

Part 1

You will hear people talking in eight different situations. For questions 1–8, choose the best answer **A**, **B** or **C**.

1 You hear someone talking about an embarrassing moment.

What happened?

A She had a row with a neighbour.

B She offended one of her guests.

C She was accused of stealing a ring.

`[ 1 ]`

2 You hear someone talking about going on holiday.

What is the speaker's intention?

A to explain how to look after your camera

B to point out the disadvantages of hotels

C to help people protect their property

`[ 2 ]`

3 You hear two people talking about queuing for a long time.

How did they feel about it?

A They thought it was worth doing.

B They were very bored with the wait.

C They would never do it again.

`[ 3 ]`

4 You hear someone talking about a cartoon character.

What does he say about her?

A She's horrible to others.

B She's popular with adults.

C She's very childish.

`[ 4 ]`

5 You hear a woman talking on the telephone.

Where is the person she is talking to?

A at a train station

B at an airport

C at a bus station

`[ 5 ]`

6 You hear part of a radio report.

Who is speaking?

A a member of a scientific committee

B a politician

C a policeman

`[ 6 ]`

7 You hear someone talking on the telephone.

What is he doing?

A making a suggestion

B criticizing

C persuading

`[ 7 ]`

8 You hear a critic talking on the radio about an art exhibition.

What is her opinion of it?

A It is shocking.

B It is of poor quality.

C It is difficult to understand.

`[ 8 ]`

That's the end of Part One. Now turn to Part Two.

Part 2

You will hear someone talking on a radio programme about how to take adults on a tour of a museum. For questions **9–18**, fill in the missing information.

TEN TIPS FOR ADULT MUSEUM TOURS

ONE

Be sure you don't forget the [_____ 9] of your adults.

TWO

To appreciate museums, adults should be taught to [_____ 10] at exhibits.

THREE

Adults need to be convinced to [_____ 11]

FOUR

Talking about exhibits will help them to [_____ 12] them.

FIVE

Get them to [_____ 13] in order to keep their attention.

SIX

It will take a lot of [_____ 14] to keep everybody happy.

SEVEN

Encourage them to use their [_____ 15]

EIGHT

Encourage them not to be so [_____ 16]

NINE

Your comments about the museum may help to [_____ 17]

TEN

If you like the museum, [_____ 18]

That's the end of Part Two. Now turn to Part Three.

Part 3

You will hear five different people talking about their obsessions with collecting things. For questions **19–23**, choose from the list **A–F** which comment each speaker makes about the things they collect. Use the letters only once. There is one extra letter which you do not need to use.

A They have entertained family and friends.

Speaker 1   **19**

B They are extremely valuable today.

Speaker 2   **20**

C They once gave pleasure to someone.

Speaker 3   **21**

D They could never be replaced.

Speaker 4   **22**

E They are not appreciated by everybody.

Speaker 5   **23**

F They are difficult to get rid of.

That's the end of Part Three. Now turn to Part Four.

Part 4

You will hear part of a radio programme about two people who changed jobs for one week. For questions **24–30**, write **J** (for Jack), **A** (for Anna), and **N** (for neither), in the boxes provided.

24 I found it difficult to use the equipment.   **24**

25 I was worried about making a mistake.   **25**

26 It was hard to do what I was asked to do.   **26**

27 I did not have the qualifications to do the job fully.   **27**

28 I wasn't asked to do anything unpleasant.   **28**

29 I did not like the work at all.   **29**

30 I was happy when the week came to an end.   **30**

That's the end of Part Four.

You now have five minutes to copy your answers onto the separate answer sheet.

NB: The complete Speaking Test in the exam takes about 14 minutes.

Part 1 The interview

(This part takes about three minutes in the exam.)

In pairs, take it in turns to answer these questions.

What are your hobbies?
What kind of restaurants do you like to go to?
What are/were your best and worst subjects at school?
What did you do for your last summer holidays?
How long have you been studying English?
What would you like to do in the future?

Part 2 The individual long turn

(This part takes about four minutes for two candidates in the exam.)

In pairs, both look at pictures 1 and 2 on page 174.
They show different places to live.

| Student A | Compare and contrast these pictures, and say what you think are the good and bad points about living in places like these. |
| Student B | Which of these places would you prefer to live in? |

In pairs, both look at pictures 3 and 4 on page 174.
They show people doing exciting leisure activities.

| Student B | Compare and contrast these pictures, and say which activity you think would be the most difficult to learn. |
| Student A | Which of these activities would you enjoy doing? |

Part 3 The two-way collaborative task

(This part takes about three minutes in the exam.)

In pairs, look at the pictures on page 169 and do the task below together.

You have been asked to choose a set of four amusing postcards to be sold in Britain's tourist shops. Look at some of the designs which have been suggested. Talk about what impression of the country the postcards give, then decide together which four postcards you think would be the most popular.

Part 4 The three-way discussion

(This part takes about four minutes in the exam.)

In pairs, discuss the questions below.

1 How popular is it to send each other postcards in your country?
2 What things can we do to remember our holidays?
3 How do you think tourism has changed life in some countries?
4 Besides tourism, what other reasons are there for people to travel?
5 What forms of transport do you think people will use in the future?

Nice just to get right away from it all -

ENJOYING OUR VIEWS OF THE COAST.

LONDON MOTORISTS ENJOYING A FEW MOMENTS RELAXATION AT A ZEBRA CROSSING

HEADING FOR THE COAST...

...DOWN BY THE SEA.

THE EASIEST WAY TO GET ABOUT LONDON IS BY TUBE...

HAVING YOUR PICTURE TAKEN

EVERYBODY SAYS

WE SHOULD HAVE BEEN HERE

LAST WEEK ...

Pair work

Unit 2

page 18

1 Open cloze

1 a	2 not	3 to
4 than	5 between	6 where
7 until/at	8 we	9 an
10 on		

page 19

6 Dreamland

1 You are having a difficult time but everything will be all right in the end.

2 You are not as successful as you thought you would be.

3 You have done something wrong and are trying to run away from the consequences.

4 You find it difficult to make other people believe what you say.

5 You are worrying about things which are not important.

6 If you feel comfortable doing this, you will succeed in what you are trying to do.

Unit 3

Page 29

4 Wordcomb

Student A

Help Student B to fill in the puzzle by giving him or her clues to 1, 3, 5, 7 and 9.

Define the words using relative clauses.

Example:

1 This is a kind of building where the ancient Egyptians used to bury their pharaohs.

```
1        P Y R A M I D
2
3    T O U R I S T
4
5        S A F A R I
6
7    H I K E R
8
9        J U N G L E
10
```

Student B will give you the clues to 2, 4, 6, 8 and 10. Complete the puzzle to find the missing word in the box.

Unit 7

Page 69

5 Personal Filofax

Student A

MONDAY **3rd**

TUESDAY **4th**
6pm doctor

WEDNESDAY **5th**
basketball training 5-9.30pm

THURSDAY **6th**
meal 8.30pm

FRIDAY **7th**

SATURDAY **8th**
4.30pm hairdresser
9pm cinema

SUNDAY **9th**
all day / evening - grandparents

Unit 9

Page 91 **Lead-in**

Student A

1   2   3

Page 100   **Talking about yourself**

Look at the points given for the five statements you have chosen and add them together to get your final score.

a 1   d 4   g 2   j 2   m 4   p 3   s 2
b 2   e 1   h 4   k 3   n 2   q 3   t 1
c 3   f 3   i 4   l 1   o 1   r 4

Now read the appropriate description saying how independent you are.

Below 6
You're independent and feel in control of your life. But you should at least listen to other people's opinions – you could learn a lot. You've got a lot of confidence and are not easily persuaded to do something you don't want to do. However this could make you seem a little selfish. Try to be a bit more diplomatic.

7–11
You have strong principles and are able to stick to them most of the time. When you change your mind, you feel disappointed with yourself. But you're not being weak, it means you're adaptable, which isn't a bad thing. When it is really important, take a deep breath and say what you think.

12–16
Although you'd like to be true to yourself, you often change your mind and then blame other people for it. You should try to be more confident and make your own decisions. You'll be surprised how often your opinions will be the right ones and you won't get into difficulties with others so often.

17+
You are always changing your mind and are terrified of disagreeing with anyone. This is because you want to be really popular and sometimes you even do the opposite of what you want to do, just to achieve this. Having an opinion won't make you any less popular and could even make your friends respect you more.

Page 120   **1 Talking together**

Student A

There are tickets for the evening of the 29th and 30th of this month.
Prices range from £20–£40.
Concerts begin at 7.30 in the evenings.

Then ask Student B

Would you like to book some tickets?

Page 139   **5 Police investigation**

Student C

Answer the questions using the information below. Use a suitable modal to complete the sentences.

1   You were having dinner in a nearby restaurant.

2   Your sister heard a loud noise which ... have been glass breaking.

3   You noticed a van parked in the street on the day of the burglary. It ... have been red.

4   You saw two men outside the house where the burglary took place. They were carrying a ladder. You thought they ... have been window cleaners.

Pair work

Unit 3

Page 29   **4 Wordcomb**

Student B

**Help Student A to fill in the puzzle by giving him or her clues to 2, 4, 6, 8 and 10.
Define the words using relative clauses.**

Example:
2   This is a place where you stay on holiday.

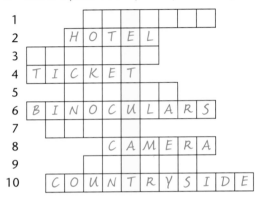

Student A will give you the clues to 1, 3, 5, 7 and 9. Complete the puzzle to find the missing word in the box.

Unit 7

Page 69   **5 Personal Filofax**

Student B

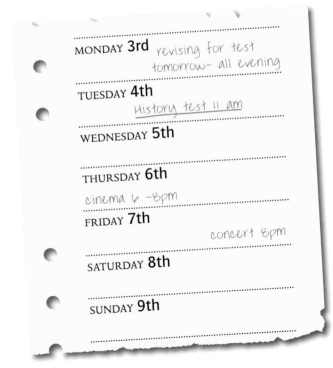

MONDAY 3rd *revising for test tomorrow- all evening*

TUESDAY 4th
History test 11 am

WEDNESDAY 5th

THURSDAY 6th
cinema 6 -8pm

FRIDAY 7th
concert 8pm

SATURDAY 8th

SUNDAY 9th

Unit 9

Page 91   **Lead-in**

Student B

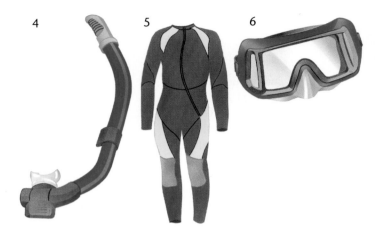

4   5   6

Unit 12

Page 120   **1 Talking together**

Student B

The musician teaches the sitar. (The sitar is a stringed musical instrument from India.)

The fees are £15 an hour.

He is free Tuesday and Thursday evenings from 6–8pm.

Then ask Student A

Are you interested in having lessons?

Unit 14

Page 139   **5 Police investigation**

Student D

Answer the questions using the information below. Use a suitable modal to complete the sentences.

1   You were having a quiet evening at home.

2   Your family ... have heard anything because you were all watching TV with the volume up.

3   On the day of the burglary you saw two men with a large suitcase which ... have been empty.

4   You heard some men in a red van, parked in the street, shouting at each other. They ... have been arguing.

Phrasal verb checklist

This list contains all the useful phrasal verbs which appear in this Student's Book. They appear here in alphabetical order and so the list can be used as a mini dictionary or to help you learn or revise these verbs. The words in *italic* give the definition of each phrasal verb as it appears in the unit.

back up	*give support to*
be fed up with	*be tired of*
be into	*be keen on sth*
blow up	*inflate*
break down	*stop working, e.g. a car*
break into	*enter by force*
bring up	*raise a child*
build up	*make larger, e.g. a business*
call on	*visit sb*
call out	*shout*
carry on	*continue*
check in	*register, e.g. at a hotel or airport*
come across	*find by chance*
come into	*inherit*
come out	*begin to appear*
come round	*regain consciousness*
come up	*occur (maybe unexpectedly)*
come up with	*think of an idea*
count on	*depend on*
cut back on	*spend less on*
cut down	*make sth fall by cutting it at base*
cut down on	*have less of sth*
cut in	*interrupt / to move suddenly in front of another vehicle*
cut off	*make inaccessible*
cut sb off	*break a phone connection*
cut sth off	*to stop the supply of sth (electricity)*
cut out	*eliminate*
fall back on	*have sth as a back up for emergencies*
get across	*succeed in making sth understood*
get ahead	*progress, be successful*
get away with	*do sth bad and not be punished*
get back (home)	*return / arrive at home*
get down to	*begin to do sth*
get sb down	*make sb feel depressed*
get out of	*avoid doing sth*
get round to	*find the time to do sth (at last)*
get together	*meet socially*
give back	*return sth to its owner*
give up	*stop doing sth*

go back over	*study again / repeat (an explanation)*
go off	*become bad, not fit to eat or drink*
go on	*continue*
go over sth	*study sth carefully (again)*
go through	*experience, endure (a bad time)*
go with	*match, combine well with*
have on	*be wearing*
hold up	*delay*
keep back	*refuse to tell sb sth*
let sb down	*not do sth you promised*
look after	*take care of*
look forward to	*feel excited about*
look in	*visit (often unexpectedly)*
look into	*investigate*
look up	*search for information, e.g. in a book*
look up to	*respect*
make up your mind	*come to a decision*
pay sb back	*get revenge on sb*
pick up sth	*go and collect sth or sb*
put sb down	*make sb feel silly in front of others*
put sb off	*make sb feel dislike for sth*
put on (weight)	*gain (weight)*
put sb through to	*connect sb by telephone*
put sb up	*provide accommodation for sb*
put up with	*tolerate sth or sb*
ring back	*return a phone call*
run into	*meet by chance / crash into*
send for	*ask to come and help*
set off	*start a journey*
stand up for	*defend*
take after	*have the same character or appearance as*
take sth back	*return to original place*
take in	*understand sth*
take on	*agree to do sth*
take off	*leave the ground, e.g. a plane*
take sth off	*remove a piece of clothing*
take over	*gain control of, e.g. a company*
take up	*start a new hobby*
try on	*put on to see if it fits*
turn back	*reverse the direction*
turn down	*refuse / reject*
turn into	*transform, change into*
turn out	*be the result*
turn up	*arrive*

Vocabulary and Grammar reference

UNIT 1

Vocabulary

Frame 3

Clothes
belt, blouse, boots, cap, cardigan, jacket, jumper, sandals, shirt, skirt, socks, tie, trainers, trousers, uniform

Frame 5

Adjectives of:

opinion and general description
fun, horrible, lovely, nice

size and weight
big, little, small

age
old, new, young

shape
round, square

colour
black, blue, brown, green, yellow

nationality
French, Italian, Norwegian, Swiss

material
cotton, denim, graphite, woolly

purpose
football (boots), walking (socks), tennis (racket)

Wordpower

Verbs of appearance and senses
feel, look, seem, smell, sound, taste

Words easily confused
try on, put on, wear, get dressed

Describing physical appearance
auburn, bright, casual, chunky, curly, elderly, expressive, flat, freckles, ginger, in his/her early/mid/late twenties, long, middle-aged, mole, mousy, oval, plump, pointed, scruffy, short, shoulder-length, slim, smart, snub, straight, tall, tiny, wavy, wrinkles

Describing personality
aggressive, ambitious, attractive, funny, hard-working, honest, independent, intelligent, jealous, romantic, sensible, sensitive

Grammar

Adjectives and adverbs

1 Adjectives: Use

a Adjectives are used to describe nouns. They come before the noun and do not change.
I've bought a green dress.

b Adjectives are also used after some verbs. These are mostly verbs of appearance or verbs of the senses.
appear, be, become, feel, get, look, seem, sound, taste,
e.g. You look nice tonight.

2 Adverbs: Formation

a Most adverbs are formed by adding *-ly* to the adjective.
beautiful, beautifully

b Some adverbs have the same form as the adjective.
hard, fast, early, late, far

c Some adverbs are very different from the adjectival form.
good – well

NB: *well* can be an adjective meaning 'in good health'.
I hope you are well.

Well can also be used as an adverb.
I sing well.

d Some adjectives ending in *-ly* do not have a corresponding adverb.
friendly, lonely, silly, elderly

So if we want to describe a verb we have to rephrase the sentence.
She smiled at me in a friendly way.

3 Adverbs: Use

Adverbs are used to describe most verbs and are also used to describe adjectives, participles and other adverbs.

Adverb + verb	*You speak English brilliantly.*
Adverb + adjective	*The new house is relatively big.*
Adverb + participle	*These cars are very well made.*
Adverb + adverb	*I passed the test fairly easily.*

4 Comparing adjectives and adverbs

a Most single-syllable adjectives and adverbs are compared using *-er* and *-est*.
old, older, the oldest
hard, harder, the hardest

b Two syllable adjectives ending in *-y friendly, wealthy, easy* and some others, e.g. *clever, quiet, narrow* also follow this pattern.
Last week's test was much easier.
My brother is cleverer than me.

c Most other adjectives and adverbs with two or more syllables are compared with *more, the most*.
Tigers are dangerous animals.
Lions are more dangerous than tigers.
Hungry lions are the most dangerous animals of all.

d Negative comparisons. We can also compare adjectives and adverbs using *not as … as*.
I do not speak English as fluently as my sister.

e Irregular comparatives and superlatives. The most common of these are:
good/better/best (adjective),
well/better/best (adverb),
bad/worse/the worst (adjective),
badly/worse/the worst (adverb)

f Present perfect. Remember that the present perfect is often used with superlatives.
She is the nicest person I have ever met.

UNIT 2

Frame 1

People
bishop, builder, cleaning lady, drummer, housekeeper, monk, owner, pilgrim, queen, servant, soldier, violinist, visitor

Places
abbey, attic, avenue, castle, cellar, hall, mansion, seaside, theatre, tunnel, wood

Uncountable nouns
advice, furniture, homework, information, luck, luggage, money, news, traffic

Frame 3

Types of entertainment
barbecue, beach party, disco, open-air cinema/theatre, restaurant

Expressing likes and dislikes
I really enjoy … , I love … , I quite like … , I don't mind … , I don't really like … , I don't find … interesting.

Asking what your partner thinks
What/How about you?, What do you think?

Frame 4

Everyday expressions
actually, I can't tell you, with any luck

Vocabulary
have time on your hands, keep your mind on, take your time, tend to

Frame 5

Formal and informal suggestions
I suggest that … , I would recommend … , Why don't you … ?

Wordpower

Talking about time
at times, fortnight, in time, leap year, midnight, month, on time, seasons, weekdays, weekend, year

Describing location
at the top, in the background, in the middle, in the bottom right-hand corner, on the left-hand side

Grammar

Present tenses

1 The simple present is used:

a to talk about things which happen regularly or are always true.
Tom starts work at 8.30 am.
The sun rises in the east.

b with adverbs of time.
never, always, usually, sometimes

c to give instructions.
First, you put the key in the lock, then you turn it very gently.

2 The present continuous is used:

a to talk about things that are happening at the moment.
Some researchers are interviewing the teachers now.

b to talk about things that are happening over a longer period of time.
The government is carrying out some research into ways of learning foreign languages.

c with *always* to express surprise or annoyance when something happens often.
That student is always coming to class late.

3 Verbs rarely used in the present continuous

Verbs of feeling
like, dislike, love, hate, need, want, prefer

Verbs of appearance
appear, seem

Verbs of possession
own, belong to, have

Verbs of physical perception
smell, see, taste, hear

Verbs of thinking
know, realize, suppose, understand, believe

These verbs refer to states or conditions, not actions.
I love music.
You seem unhappy today.

UNIT 3

Vocabulary

Frames 3 & 4

Holiday types
motoring holiday, pilgrimage, safari, sightseeing trip, walking tour

People
astronaut, backpackers, guide, hikers, passengers, tourists, travel agent

Places
beach, campsite, castle, countryside, desert, desert island, gallery, hotel, jungle, monastery, museum, restaurant

Travel
airport, bus, boat, coach, ferry, flight, foot, helicopter, hire car, hovercraft, motorway, plane, rickshaw, taxi, train, tube, underground

Wordpower

Uses of *get*
get angry, get a new car, get a new job, get a present, get away, get a phone call, get better, get cold, get home, get on the bus, get to London, get old

Words easily confused
excursion, journey, tour, travel, trip, voyage

Word grades
*boiling, cold, cool, freezing, hot, warm
busy, crowded, deserted, empty, packed, quiet*

Grammar

Relative clauses

1 Defining relative clauses

These relative clauses contain important information that helps to define or identify the person or thing we are talking about.

a   We can use relative pronouns such as *who, which,* or *that* to refer to people or things.
*The man who/that helped us spoke excellent English.
I've bought Jack a present which/that he will like.*

b   The relative pronoun can be left out if it is the object of a verb.
I've bought Jack a present (–) he will like.

c   The relative pronoun *whose* refers to possession.
I met a woman whose car is over 50 years old.

d   *Where* means *in which* or *to which*.
Can you remember the name of the hotel where we stayed?

e   *Whom* can be used as an object pronoun referring to a person, but *who* is also acceptable.
The man who(m) I talked to was very interesting.

f   If the relative pronoun comes after a preposition such as *to, from, with,* etc. *whom* must be used.
*The man who I was talking to was very interesting.
The man to whom I was talking was very interesting.*

g   *What* can be used to mean *the thing that* or *the things that*.
*What annoyed me was the way he spoke to the teacher.
I don't know what you are talking about.*

2 Non-defining relative clauses

These contain additional information, and are used when the person or thing we are talking about is already defined or identified.
My mother, who was 50 last week, has worked all her life.

a   Commas are always used around the non-defining relative clause.

b   The pronoun cannot be left out and it is not possible to use *that*.

c   You can use *which* to refer to things, *when* to refer to time, *where* to refer to place.
*My passport, which was here a minute ago, seems to have disappeared.
October, when the weather is a bit cooler, is a good time to visit Cyprus.
I always go to Spain, where my parents have a holiday home.*

UNIT 4

Vocabulary

Frame 1

Age groups
*adult, baby, child, elderly person, middle-aged person,
pensioner, teenager, toddler*

Frame 2

Words connected with entertainment
*act, cast, curtain, film, interval, performance, play, scene,
scenery, stage, star*

Words connected with life in the past
*candles, gramophone, open fire, penny-farthing, quill pen,
stagecoach*

Frame 3

TV programmes
*cartoons, chat show, comedy, current affairs, documentary,
drama, game show, nature programme, soap opera*

Giving yourself time to think
*Now, let's see …
Well, I suppose we could …
Let's think about this for a moment …*

Frame 4

Words connected with time
*at the time, behind the times, for the time being,
keep up with the times, some time ago*

Wordpower

Countries, people, and languages
*Argentina/Argentinean, Brazil/Brazilian, Britain/British/
English/Scots/Gaelic/Welsh, France/French,
Germany/German, Greece/Greek, Holland/Dutch,
Italy/Italian, Japan/Japanese, Spain/Spanish*

Words easily confused
whole/all/both, alone/lonely, raise/rise, lie/lay

Numbers
*centigrade, dates, decimal point, degrees, first, fraction, half,
million, per cent, three quarters*

Grammar

Past tenses

1 The simple past is used:

a   to talk about completed actions in the past.
    *A group of musicians suddenly appeared.
    The musicians started to play jazz.*

b   with expressions that refer to points of time.
    *at 6 o'clock, on Wednesday, in May, two days ago,
    last week, the day before yesterday, when I was a child*

c   to describe a number of actions happening one after
    the other.
    *Theatre-goers put money into a box, entered the theatre,
    then found their seats.*

2 The past continuous is used:

a   to talk about things that were happening when another
    action took place.
    *As we were waiting for the film to start, the lights in the
    cinema suddenly went out.*

b   to set the scene in a story.
    *I was standing in a queue for the cinema. It was raining
    heavily and a cold wind was blowing.*

3 *Used to* (+ infinitive) is used:

a   to describe past habits.
    *Poorer theatre-goers used to stand and watch plays. If it
    rained, they used to get wet.*

b   to talk about an action which didn't happen in the past
    but does now.
    I didn't use to live in Washington.

c   to describe past states or conditions.
    *Theatres used to be open in the middle to let in the
    daylight.*

4 *To be used to* (+ -ing) is used:

to talk about an action which (you) were accustomed
to doing.
*Actors were used to audiences throwing apples and nuts
at them.*

5 *To get used to* (+ -ing) is used:

to talk about an action which you became accustomed
to doing.
*It was cold but after a while I got used to standing in the
open air.*

UNIT 5

Vocabulary

Frame 1

Word pairs connected with earning a living
employers/employees, job/work, salary/wages, staff/bosses

Words in text
controls, founder, grim, in debt, miniature estate cars, precision, scary, taking people on

Frame 3

Adjectives describing qualities for jobs
confident, co-operative, courageous, dedicated, kind, patient, strong, sympathetic

Jobs
archaeologist, artist, engineer, pianist, politician, surgeon

Showing you are listening
Oh, really! Right/I see! That's interesting!

Frame 4

Everyday expressions
I have to admit, I can honestly say, to tell the truth, to be honest

Wordpower

Talking about computers
CD-ROM, computer operator, keyboard, monitor, mouse, mouse mat

Jobs
astronaut, detective, explorer, homework, housework, job, journalist, surgeon, vet

Words connected with work, not having a job or looking for a job
applicant, career, contract, interview, pensioner, promote, redundant, reference, retire, training, unemployment

Negative prefixes *un/in/im*
impatient, inexpensive, unambitious, unco-operative, unemployed, unfriendly, uninteresting, unlucky, unsuccessful, unusual

Grammar

The present perfect

The present perfect simple is used:

a   to talk about a non-specific time in the past,
i.e. when no time is mentioned.
My brother has been to Australia.

b   to talk about a present situation which is the result of a previous action.
Someone has spilt some coffee on the cloth.

c   with adverbs of time, e.g. *just* (recently), *already* (before now) – in positive sentences or questions.
Have you (already) done your homework (already)?
Yes, we've just finished it.

still (continues not to have happened) – in negatives and questions.
Mary still hasn't telephoned me.

yet (hasn't happened, but is expected to) – in negatives and questions.
Has Peter contacted you yet?

ever (at any time up to the present) – in questions.
Have you ever been to Florida?

never (at no time in the past) – to talk about personal experience.
No, I've never been there.

d   with prepositions or prepositional phrases, e.g. *this morning/week, so far, up to now*, to talk about actions which are still going on or which have just finished.
We've studied two different books this term.
I've worked hard over the last two days.

e   with *been* and *gone* to convey a different meaning.
Maria has been to New Zealand. (She is not there now.)
Paul has gone to New Zealand. (He is there now.)

f   with *for* and *since* to talk about how long something has lasted and when it began.
Mr Thomas has worked here for a month.
He has been here since the end of last month.

UNIT 6

Frame 1

Sports
air chair, B.A.S.E. jumping, basketball, football, golf, ice-skating, jet belting, street luge, paragliding, skydiving, tennis

Frame 2

People
amateur, captain, coach, fan, goalkeeper, instructor, judge, official, player, professional, referee, substitute, supporter

Frame 3

People
bull fighters, figure skaters, football teams, jockeys, riders, wrestlers

Places
bullring, countryside, course, pitch, ring, rink

Activities
dancing, fighting, galloping, hunting, playing

Injuries
be knocked out, break an arm or leg, cut, pull a muscle, sprain a wrist, twist an ankle

Treatments
bandage, medicine, operation, pills, plaster cast, sling, splint, sticking plaster, stitches, X-ray

Frame 4

Sports related word sets:

boxing
hit, punch, ring, 15 rounds, strong

motor racing
brake, change gear, engine, rev up, spin off, steer

swimming
competitions, gold medal, 100 metres, Olympics

football
captain, goal, pitch, score, team

basketball
athlete, defence, player, point, professional, shoot, tall

Frame 5

Similarities and differences
a combination of, a cross between, like, unlike, the same as, different to/from

Sports
American football, 'Australian Rules' football, gliding, judo, karate, parachuting, rugby, soccer, volleyball

Wordpower

Adjective and preposition combinations
capable of, enthusiastic about, excited about, fed up with/of, frightened of, good at, interested in, keen on, responsible for, serious about, sick of, tired of

Words easily confused
beat/win/gain, lose/miss/fail

Grammar

Verbs followed by -*ing* or the infinitive

1 Verbs + -*ing* form

a A number of common verbs and expressions are usually followed by the -*ing* form rather than the infinitive.
I enjoy playing basketball.

Other common verbs that follow this pattern are:
appreciate, avoid, can't help, can't stand, consider, deny, dislike, enjoy, feel like, finish, give up, it's not worth it, it's no use, keep on, look forward to, mention, mind, miss, object to, practise, put off, risk, suggest, there's no point

(Remember that all verbs usually take the -*ing* form after a preposition.)

b Some verbs are followed by an object + preposition + -*ing* form.
They congratulated him on winning the race.

Other common verbs that follow this pattern are:
apologize to sb for, accuse sb of, blame sb for, prevent sb from, protect sb from, thank sb for

2 Verbs + infinitive

a Some verbs are followed by the infinitive rather than the -*ing* form.
I want to play tennis this afternoon.

Other common verbs that follow this pattern are:
afford, appear, arrange, decide, expect, fail, happen, hope, intend, learn, manage, offer, plan, prepare, pretend, promise, refuse, seem, threaten, want

b *Make* and *let* are followed by an infinitive without *to*.
They made the players train every day and did not let them have much time off.

c Some verbs are followed by an object + infinitive.
They have asked me to join the team.

Other common verbs that follow this pattern are:
advise, allow, enable, encourage, force, invite, order, persuade, remind, teach, tell

3 Verbs + -*ing* or + infinitive

a Some verbs can be followed by either the -*ing* form or infinitive, and there is no difference in meaning.
We started to train/training last week.

Other verbs like this are:
begin, intend, continue

b Verbs of perception (*see, hear, watch*, etc.) are usually followed by the -*ing* form if we see part of the action, and by the infinitive if we see all of the action.
I saw the children playing in the field.
(I noticed that they were there.)
I saw Manchester United play Newcastle on Saturday.
(I saw the whole match.)

c Some verbs change in meaning when followed by the -*ing* form or infinitive.
I like going for a run every day. (I enjoy doing it.)
I like to go for a run every day. (I choose to do it.)

UNIT 7

Vocabulary

Frame 2

Expressing probability
I'm absolutely convinced that ... will ,
I think ... is/are (probably) going to ... ,
I think ... will ...

Expressing improbability
I don't think it's very likely that ... ,
I don't think ... will ... ,
There definitely won't be ...

Frame 3

Expressing anticipation
I can't wait ... , I'm dreading ... , I'm excited about ... ,
I'm nervous about ...

Environmental problems
acid rain, air pollution, global warming, natural disasters, oil spills, skin cancer, traffic congestion, wasting natural resources

Solutions to environmental problems
electric cars, public transport system, recycling, smokeless fuel, solar energy, unleaded petrol

Expressing uncertainty
I can't say for certain ... but ... is going to be ... ,
I'm not really sure ... but I think ... would be ... because ...
It's difficult to say exactly ... but perhaps ... would be ...

Frame 4

Everyday expressions
You know ... , You mean ... , You see ... ,

Wordpower

Words easily confused
neither ... nor, no, nobody, none, no one, nothing

Extreme weather conditions
blizzard, drought, flood, gale, hurricane

Grammar

The future

1 *Going (to do)* **is used:**

a   to talk about an intention.
    I'm going to study French at university.

b   to discuss a probability based on evidence now.
    The course is going to be interesting.

2 **The present continuous is used:**

to talk about a future arrangement.
I'm having an interview at 10.30 am tomorrow.

3 **The simple present is used:**

to talk about a future event, e.g. on a timetable.
The course begins on the 1st of October.

4 *Will* **is used to express:**

a   to express a willingness or offer to do something.
    I'll show you how to use the computer.

b   to make a request.
    Will you help me with my homework?

c   to make a snap decision (made just now).
    I'll phone you tonight!

d   to express an inability or refusal to do something
    The video won't work.
    I won't tell you what Paul said!

e   to make a promise
    I'll buy you a really nice present!

f   to express determination
    I will study harder!

g   to make a prediction
    Natural resources will gradually disappear.

5 *Shall* **is used:**

to make a suggestion.
Shall we go for a pizza?

UNIT 8

Vocabulary

Frame 1

Words in text
charity, consumer goods, fortune, inherit, mansion, millionaire, over-ambitious, sob story, the 'haves' and the 'have-nots', the rat race, wealth

Frame 3

Shopping
bargain, cash, credit card, look for, market stall, pay by, pay in, price, queue up, the sales, a till

Asking for advice
If you were me, what would you buy … ?
What would you advise me to buy … ?

Giving advice
If I were you, I'd buy …, because …
I certainly wouldn't spend my money on … if I were you.
How about buying … ?

Frame 5

Linking words
also, finally, firstly, however, in addition, in my opinion, on the other hand, what is more

Wordpower

Words connected with money
afford, a good salary, a fortune, borrow, cost, earn, lend, make, owe, pay, spend, the bill

Grammar

1 Too (much)

We can use *too* + adjective, *too much* + uncountable noun, *too many* + countable noun to talk about a problem of some kind.
They're not too expensive, are they?

2 Not enough

We use *not* + adjective + *enough* or *not enough* + noun in a similar way.
Andy is not old enough to have a credit card. He does not have enough money anyway.

3 Conditionals

a   Zero conditional. *If* + present tense, + present tense. This is used when *if* means *whenever* or *every time.*
If you borrow money, you pay interest to the bank.

b   First conditional. *If* + present tense, *will* + infinitive. This is used to talk about real plans and possibilities.
If I see Peter tomorrow, I will invite him to the party.

In the *if* clause, it is also possible to use the present continuous or present perfect. In the other clause, it is possible to use other modals, e.g. *may, can, must,* etc.
If it's still raining, he must be really wet by now.
If he's missed the train, he may be late.

The first conditional can also be used to give instructions.
If you need something from the fridge, help yourself.

c   Second conditional. *If* + past tense, *would* + infinitive. This is used to talk about imaginary or unreal situations.
If I had a year's holiday, I would travel round the world.

It is possible to use other modals, e.g. *might, could,* etc. in the second part of the sentence.
If we spent more time studying, we might get a really good mark.

4 Unless and in case

a   *Unless* means *if not.*
He would not ring unless it was an emergency.

b   *In case* is quite different to *if. If* is used to explain that you do B if A happens.
A   *If it rains,*
B   *I'll take an umbrella.*

In case is used to explain that you do A anyway to prepare for the eventuality of B happening.
A   *I'll take an umbrella,*
B   *in case it rains.*

UNIT 9

Vocabulary

Frame 1 & 3

Animals
camels, canary, dog, dolphin, elephant, fox, gorilla, hippo, huskies, monkey, oxen, race horses, rat, rhino, squirrel, St Bernard dog, tiger

Frame 3

Asking if someone agrees
Do you agree? Do you think so too? Don't you think that … ?

Agreeing
I agree with … , I think … is right, I quite agree.

Disagreeing
Actually, I don't agree.
I don't think that's (true, right, correct).
Well, I'm not sure if that's (true, right, correct).

Frame 4

Words connected with diving
aqualung, flippers, life jacket, mask, snorkel, wetsuit

Paraphrasing
It's a kind of/sort of … , It's something that … ,
What I mean is … ,

Wordpower

Ways of talking
argue, discuss, gossip, mumble, whisper, yell

Words easily confused
asleep/exhausted/sleepy/tired,
close/near/nearby/next
country/countryside/nature/wildlife,
damage/harm/hurt/injure,
dead/died/endangered/extinct,

Irregular plurals
butterflies, calves, deer, fish, geese, mice, sheep, wolves

Grammar

Past tenses

1 The simple past is used:

a   to discuss events which were completed at a particular time in the past.
   I went on a safari to Africa last year.
   The bus was late this morning.

b   to talk about a series of events in a story.
   Sally bought a ticket and caught the next train home.

c   to talk about a past habit.
   Henry got up every morning at 6.30 am.

2 The past continuous is used:

a   to talk about an action which was happening when another occurred.
   Brian was driving home when he saw something in the middle of the road.

b   to talk about an action which was going on for some time.
   William was studying Art in Paris.

c   to set the scene for a story.
   The wind was howling and it was snowing hard.

3 The past perfect is used:

to talk about an action which happened before another in the past.
   Ashley thought the creature had probably escaped from a zoo.

UNIT 10

Vocabulary

Frame 1

Phrases in the text
a monster at school, a genius at, to expel, for its own sake, in my own way, mad keen on, set to continue in my old ways, the trouble was, to calm down a little, what stuck out instantly

Frame 3

Persuading and convincing
I'm sure you'd agree that the (people) in picture … couldn't manage without each other.
Surely the (people) in picture … don't really need each other?
Don't you think the (people) in picture … need each other the most?
The (person) in picture … really needs (help), doesn't he/she?
But the (people) in picture … don't, do they?

Frame 4

The same or different?
caught/court, copying/coping, prices/prizes, stare/stair, threw/through, wear/where, whether/weather, wondering/wandering

Wordpower

Words connected with education
go to university, get a degree, graduate from university, pass an exam, take an exam

Words easily confused
allow/let/make, avoid/prevent

Question tags
You do, don't you?
You don't, do you?

Grammar

1 *So* and *such*

So is used before adjectives and adverbs.
The dress was so expensive that I couldn't afford it.

Such is used before nouns.
It was such an expensive dress that I couldn't afford it.

Both are emphatic.

Modals

2 *Can/could* are used:

a to say that somebody knows how to do something.
   Gill can play the piano very well indeed.

b to ask for permission informally.
   Can/Could I ask you a personal question?

c to talk about a possibility.
   I suppose it could be true.

d *can't* is used to express a disbelief that something is true or could be possible.
   You can't be hungry. You've just eaten.

3 *Have(n't) (got) to/have (don't have) to* are used:

to talk about what is necessary or obligatory. The negative form has the meaning of lack of obligation (not to be confused with *must not* which means prohibition).
We've got to be at the theatre at 6pm.
They've got to do their homework.
We haven't got/don't have to finish the homework now.

4 *May/might* are used:

a to talk about a possibility.
   It may/might rain this afternoon.

b *may* gives the idea that you have permission to do something.
   You may have a short break if you wish.

5 *Must/mustn't* are used:

a to say that it is very important (not) to do something.
   Students must come to the lessons on time.
   Students mustn't cheat in exams.

b *must* is used to express that something is highly probable.
   You've been up all night – you must be exhausted.

6 *Needn't* is used:

to talk about what isn't necessary.
You needn't phone Peter. I've already done it.
You needn't tell me if you don't want to.

7 *Should(n't)/ought (not) to* are used:

a to say that this is (not) the right thing to do.
   We shouldn't/ought not to tell lies.
   We should/ought to tell the truth.

b to give suggestions or polite orders.
   You shouldn't/ought not to go to work with that cold.
   You should/ought to see a doctor about that cough.

c to express that something will almost certainly happen, unless something unforeseen prevents it.
   We should arrive at the airport about midnight.
   We ought to be there in five minutes.

UNIT 11

Vocabulary

Frame 1

Words connected with flying
aircraft, air force, air traffic control, altitude, balloon, breeze, climb, cockpit, co-pilot, crash, drift, flight, float up, helicopter, helium, jumbo jet, level off, pilot, propeller, radar, rise, unidentified flying object (UFO)

Frame 3

Comparing and contrasting photographs
Although all the photographs are …, only one or two … .
This photograph seems … whereas this one … .

Frame 4

The same or different?
angry / hungry, possible / passable, seat / sit, site / sight, thirty / thirteen

Wordpower

Word grades
cry, delighted, dissatisfied, ecstatic, frown, giggle, laugh, miserable, pleased, satisfied, smile, sob, unhappy

Phrases with *fun* and *funny*
do something for fun, feel a bit funny, funnily enough, have a funny feeling, have fun, make fun of, so funny

Grammar

The present perfect continuous and present perfect simple

1 The present perfect continuous is used:

a to talk about activities that began in the past and are still going on.
Alex has been waiting for a bus for ages.

b to talk about an uncompleted activity.
He has been making a film in the USA. (It is not finished.)

c to talk about a recently completed activity.
I've been painting the bedroom.

2 The present perfect simple is used:

a to talk about a finished action.
He has made a film. (It is finished.)

b with stative verbs.
I have known Anna for years.
NB: *not* have been knowing …

c If we want to concentrate on how long it is since something happened, we usually use the present perfect simple in the negative.
I haven't written to my parents for ages.

UNIT 12

Vocabulary

Frame 1

Words connected with music
*album, bass player, blues, classical, concert,
country and western, fan, heavy metal, jazz, on tour,
reggae, rock, stage, traditional music*

Words from the text
*at full volume, autographs, band, bloke, bother, convert,
cuttings, depression, devoted, obsession*

Frame 4

Listening text
*banjo, bongo, carnival, ceremony, dance, drum, conga, guitar,
rhythm, steel band*

Frame 5

Indirect questions
*Could you let me know … ?
Could you tell me … ?
Do you know … ?
Do you think … ?*

Wordpower

Words easily confused
say/talk, speak/tell

Reporting verbs
*admit, advise, agree, deny, encourage, promise, refuse,
remind, threaten, warn*

Verb and preposition combinations
*believe in sth/sb, call sb up, consist of, depend on sth/sb,
dream about/of sth/sb, go on, go out, go off, listen to sth/sb,
pay for sth/sb, ring sb up, spend on, talk about sb/over sth,
write down sth, write to sb*

Grammar

Reported speech

1 No change

There is no need to make any tense changes if the
reporting verb is in the present tense and the statement is
still true.
Claire says she loves going to concerts.

2 Tense changes

If the reporting verb is in the past tense, we usually have to
change the tenses.

Actual words	Reported speech
Imperative	**Infinitive**
'*Sit down!*'	*She told them to sit down.*
Simple present	**Simple past**
'*I am happy to be back.*'	*He said he was happy to be back.*
Present continuous	**Past continuous**
'*You are talking too loudly.*'	*They said she was talking too loudly.*
Simple past	**Past perfect**
'*She borrowed my bicycle.*'	*He said that she had borrowed my bicycle.*
Past continuous	**Past perfect continuous**
'*We were dancing all night.*'	*They said that they had been dancing all night.*
Present perfect simple	**Past perfect simple**
'*No one has ever spoken to me like that before.*'	*She said no one had ever spoken to her like that before.*
Present perfect continuous	**Past perfect continuous**
'*You have been driving around for ages.*'	*She said that they had been driving around for ages.*
Past perfect	**Past perfect (no change)**
'*I had never seen anything like it.*'	*He said that he had never seen anything like it.*
to be going to	**was/were going to**
'*They are going to have a party soon.*'	*I said that they were going to have a party soon.*
can, will, etc.	**could, would, etc.**
'*I can't hear myself think.*'	*She said that she couldn't hear herself think.*

3 Other changes

If dates and locations have been mentioned, make the
following changes.

today	*that day*
yesterday	*the day before, the previous day*
tomorrow	*the next day, the following day, the day after*
the day after tomorrow	*in two days' time*
here	*there*

4 Reported questions

a   The tense changes in reported questions are exactly the
same as in reported speech.

b   When reporting direct questions, we use the word *if*
before the question.
Did you enjoy the party?
She asked me if I had enjoyed the party.

c   When reporting a question which begins with a
question word, e.g. *who, which, where, why, when, how*,
we repeat the question word.
Where did you learn to play the piano?
He asked me where I learnt to play the piano.

d   The word order in reported questions is reversed to
subject + verb (not verb + subject).
They wondered if I was feeling OK.
NB: **not** *They wondered if was I feeling OK.*

e   Indirect questions also follow this pattern.
Could you tell me where the station is?
NB: *Question marks are **not** used in reported questions.*

UNIT 13

Vocabulary

Frame 1

Words and phrases from the text
accident-prone, go wrong, lose count, near-miss, side effect, traffic jam

Frame 2

Negative prefixes
illogical, irresponsible, unfashionable, unfortunate, unlucky, unreasonable, unsuccessful, unsympathetic

Frame 3

Asking someone to repeat
Could you say that again please?
I'm sorry, I didn't quite catch that.
Would you mind repeating that, please?

Checking you've understood
Am I/Are we supposed to … ?
Do you want me/us to … ?
Should I … ?
So, I/We have to … ?

Frame 4

The same or different?
career/carer, fair/fare, heat/hit, reel/real, scene/seen, some/sum, steal/still, wrote/rode

Wordpower

Words easily confused
chance, occasion, opportunity, possibility

Neutral and negative adjectives
arrogant, confident, famous, interested, notorious, obsessed, pleased, shocked, shy, skinny, slim, smug, surprised, timid

Phrases with *have* and *take*

have	*a good idea, a good time, fun, sth for lunch, sth in common with sb*
take	*action, a photo, care of sb, part in sth, place*

Grammar

Wishes and regrets

1 *I wish/If only* are used:

> I wish you wouldn't eat with your mouth open.

a to complain about someone's behaviour. In this case we use *would (not)* + infinitive.
I wish you wouldn't eat with your mouth open.

b to express regret about a present situation. In this case we use the past tense.
I wish I was/were better at maths.
If only I knew where those keys were.

c to express regret about a past action. In this case we use the past perfect.
I wish I had stayed at home today.
If only I had been more careful.

2 Third conditional

The third conditional is used to speculate about the past. We use it to talk about the imaginary past results of things that did not happen, so it is sometimes called the 'unreal conditional'.

a In the *if* clause, we use the past perfect, and in the other we use *would have* + past participle.
If I had left home on time, I would not have missed the bus.

b In the *if* clause, we can also use the past perfect continuous. In the other part, we can use other modal verbs such as *might*.
If I had not been wearing my seat belt, I might have hurt myself badly.

c If we want to talk about a result in the present of something that did not happen in the past, we use a mixed conditional structure *if* + past perfect and *would* + infinitive.
If you had done your homework, you would know the answer.

UNIT 14

Frame 1

Words from the text
ancient, astonishing, carry out, case, circumstantial evidence, corpse, cover-up, dangerous, examine, forensics, identify, investigation, interview, lead, magnificent, pathologist's report, reveal, startling, witness

Frame 3

Punishments
electronic tagging, fine, imprisonment, probation, warning, working in the community

Saying you don't know
I have to say I know very little about … , but …
I don't actually know a great deal about … , but …
… is something I don't know very much about, but …

Frame 4

The same or different?
brakes / breaks, breathe / breath, past / passed, place / plays, raising / rising, sick / six, warn / worn, week / weak

Everyday expressions
No, sorry … , Well, maybe … , On second thoughts … , or was it …

Frame 5

Presenting an argument
It's generally accepted that …
It's safe to say that …
Most people would agree that …

Wordpower

Words connected with crime and punishment
criminal / petty thief, defence / prosecution, guilty / innocent, in jail or prison / under arrest, judge / jury, murder / manslaughter, rob / steal, robbery / burglary

Expressions with good and bad
as good as gold, do someone good, do someone a good turn, go through a bad patch, it's no good, it's too bad, make the best of a bad job, too good to be true

TOO GOOD TO BE TRUE!

Past modals

1 *Must have (done)* is used:

to offer a logical explanation for what happened.
The thieves must have got into the bank by the back entrance. They must have stayed in the bank overnight.

2 *Can't / couldn't have (done)* is used:

to express that it was impossible that this was the case.
The thieves couldn't have entered the bank by the front entrance. They can't have got past the security guards.

3 *Could / may / might have (done)* are used:

to give a possible explanation for what happened.
The thieves might have known one of the bank employees.
The employee could have let them in.
The employee may have known how to stop the alarm ringing.

4 *Should(not) have (done)* is used:

a to express that it was the right thing to do but it didn't happen.
There should have been a security guard at the back entrance to the bank.

b to say that it was the wrong thing to do but it happened.
The money shouldn't have been so easy to steal.

5 **Needn't have (done)** is used:

to say that it was unnecessary but it happened.
The bank employees needn't have come into work the next morning as the bank was closed.

6 **Didn't need to (do)** is used:

to express that it was unnecessary so it didn't happen.
The police didn't need to look for the thieves as they were identified by the security cameras.

UNIT 15

Vocabulary

Frame 1

Movements
bend, curl up, emerge, lift, lower, stick out, waggle, wriggle

Frame 3

Words associated with sporting activites
camera, diving mask, hot air balloon, mobile phone, parachute, snorkel, surfboard

Describing how something works or how to use something
First, you …
Then you …
Next, the … can/should be …
Finally, you …

Frame 4

The same or different?
bored/board, damp/dump, hit/heat, our/hour, right/write, sell/cell, slip/sleep, wear/where

Wordpower

Which way?
back to front, bumper to bumper, inside out, round and round in circles, side by side, upside down

Grammar

1 **The passive is used:**

a when we are more interested in the subject of the sentence than in who did it.
The video was made in Japan.

b when we do not know who did the action.
Our neighbour's car was stolen last night.

c when the action and the person who did the action are important.
A statement was made by the Chief of Police.

d in newspaper reports.
Two men were hurt in an accident today.

e to describe scientific experiments or processes.
The liquid was placed in a glass container and heated slowly.

f to describe what people think generally.
It is thought that the new road will solve the city's traffic problems.

g it is obvious or unimportant who does the action.
Our computers are sold all over the world.

2 **The causative *have* or *get something (done)* is used:**

when somebody else does something for you. They are quite often used when describing a service which you pay for.
We had a new central heating system put in last week.
I got my hair cut yesterday.
Bill's going to get the car serviced tomorrow.

Oxford University Press
Great Clarendon Street, Oxford OX2 6DP

Oxford   New York
Auckland Bangkok Buenos Aires Cape Town
Chennai Dar es Salaam Delhi Hong Kong Istanbul
Karachi Kolkata Kuala Lumpur Madrid Melbourne
Mexico City Mumbai Nairobi São Paulo Shanghai
Singapore Taipei Tokyo Toronto

with an associated company in   Berlin

OXFORD and OXFORD ENGLISH
are trade marks of Oxford University Press

ISBN 0 19 453352 2

© Oxford University Press 1999
First published 1999
Ninth impression 2002
Printing ref. (last digit): 6 5 4 3 2 1

Acknowledgements

The authors would like to thank their families for their help and support and
in particular Mark Gude.

The authors and publisher are grateful to those who have given permission
to reproduce the following extracts and adaptations of copyright material:
p7 'Face Facts' by T. Unsworth from the *Sunday Times Magazine* 15 December
1996 © Times Newspapers Limited, 1996; p16–17 'Things that go bump in
the night' by Anthony Edwards, with his permission. Appeared in *XC
Magazine,* Summer/Autumn 1996 issue, published by the BLA Group;
p18 'This article will send you to sleep' © *The Observer;* p27 In Search of
Happiness by Angus Deayton and Lise Mayer by permission of Macmillan;
p36–37 'Antonio: The boy's done well' by Gabrielle Donnelly, with her
permission. Appeared in *Now* on 6 March 1997; p38 'All the world's a stage'
by I. Hussain © *The Guardian;* p46 'Megabucks, megabytes and the
expansion of a mansion' by L. van der Post, from *Financial Times How to
Spend It Magazine,* September 1995. Reproduced by permission of the
Financial Times Syndication; p48 'The cavewomen of Coober Pedy' by
A. Haworth. Appeared in *Marie Claire,* reproduced with their permission;
p57 'Adrenaline Overload' by B. Borrows from *Bizarre* March/April 1997
edition. Reprinted by permission of John Brown Publishing Ltd; p57 'You'll
believe a man can fly'. Appeared in *Focus* April 1997 edition, and reproduced
by permission of Gruner & Jahr (U.K.) Partners; p58 The World's Most Bizarre
Facts Ever, a supplement to *Bizarre* magazine April 1997. © 1997. Reprinted
by permission of John Brown Publishing Ltd; p58 The Return of Heroic
Failures by S. Pile, published by Secker & Warburg. Reproduced with
permission of Random House UK Limited; p66–67 'Ten things you won't be
doing in fifty years' by R. Hood. Appeared in *Focus* September 1996 edition,
and reproduced by permission of Gruner & Jahr (U.K.) Partners; p76 In
Search of Happiness by Angus Deayton and Lise Mayer by permission of
Macmillan; p88 'Blow me! It's an Iguana!' by Simon Wright, with his
permission. Appeared in *Bella* issue 18, May 1997; p89 'The bundle of fun
who turned my house into a zoo' by K. Ginn © *Daily Mail;* p95 'The bobby
snatched from his beat' © *Daily Mail;* p96 'My Inspiration: Benedict Allen'
by E. Moore © *The Guardian;* p96 & p163 'My Inspiration: Siobhan Redmond'
by E. Moore © *The Guardian;* p96 'My Best Teacher: Rory Bremner' by
H. McGavin from the *Times Educational Supplement* 28 February 1997
© Times Supplements Limited, 1998; p96 'My Best Teacher: Darcus Howe' by
H. McGavin from the *Times Educational Supplement* 14 March 1997 © Times
Supplements Limited, 1998; p98 'Surviving your teenagers' by J. Warren with
permission of *The Express;* p116–7 In Search of Happiness by Angus Deayton
and Lise Mayer by permission of Macmillan; p126 'Is this the unluckiest
woman in Britain?' by M. Driscoll from *The Sunday Times* 1 January 1995
© Times Newspapers Limited, 1995; p136–7 'Who killed King Tut?' by S.
Kinnes. Appeared in the Museums and Galleries Magazine, May/June 1997
edition, and reproduced with their permission; p138 'Netball coaches caught
their man' appeared in *Eva magazine.* Reproduced by permission of Rex
Features; p146–7 'Promise you won't tell how it's done'. Appeared in *Focus*

September 1996 edition, and reproduced by permission of Gruner & Jahr
(U.K.) Partners; p148 'The X-Ray Picture Book of Everyday Things' by
P. Turvey, by permission of the Salariya Book Co. Ltd; p156 'Teenage hacker
started a spy hunt in US and London' by C. Elliott © *The Guardian;* p157
'The man who walks with lions' by T. Shubart, first printed in British Airways
High Life; p158 'The Washerwoman philanthropist' by K. Chappell. Reprinted
by permission from *Ebony* magazine, © 1995 by Johnson Publishing
Company, Inc; p159 'Costa-not-much' appeared in *New Woman* May 1997
edition, and reprinted with their permission; p161 'The Story of Thomas
Cook – The First Travel Agent' based on information supplied by the Thomas
Cook Archives; p162 'Susceptible to spirits' by Gillian Thornton, with her
permission. Appeared in *My Weekly.*

Although every effort has been made to trace and contact copyright holders
before publication, this has not been possible in some cases. We apologize for
any apparent infringement of copyright and if notified, the publisher will be
pleased to rectify any errors or omissions at the earliest opportunity.

Illustrations by:
Kathryn Adams/*Three in a Box Inc.* pp10, 42, 103, 127, 138; Adrian Barclay
pp19, 30, 50, 63 (sports objects), 82, 133; Mark Bergin pp38, 39 (actors);
Vanessa Card p129; David Downton p11; Mark Draisey pp49, 97, 106, 107;
Nicki Elson pp20, 92, 139, 142, 163; Michael Fisher/ *Illustration* pp39
(quill pen, gramophone, stagecoach, candles, open fire, penny farthing), 40;
Jon H Hamilton/*Debut Art* pp 56, 81; Jon Jackson pp9, 60, 66, 67 (electric car),
75, 123, 149, 154, 170, 172; Ed McClachlan p17; Reneé Mansfield/*Three in a
Box Inc.* pp13, 37, 83, 87; Julie Nicholls p126; Sheilagh Noble pp80, 86, 90,
140; OUP Tech Graphics dept. p44; Nigel Paige pp 67 (floods), 101, 111, 118;
Scot Ritchie/*Three in a Box Inc.* pp54, 63 (paragliding), 69; Timothy Slade p18;
Gary Swift pp44, 77, 94; Harry Venning pp8, 18, 59, 68, 79, 89, 99, 109,
128, 148, 178, 179, 180, 181, 183, 184, 185, 186, 187, 189, 190, 191.

Commissioned photography by:
Gareth Boden p102; Trevor Clifford p152

The publishers would like to thank the following for their kind permission to
reproduce photographs and other copyright material:
Pictor International *Cover photograph;* AC Press Services p57 (jet belting);
AKG Photo, London p146; Action Plus p60 (N Tingle/horseracing,
S Bardens/skating), p150 (photographer), p174 (R Francis/scuba diving,
D Young/sky diving); Advertising Archives p9 (jeans), p150 (camera, mobile
phone); Allsport p10 (P Cole/Arsenal), p57 (S Bruty/ street luge), p60
(P Rondeau/bull fighting, P Cole/football), p61 (M Powell/ Muhammed Ali,
J Daniel/Michael Jordan, Ferenc Puskas, G M Prior/Pete Sampras, Johnny
Weismuller); Aquarius Picture Library p6 (101 Dalmatians), p110 (Bart
Simpson); Rupert Besley p169; ©BBC p96; Camera Press p96
(R Gill/Siobhan Redmond); Capital Pictures p6 (H Thompson/Liz Hurley), p36
(P Loftus/Antonio Banderas), p78; Collections p28 (R Scruton/York rickshaw);
Colorific! p120 (M B Camp/Matrix/choir); Corbis pp23, 57; Mary Evans
Picture Library pp136, 137; *The Ronald Grant Archive* p6 (Big Chill, Hamlet),
p113 (Honey I Shrunk the Kids); The Guardian p156; Robert Harding Picture
Library pp30, 31 (Land Rover, travel agent); Idols p91 (A Houston); The
Image Bank p22 (M E Newman/restaurant), p31 (S Krongard/Concorde),
p40 (W Sallaz/judo), p85 (D Berwin), p100 (A Upitis/ orchestra), p110
(R Whitaker/children, K Tannenbaum/comedian, S Wilkes/ theatre); Katz
p110 (K Kuehn/Matrix/Oprah Winfrey); London Features International p10
(G Knaeps/The Verve); Magnum p30 (M Parr/backpackers), p38
(G. Pinkhassov/ballet), p100 (Abbas/Benazir Bhutto), p120 (S McCurry/Rock
music); ©1992 by Dr. Stephen R. Marquardt. All rights reserved. p6 (mask);
The Natural History Museum, London p71; Pictorial Press p6 (The Paper),
p108 (Polygram/Mr Bean), p110 (Bugs Bunny, The Flintstones, Tom & Jerry);
Powerstock p18 (C Rossini/man); Rex Features p10 (W Boxce/military,
J S Hibbert/schoolchildren), p31 (catamaran), p36 (baby), p38 (cinema), p40
(arcade, N Stevenson/ night-club), p58, p60 (C Ommaney/wrestling), p61
(P/Ayrton Senna), p62 (The Times), p71 (Butler/Raver/earthquake), p80
(P J Jorgensen/ Harrods), p96 (Rory Bremner, Nils Jorgensen/Darius Howe),
p108 (Mr Bean), p110 (Beavis and Butthead), p113 (Mrs Doubtfire), p120
(folk dancing), p128, p130 (aeroplane, fallen tree, mountain rescue), p150
(Sunstar/surfer); Salariya Book Company p148; Science Photo Library
(ESA/ozone, J Heseltine/sunbathing); Solo Syndication p89; Paul Stokes p88;
Tony Stone Images p6 (J Darell/male), p14 (D Durfee/man, S Rose/ woman),
p20 (M Mouchy/fireworks, S Peters/telescope), p26 (R Talbot/Cotswolds,
E Pritchard/aerial view, J M Truchet/islet, K Biggs/skyline), p28 (J Lamb/
rickshaw), p40 (T Arruza/teenagers, J Walker/theatre), p51 (J Darrell/man,
L Page/man in sweater), p57 (K Fisher/base jumping), p70 (R Iwasaki/flood,
B Osborne/smoke, E Pritchard/traffic), p71 (S Wayman/eruption), p100
(B Lewis/nurse, J Darrell/woman and child), p110 (B Thomas/beach,
D Kitchen/decorating, T Davis/orang-utans), p120 (A Sacks/piano), p121,
p130 (J Darling/ helicopter), p150 (D Olsen/diving mask, J Warden/hot air
balloon, P Correz/ mobile phone); Talkback Productions pp27, 76, 116, 117;
Telegraph Colour Library p12 (Benelux Press/teenagers), p26 (VCL/
Switzerland), p40 (B Tanaka/pool, VCL/horseriding), p51 (R Chapple/woman,
J L Fornier/woman, Masterfile/woman), p60 (P Ward/hunting), p70 (Planet
Earth/R A Jureit/acid rain, Planet Earth/M Mattock/logging, C Ladd/oil spill),
p110 (VCL/clown), p147 (Bavaria Bildagentur/levitation), p150 (D Waterman/
parachuting), p174 (G Hanson/Cotswolds, I McKinnell/Oxford Street);
John Walmsley p40 (band), p80 (market), p100 (lollipop lady).

We are unable to trace the copyright holders of:
p46 (Larry Lacerte), p48 (The Cave Women of Coober Pedy), p151 (BOB),
p157 (Gavin Ford) and would be grateful for any information which would
enable us do so.